Punishing Schools

Law, Meaning, and Violence

The scope of Law, Meaning, and Violence is defined by the wide-ranging scholarly debates signaled by each of the words in the title. Those debates have taken place among and between lawyers, anthropologists, political theorists, sociologists, and historians, as well as literary and cultural critics. This series is intended to recognize the importance of such ongoing conversations about law, meaning, and violence as well as to encourage and further them.

Series Editors: Martha Minow, Harvard Law School
Elaine Scarry, Harvard University
Austin Sarat, Amherst College

Narrative, Violence, and the Law: The Essays of Robert Cover, edited by Martha Minow, Michael Ryan, and Austin Sarat

Narrative, Authority, and Law, by Robin West

The Possibility of Popular Justice: A Case Study of Community Mediation in the United States, edited by Sally Engle Merry and Neal Milner

Legal Modernism, by David Luban

Lives of Lawyers: Journeys in the Organizations of Practice, by Michael J. Kelly

Unleashing Rights: Law, Meaning, and the Animal Rights Movement, by Helena Silverstein

Law Stories, edited by Gary Bellow and Martha Minow

The Powers That Punish: Prison and Politics in the Era of the "Big House," 1920–1955, by Charles Bright

Law and the Postmodern Mind: Essays on Psychoanalysis and Jurisprudence, edited by Peter Goodrich and David Gray Carlson

Russia's Legal Fictions, by Harriet Murav

Strangers to the Law: Gay People on Trial, by Lisa Keen and Suzanne B. Goldberg

Butterfly, the Bride: Essays on Law, Narrative, and the Family, by Carol Weisbrod

The Politics of Community Policing: Rearranging the Power to Punish, by William Lyons

Laws of the Postcolonial, edited by Eve Darian-Smith and Peter Fitzpatrick

Whispered Consolations: Law and Narrative in African American Life, by Jon-Christian Suggs

Bad Boys: Public Schools in the Making of Black Masculinity, by Ann Arnett Ferguson

Pain, Death, and the Law, edited by Austin Sarat

The Limits to Union: Same-Sex Marriage and the Politics of Civil Rights, by Jonathan Goldberg-Hiller

From Noose to Needle: Capital Punishment and the Late Liberal State, by Timothy V. Kaufman-Osborn

Communities and Law: Politics and Cultures of Legal Identities, by Gad Barzilai

The Jurisprudence of Emergency: Colonialism and the Rule of Law, by Nasser Hussain

Jurors' Stories of Death: How America's Death Penalty Invests in Inequality, by Benjamin Fleury-Steiner

Transformative Justice: Israeli Identity on Trial, by Leora Bilsky

Suing the Gun Industry: A Battle at the Crossroads of Gun Control and Mass Torts, edited by Timothy D. Lytton

Punishing Schools: Fear and Citizenship in American Public Education, by William Lyons and Julie Drew

Among the Lowest of the Dead: The Culture of Capital Punishment, by David Von Drehle

Punishing Schools

Fear and Citizenship in American Public Education

William Lyons and Julie Drew

The University of Michigan Press

Ann Arbor

For Philip and Brian

Published in the United States of America by
The University of Michigan Press
Manufactured in the United States of America
⊗ Printed on acid-free paper

2009 2008 2007 2006 4 3 2 1

A CIP catalog record for this book is available from the British Library.

Library of Congress Cataloging-in-Publication Data

Lyons, William, 1960–
Punishing schools : fear and citizenship in American public education / William Lyons and Julie Drew.
p. cm. — (Law, meaning, and violence)
Includes bibliographical references and index.
ISBN-13: 978-0-472-09905-4 (cloth : alk. paper)
ISBN-10: 0-472-09905-1 (cloth : alk. paper)
ISBN-13: 978-0-472-06905-7 (alk. paper)
ISBN-10: 0-472-06905-5 (pbk. : alk. paper)
1. Education and state—Ohio—Case studies. 2. School violence—Ohio—Prevention—Case studies. 3. High schools—Security measures—Ohio—Case studies. 4. Social control—Ohio—Case studies. I. Drew, Julie. II. Title. III. Series.

LC90.O3L96 2006
379.73—dc22 2005026387

Contents

Tables

Acknowledgments

We would like to express our appreciation to the University of Michigan Press and to Jim Reische in particular. The research for this book would not have been possible without the support we received from the Buchtel College of Arts and Sciences, the Department of English, the Department of Political Science, and the Center for Conflict Management, all at the University of Akron. We want to thank the teachers and administrators we were privileged to speak with, for the important work they do, for their willingness to give of their limited time, and for all that we learned from them. Our students, always a source of inspiration, and the students we spoke with as part of this project consistently impressed us as we examined the conflicts central to punishing schools, and we thank them for their participation and support.

Our most heartfelt appreciation is reserved for our sons, Philip and Brian. While we could not imagine a world where we could be any more proud of the gentle and loving, passionate and caring, curious and thoughtful young men that they have become, we were nevertheless routinely impressed by their patience and willingness to support us as we worked on this book, even when it meant fish sticks or leftovers for dinner yet again. For these and countless other reasons we would like to dedicate this book to them.

Chapter 1

Punishing Schools and a Zero Tolerance Culture

Our fear grows, I suggest, proportionate to our unacknowledged guilt. By slashing spending on educational, medical, and antipoverty programs for youths we adults have committed great violence against them. Yet rather than face up to our collective responsibility we project our violence onto young people themselves, and onto strangers we imagine will attack them.

—Barry Glassner (1999)

The defining purpose of education is not to train students to take their place in either the corporate order or the existing society, but to encourage human agency as an act of social intervention.

—Henry Giroux (2003b)

On a chilly November morning we approached the side entrance doors at Suburbia High School (SHS) in Ohio to conduct half a dozen prearranged student and teacher interviews.[1] We were met at the door by a teacher who told us in a tense, excited voice that the school was "in lockdown" for a random drug search and that if we came in we would be unable to leave for several hours. He asked if we still wanted to come in. We assured him that we did. We walked quickly through the halls, following our teacher-guide, as he explained to us that lockdowns were always a surprise and that this one had been announced only moments before our arrival. He said that once a lockdown was announced, it usually took about five minutes for every exit to be secured, including interior doors, effectively separating sections of the school and making movement between those sections difficult, if not impossible. When we asked him what the lockdown would mean in terms of procedure, he replied, "It means dogs. Uniforms. Nobody gets in or out."[2]

This teacher offered to accompany us if we wanted to try to walk around during the lockdown; we did. We walked quickly through the school and between floors, hoping to catch a glimpse of the police officers and their dogs and listening to our companion describe the procedures he had witnessed on prior occasions: "It's really quite something when you see all of them lined up in military formation. The dogs are unbelievable—the training! They're all German shepherds, big, and it's really sort of bizarre to see them right before they come into the school, perfectly still, and at a word they split up because they have different things to do."[3]

Moments later, through an interior window, we saw an officer with a dog walking around in a classroom; as we turned the corner we saw the students from that classroom standing outside the door. They had been instructed to leave their backpacks in a pile, and the officer brought the dog in to search the room and their belongings while the students waited in the hall. If the dog sniffs any contraband, we were told—if the dog "tags" anything—the owner of the offending backpack is asked to come into the classroom and the door is shut. The student is then questioned by the officer and an administrator or teacher while the backpack is searched and the substance examined. If further action is deemed necessary, it is taken after the student has been escorted to the principal's office, where parents, police officers, or other officials might be called.[4]

Most of the students waiting outside their classroom chatted quietly; we moved on to a large open area, the Senior Commons, which looks like the atrium café of a five-star hotel, with huge panes of glass, sunshine streaming in, brand new tables and chairs, and gleaming tile floors. We arrived just as three officers with dogs approached from the opposite hallway. We stopped about thirty feet from the nearest tables and watched.

There were fifty to sixty students occupying the tables, and the officers stopped a moment to speak with each other before proceeding. We were immediately struck by an overwhelming impression: this was a paramilitary unit. There's no other way to describe it. Their uniforms are designed on a military model, and every officer we saw was physically imposing: big shoulders and chests with weight-lifter arms that strained the fabric of fitted, button-down black shirts. We did not see any women or thin, small men. Every officer we saw was a white male with a short, military-style haircut. They wore no hats, and their paratrooper pants were tucked into black, lug-soled, lace-up jackboots. Their heavy belts held various pieces of equipment, including a nightstick, gun, radio, and other items we could not identify because they were encased in closed, individual compartments. Most imposing of all their tools and accessories, however, and far more redolent of a fear-inducing, social-control operation were the dogs.

Each dog weighed an estimated 100–120 pounds; they were all fully grown German Shepherds, and one of them was so big that his head reached the lower torso of the tall man who held him on a short leash. We watched while the officers instructed the students to deposit their backpacks in a pile in the middle of the floor and to line up against the walls on the perimeter of the Senior Commons. There were two administrators present, who said nothing but observed the entire search. The dogs were led to the backpacks, and they sniffed them all, quickly and quietly. They did not tag anything. Then, without speaking to anyone, one of the officers took his dog over to the line of students and, beginning at one end, walked the dog along the line of students. The dog's head reached anywhere from crotch to abdomen on the students, and as he was led down the line by the officer, he sniffed each student. We had observed another dog sniffing a row of lockers earlier, and the procedure is exactly the same: the dog approaches and remains very close to the object or objects of the search, with its nose within an inch of—or actually touching—what it's sniffing. The teacher, who was still with us, turned and whispered, "Holy shit! They're not supposed to go near the kids—the dogs are not allowed near the kids!"[5]

Having finished their search and finding nothing, the officers and dogs moved on. We asked the teacher about the policy prohibiting dogs touching the students, and he assured us that this was indeed the rule[6] and with good reason:

> *I've seen them when they tag something. When they tag a locker, or they tag a backpack, the dog goes nuts, the dog claws and jumps up and barks. That's what they're trained to do. That's how the dog gets rewarded, and the dog really freaks out. My god! What if somebody stuck something in their jeans pocket, or down their shirt? What if the dog made a mistake?*[7]

The entire operation in the Senior Commons took no more than ten minutes, but its visual impact was so powerful, so filled with social, political, and historical implications, that we found ourselves trembling as the narcotics unit left the area. We had witnessed fifty young people being told to relinquish their property for inspection and to stand quietly against a wall. We had watched several physically intimidating men wearing military uniforms and haircuts, combat boots, and radios, with visible weapons and huge, eager German Shepherds straining on short leashes, search that property for contraband. We stood by while one of these men and his dog searched the bodies of students, who said nothing and did as they were told. No one appeared afraid—except us. While the students, teachers, and administrators appear to have internalized punishing schools and the zero tolerance political culture upon which they are based as normal, we agree with scholars in the fields of education, criminal justice, and cultural studies, among others, who point out a troubling and growing trend toward enforcement as education.[8]

This book is about punishing schools—about the ways schools are punished as both focal points of particular, power-poor neighborhoods and, in a more general sense, the ways schools are increasingly being punished regardless of the economic and political power status of their communities by the steady, increasing disinvestment in public education. Our schools are being victimized, our children's futures as participants in a democratic society literally *looted* by a political leadership that privileges corporate interests at the expense of neighborhoods, families, and children. And schools have also become instruments of punishment themselves, as the criminalization of youth and difference, the mass-mediated amplification of some citizen fears and the muting of others, and a zero tolerance approach to difference and conflict increasingly erode the conceptual and material distance between the prison and the school.[9]

We examine here the complex relationships between these political, economic, and cultural forces through a detailed analysis of the leadership and political struggles over educational funding and policy at the national, state, and local levels as related to two schools in one midwestern state. We collected and analyzed thousands of pages of school district documents, local newspaper accounts, and narrative descriptions of conflict by students, teachers, administrators, and parents who were interviewed at an urban and a suburban high school—narratives that focus on fear, identity, and the role of community in education. We analyzed the narratives of school violence, in these and popular culture texts that constitute a rhetorical context in which meaning is produced for both state politics and individual experience, in order to shed light on a pervasive cultural fear—fear of youth and fear of difference—and its utility for political leaders seeking to divest from any notion of public education as a democratic social good. We bring these historical, political, popular-cultural, and individual narrative texts together in an attempt to thicken our understanding of "zero tolerance" as both punishment and pedagogy—zero tolerance approaches to conflict and ongoing struggles over identity teach us to reproduce the social stratifications in school culture that are predicated on race, class, and gender subordination. Further, we make the case here that zero tolerance policies are a part of a larger political culture, which is reflected in punishing schools—as one dimension of a more generalized impoverishment of democratic public spheres—and a zero tolerance culture, which amplifies the fears of privileged publics to justify the more aggressive and less accountable punishment of other publics in ways that ultimately disempower both.[10]

We begin the study, in chapter 2, in the suburbs, where we find one aspect of punishing schools in a brand new, affluent high school where the conflicts central to that school culture are generated largely from within the school building—conflicts that indirectly reflect the mass-mediated impact of consumer culture and mobilize prevailing gender, sexual orientation, and racial prejudices. This chapter examines the identity construction going on in SHS and its surrounding community and the ways in which it is influenced by nostalgic representations of small-town life; amplified fears of association with black, urban, and poor schools, and the punishing attention these schools receive from the media and political leaders. Mass-mediated images of diversity and chaos and the decay of urban locations abandoned by political and economic leaders encourage the town of Suburbia and its high school to distance themselves as far from their urban counterparts as possible. Through over sixty in-depth interviews of students, teachers, administrators, and parents and an analysis of the texts of those interviews,[11] we find a widespread belief among members of SHS that this distance and the physical absence of black bodies it makes possible—that is, the *absence* of difference—account for their shared expectation that they are entitled to live the kind of no-conflict existence found in fictionalized, popular images of the small town. The result of these beliefs may be found in the punishing policies justified by amplified fears of absent (virtual) black bodies and in the informal mechanisms of social control at SHS that seek to identify and eradicate difference among students, because it is the invisible differences among students in the halls of the school that are constructed as the greatest threat to Suburbia—the threat to property, to community, and to the carefully constructed identity of SHS as a nonblack, nonurban, nonpoor school that is thus not deserving of punishment.

Teachers' fears that "those potentially violent students are unrecognizable," unknown, and possibly unknowable are fueled by the kind of fearmongering that Barry Glassner discusses in *The Culture of Fear.*[12] But whether or not such fears have a basis in empirical reality, they have material consequences for schools and the students (and teachers) who attend them. Chapter 2 reveals the extent to which SHS, despite its palatial building and (initially) well-funded curriculum, operates in many ways as a prison, including continual surveillance by cameras and patrolling adults carrying walkie-talkies, locked exits, random drug searches, and a "shock and awe" police and K-9 unit presence in the school. Many of those interviewed expressed the belief that only "rule breakers" would object to such surveillance and discipline, and the official administrative rationale for an increasing number of lockdowns is that surveillance *itself* is a success, regardless of how little crime such surveillance might reveal. Procedures put in place to detect the possibility of random violence, à la Columbine, and thus to prevent it, as well as to detect what many *believe* to be the overwhelming presence of illegal drugs in all schools, contrary to the best evidence available, appear to be most useful in catching kids who skip class, tear down posters, and occasionally steal from lockers; such procedures also construct students as either potential victims in need of protection or perpetrators—and both identities, importantly, are premised on renouncing agency.

In chapter 3 we move beyond questions about why we fear young people—and how those fears become manifest in the offices, classrooms, and hallways of SHS—to an examination of the broader cultural contexts in which such fears are generated and reproduced. Popular films and television often present images and stories of educating youth in both urban and suburban sites, and audiences are made to understand those sites as either dangerous or safe; such images and stories have everything to do with the visual and meaningful markers of *black, urban,* and *poor.* Teenagers are often depicted in such films as threatening to the social order: young women disturb and disrupt sexual mores; sexual difference awakens chaos and violence; and race (read as nonwhite) is juxtaposed to law and authority and associated with crime, poverty, and a war on drugs that both produces and supports fears *for* our children and, simultaneously, *of* our children. Such images, and the stories they implicitly or explicitly tell, support the further abandonment of those schools and communities already most vulnerable to the escalating failure of the state to fulfill its obligations to provide equal public education and the increasing isolation of the most powerful schools in fortress communities whose privilege depends upon constructing and maintaining an identity over and against the Other.

This chapter offers a detailed examination of the 1999 film *Pleasantville* and its narrative account of education, youth, sex, and racial difference. On its face, *Pleasantville* offers a critique of sexual repression, limits on free speech, and gender and racial oppression; it promotes a post–civil rights celebration of human sexuality, racial and cultural difference, and secular-humanist education. But it undermines its own critique by also defining sexual agency in young women as dangerous, social change as properly authored by white men, racial conflict as devoid of a lived history and easily resolvable, and youth in general as in need of containment and control, for their own sakes as well as for the sake of the larger community. The pedagogical force of *Pleasantville* encourages audiences to understand that conflict is best managed and ultimately resolved by heroic (white, male) individuals, obscuring the presence of oppressive institutions and traditions and, by doing so, supporting them. *Pleasantville* confirms popular beliefs and fears that young people are at risk in the contemporary family, where Mom has lost her way, both sexually and maternally; Dad is absent; and the kids are fending for themselves, without guidance or control. In reproducing these fears, *Pleasantville* participates in the promotion of a conservative call for traditional family values, the criminalization of youth, and the resulting war on *real* families and youth culture.

We move from examining the film's narrative structure to making connections between that text and the previous chapter's reading of SHS narratives, reading them with and against each other in order to better understand a wider set of cultural associations and meanings that shift the discourse of fear from the state's failure to meet its obligation to invest in social welfare and public goods, and the systematic abandonment of the poor and the nonwhite, to an uncritical celebration of individualism and a liberal discourse of diversity that remains complicit in defining youth and difference as dangerous. Mass-mediated images of our failure to keep children safe—a failure that results, such images warn us, in children facing a more dangerous world and, importantly, becoming dangerous themselves—resonate with and through other cultural texts, including the narratives of students, teachers, and parents, in ways that reproduce fear, construct particular identities, and result in punishing schools.

The next two chapters present the voices of students, teachers, administrators, and parents from SHS's inner-city counterpart, Urban High School (UHS), and attempt to make sense in particular of the data presented in those texts about the relationship between neighborhood and school conflict at UHS. We focus especially on media portrayals and political decisions, noting the central role they play in the perceptions that students, parents, and teachers share about the most common conflicts at UHS. UHS's members describe a complex picture of conflicts that seep in from their neighborhoods, connecting school conflict and disciplinary policies with varying experiences of family and community life. The results of local and statewide school funding conflicts have sent a clear message to UHS: they must do more with less, and government support will increasingly come in the form of a variety of punishments that increase the burdens on their already struggling school.

Chapter 4 examines the social foundations of what we call punishing schools: current approaches to education and order that include some communities and exclude others in ways that disempower both. We provide here a detailed historical context of the political and economic struggles over schools and educational funding that frame the widely accepted, negative identity of UHS and construct it as a punishing school. We trace electoral contests and antitax fearmongering by state officials working in concert with private sector leaders to decimate city neighborhoods; to disrupt, disable, and relocate families; and then to continue to punish these already power-poor citizens because their schools have been left with no neighborhood. We offer a broad, cross-disciplinary array of evidence to support our contention that state leadership has dismissed the value of public education; dismissed the importance of intellectual inquiry; encouraged an anti-intellectual culture based on a nostalgic and vanishing sense of blue-collar community; and dismissed investment in the public sphere, leaving citizens with a legacy of public impoverishment and a school system so seriously neglected that the only viable response to unsafe buildings has been for the state legislature to exempt schools from building code requirements. The situation at UHS, this chapter argues, is not the result of a "school gone bad" but rather one foreseeable consequence of a series of choices made by public and private leaders at the national, state, and local level: the construction of a punishing school.

While SHS's students and teachers experience their palatial building as a prison, the students, teachers, and parents of UHS experience their school as a target for punishment from state and local leaders, who continue to punish the school for the challenges its students face—challenges created in part by the decisions of those same leaders. But conflicts among leaders did not receive the kind of media attention that youth conflicts received; youth conflicts were routinely represented as dramatic and frightening threats to community and family. Elite-amplified fears of permissiveness and unruly youth were represented as central explanations for our failing educational system rather than consistent underfunding; we are increasingly encouraged to focus our fears and anxieties on the children of frightening Others, on amplified images of rising school violence, and on the "excessive permissiveness" of a criminal justice system with more inmates per capita than any civilization in the history of time rather than on leaders constructing punishing schools and a zero tolerance political culture that sustains and justifies them.

Chapter 5 presents an examination of the widely held belief that UHS is a frightening school without a neighborhood. This chapter details the fairly consistent, local support for school levies that mitigate somewhat against statewide forces hostile to educational funding and the powerlessness of residents to combat federal dollars made available to industry and development for the renewal of "blighted," mixed-race, working-class, inner-city neighborhoods. In this chapter we argue that local and state political decisions have constructed UHS as expendable if not outright dangerous and the fears of UHS parents as therefore unreasonable; this identity, constructed *for* UHS, amplifies fears of (their own) black children and of difference already circulating in broader cultural discourses and mutes the fears of UHS parents, making it much more difficult for UHS to challenge its steady decay and marginalization as a frightening, inner-city, punishing school without a neighborhood.

This chapter reveals how changes in the city and its neighborhood—changes made by political and economic leaders—were soon mirrored in the rhetorical changes of news stories covering the school. The diversity of UHS became a threat; UHS literally and rhetorically *became* "a school without a neighborhood." The media increasingly created frightening images of a blackening inner city that required more punishment than pedagogy. Zero tolerance policies came to permeate the school, including not only disciplinary policies but academic policies as well, as schools were increasingly asked to focus on outcomes and accountability measures in the form of state-mandated examinations or unfunded federal mandates in the No Child Left Behind Act.

A zero tolerance *culture,* we argue, undermines the problem-solving efforts of many teachers, parents, and administrators, efforts whose success requires a culture in which there is at least the possibility of cooperation, negotiation, and compromise. Instead of promoting leaders who utilize problem solving and conflict management, a zero tolerance culture promotes leaders who choose discipline to displace democracy, surveillance instead of deliberation, and enforcement instead of education, further compounding the conflicts we face as a nation and disproportionately victimizing our already most disadvantaged communities. Chapters 4 and 5, then, examine a second, complementary school, where conflicts central to the school culture are identified by its members as coming directly from outside the school building, encouraging the unmediated and disruptive colonization of education by enforcement and reflecting larger trends—and their consequences—of our collective unwillingness to address inner-city problems. Leadership choices on school funding, taxation, and the role of public schools provide an explanation for salient but muted UHS concerns about the conflicts that students, teachers, and the community face—concerns that are further muted by unfunded mandates that they cannot fund themselves as a suburban school might and that together punish their children for living in, and attending schools within, neighborhoods of concentrated disadvantage (Sampson and Bartusch 1998).

In chapter 6, we conclude by arguing that Suburbia's fear of association with the challenges, conflicts, and subsequent punishment of black, poor, urban schools—a fear that is echoed in *Pleasantville*'s story of fear of youth, difference, and conflict—begins a process of constructing both SHS and UHS as punishing schools. As punishing schools within a growing zero tolerance culture, both institutions help to produce less resilient communities and citizen identities that renounce agency as either unnecessary or impossible in a context where political leadership patronizes some of our fears and punishes others. We argue that the pedagogical force of a zero tolerance culture sends the message that diversity *is* conflict, and this results in official and unofficial approaches to conflict that focus on making differences invisible and on isolating privileged individuals from experiencing difference. Importantly, such isolation limits opportunities to develop the practical and intellectual skills needed to effectively prevent, resolve, or reduce the harms associated with these conflicts in school and beyond. Instead, the weakness of deskilled student-citizens is manifest in identities without effective agency, leaving individuals (and Others more than some) subject to more aggressive and less accountable forms of power and an increasingly impoverished public sphere. There is a clear and powerful political utility in identities that distract our attention from fears that point to the powerful and draw our attention instead to fears for our children that target teachers' unions, stranger predators, and "political correctness," as Glassner (1999) argues; a zero tolerance culture cultivates citizen identities as inattentive to failed leadership and amplifies fears that divide and paralyze us.[13]

The combination of punishment and patronage constitutive of what we call the "zero tolerance coalition" relies on a right-utopian vision of limited government manifest in increasing privatization of public schools through starvation and deregulation; in punishment and patronage found in the charter school movement, which is neither innovative nor educationally defensible; in rhetoric about unsafe schools that focuses on crime rather than unsafe buildings resulting from decades of disinvestment; and in rigid antitax ideologues who insist—despite the rapid and ongoing flight of capital and jobs on their watch—that shifting funds from education to prisons and corporate welfare is fiscally responsible leadership. We insist here that democratic governments can only "provide for the general welfare" when they are built on informed, thoughtful, cooperative, prudent, and innovative forms of citizenship—and these depend on investing more in a democratic information system that begins with a vigorous education and resilient civic organizations and less in prisons and punishing schools.

Chapter 2

Talking Out of School
Living and Learning in Suburbia

Our careful analyses, together with those conducted by components of the justice system, have demonstrated the pervasiveness of youth violence in our society; no community is immune.

—David Satcher, Surgeon General (2001)[1]

Remember why you came to Suburbia? It was because of the schools and the style of life that this community afforded.

—Superintendent of Schools, Suburbia, Ohio

The misbelief that every child is in imminent risk of becoming a victim has as its corollary a still darker delusion: Any kid might become a victimizer.

—Barry Glassner (1999)[2]

I. *Introduction*

The small town of Suburbia, Ohio, is lovely. The visual impact of its rolling hills, spacious green lawns, and renovated town square, where band concerts are staged in the gazebo on summer nights and everyone turns out to see the high school homecoming parade, is amplified by our collective, willful nostalgia for the small town.[3] Such nostalgia, with its concomitant belief that the rare quality of small-town life depicted in our popular culture is fast disappearing, is founded in part on our sense of its familiarity—regardless of whether we have ever lived in such a setting. We *know* Suburbia. Such spaces are sentimentalized and commonly depicted in popular media and in twentieth-century film and literature as the locations of "real" community: shared values, common goods, and an absence of fear.[4]

Towns like Suburbia are also, however, relatively homogenous spaces, where community identity appears on the surface to be both obvious and unified, in part because "difference" is less visually present and power relations are often less disorderly—less openly contested—than in more heterogeneous communities. But while such tensions and struggles may be more subtly articulated in places like Suburbia, difference is no less widely understood as dangerous. In fact, in such culturally idealized spaces, it is the *absence* of difference that is often deemed responsible for those shared values and common goods, as well as the collective sense of security enjoyed by residents. Therefore, a seemingly civil, but ongoing, concerted effort to eradicate difference and its markers is often waged aggressively and effectively within smaller, relatively homogenous communities—and nowhere are such efforts more apparent today than in the schools, where the community's greatest hopes, as well as its worst fears, reside.

II. Suburbia County, Ohio

Suburbia County's rural townships, as well as the small city of Suburbia (the seat of Suburbia County), have become suburbs of a nearby metropolitan area. Suburbia County's rapid population increase (growing over 20 percent in the past ten years), housing boom, and subsequent immediate need for schools to accommodate the children of the working professionals moving into the area indicate how quickly the county is changing from a quiet, rural area devoted to regional manufacturing enterprises and family farming to a quaint, wealthy suburb of several surrounding urban centers. The 2000 census ranks Suburbia County in the top ten fastest growing counties in Ohio, a fact that is reflected not only in population but in construction, per capita income levels, and tax revenue, as well as school construction and funding. While the state population was 11.5 percent black, the county was less than 1 percent black.

Private home construction increased more than 100 percent in Suburbia County in the 1980s. During that same period, new homes in all of Ohio increased by 43 percent, while, nationally, new home construction *decreased* by 0.4 percent. Suburbia County has conspicuously outstripped both state and national growth rates regarding population, private home construction, and average home value—a figure that speaks not only to growth but to the economic status of the majority of families relocating to Suburbia County.

All available indicators suggest that Suburbia County enjoys an impressively strong economy as compared to both state and national data. The relatively high income and construction levels and the increasing value of the homes being built and occupied by Suburbia's growing number of residents translate into increased revenues for the county. And though the tax rate is low compared to statewide figures—another reason why residents find Suburbia County an attractive place to live—the revenue generated from property taxes is comparatively high, providing the kind of funding for the county's schools that urban areas, hit hard by white flight and a shrinking tax base, cannot approximate.

Suburbia County's housing boom, rapid increase in private home value, and steadily rising per capita income, as well as its related property tax revenue, have helped to create a context within which we can examine the community's efforts to construct and maintain a singular and unified identity and investigate the degree to which residents of the city of Suburbia feel a sense of ownership and agency in regard to their schools, as they strive to shape and control the institutional spaces in which their children spend the vast majority of their time.

III. Suburbia High School

Suburbia High School was established in the late nineteenth century, but by the mid-1990s it had long since ceased to accommodate the growing number of students in attendance; it was clear that SHS could not keep up with the alarming rate of new student enrollment as more and more families moved into the area. Suburbia County was growing and so was its high school population.[5] In 1996, therefore, members of the community began a two-year-long series of public discussions and focus groups designed to find a solution to the problem of their now inadequate high school structure. Eventually, participants decided upon "a set of core community values" that would guide all future decisions about the school—decisions regarding whether or not they would renovate, add on, or start from scratch with a new property; the design of the school itself; how spending was to be approached; and to what degree the community would both participate and benefit. Participants in the discussions determined that their highest priority was "to maintain a sense of community."[6]

In addition, "members from the school district and the community [that] gathered in a variety of forums" identified "a personalized education for all students," "equity," "long-term solutions," "frugality," and "community involvement" as the underlying vision for SHS. One of the biggest challenges faced by the community and planners was how to retain one high school—deemed preferable in order to allow the entire community to invest in a single school for all students, regardless of residential location and income level—and still provide a personalized education.[7]

Much research and discussion later—as well as an initial set of proffered plans that was discarded as unsatisfactory—the "House Concept" was agreed upon. The architectural design that was finally approved utilizes a "school-within-a-school" concept in which

> the building is divided into two Neighborhoods each comprised of two Houses. Each House serves approximately 600 randomly assigned students in grades 9 through 12. Each House is staffed with its own House Principal, guidance department, and core academic teaching staff. . . . [The] goal is for students to remain in their House and Neighborhood to the greatest extent possible for all core academics.[8]

SHS had over 2,000 students enrolled for the 2003–4 academic year, divided into four Houses and distributed relatively evenly across grades 9–12. And while on paper this appears to address community concerns about discipline, order, and safety in this overwhelming population of teenagers housed in a single building, teachers and students express doubt about its effectiveness in the interviews discussed in the following section. Two problems were identified with the House Concept by interviewees: first, 600 students in each house are still too many for adults to know individually and to keep under surveillance in a manner sufficient to quell fears about unknown students; and second, students do not remain in their House and Neighborhood to the extent imagined in the school's planning stages.[9]

In addition to the House Concept, Suburbia appealed to residents for support with a vision of "an educational facility that would be closely integrated with community programs." Suburbia city schools therefore initiated a series of partnerships with public and private community institutions that have turned the school into a "'hub' for the community" that provides a central location for all residents to participate in educational, social, and performing arts activities.[10] Residents were persuaded that the expensive new school's "value" to the community was therefore not restricted to high school students and their families; the value of the new school could potentially be extended to everyone in the community, through access to the school and its health and recreational facilities, as well as through its partnership with the city of Suburbia.[11]

In addition to classrooms, the school facility includes science labs and prep rooms, business labs, special education classrooms and tutorial rooms, project labs, computer labs, and large and small group instruction areas. SHS has partnered with nearby Central City University in a distance learning (DL) program; SHS has several DL-dedicated classrooms and currently has over $3 million invested in instructional technology, including voice, video, and data technology infrastructure.[12]

The newly completed school facility includes two theater-auditoriums with a total seating capacity of over 1,600: the larger auditorium with separate public access "seats 1,200 on the floor and balcony, and includes an orchestra pit, full fly loft, dressing rooms, green room, scene shop, and storage." A "renovated 400-seat theater is used as a drama classroom, rehearsal hall, and performance stage" and includes "orchestra, band, and choir spaces" for the purposes of instruction, rehearsal, and sound control. The Suburbia County Performing Arts Foundation has partnered with the school, booking live productions and providing "workshops with guest artists" for both students and community members.[13]

SHS is also partnered with a local television cable channel, enabling the new school addition to "incorporate a television studio located adjacent to the media center and multimedia production studio," which is used by both station staff and the school's journalism program. These spaces "provide another opportunity to integrate student curriculum and activities with those of a community-based operation."[14]

The large recreation center is utilized by both the community and SHS students and is supported in part by the membership dues paid by community members.[15] It includes a competition pool with "a diving well and spectator seating for 280"; a leisure pool "visually open to the outdoors," with a whirlpool, slide, and other features; an elevated track; a 24,000-square-foot field house with basketball, volleyball, and tennis courts; batting and golf cages; aerobic rooms; fitness and weightlifting room; physical therapy rooms; "community rooms" available to rent for social events; a food service area, a senior center, and an area for babysitting.[16] The local hospital, including its sports medicine and rehabilitation services, is also partnered with the high school and has facilities in the recreation center. Attaching this community recreational center to the school's physical education facilities, argued educational and city and county political leaders, expands students' access to quality health care, as well as nearby residents' access to both physical education and therapy.[17]

Clearly, these partnerships reinforce and even increase the level of residents' commitment to a first-rate educational facility for students—as well as their willingness to pay for its construction and ongoing maintenance. How much less likely that willingness might have been without granting community access to SHS's facilities is difficult to gauge but equally difficult to dismiss when one actually visits the school; what is not captured by these lists of SHS's partnerships, equipment, and square footage is the powerful visual impact of the facility itself.

We made regular trips to SHS over a four-month period in order to interview students, parents, teachers, counselors, and principals. The grandeur of the school complex is undeniable, and we felt aesthetic appreciation, approval, even awe on our first visit—and those feelings did not entirely disappear, even after many visits and much time spent within the school. In our thirty-five years each of nearly constant presence in school buildings (as students, parents of students, and teachers), we have rarely been in an educational facility as beautiful, spacious, functional, or technologically advanced in design or execution.

The size of the school, from the outside, is rather astonishing, regardless of one's prior knowledge of its square footage and the number of students and teachers who fill it every day. It is simply enormous. Set a short distance from the town square on gently rolling acres whose athletic fields are surrounded by trees on the edges of the ample property, the building is constructed of a warm sandstone-colored block characterized by an uneven, pale terra-cotta hue. The two-plus stories (ceilings are higher than standard on both floors) are made dramatic by huge off-white pillars at the entrances; wide, sweeping staircases; and windows that span twenty feet or more in height. Stately rooflines and banks of heavy glass doors indicate entrances to the school, and each time we walked inside, we were struck by the beauty of the materials used here: imported-tile floors, richly veined marble walls, and pillars supporting twenty-foot ceilings in the many common areas—all in pale, warm colors made sumptuous by the natural light pouring in from the soaring windows (sunlight is no small luxury in this region). The hallways are wide, and windows are seemingly everywhere in this institutional space—windows looking outside from classrooms, hallways, and public spaces such as the cafeterias and the Senior Commons and windows looking into the classrooms from the hallways. The television production studios and DL classrooms are plush (carpet, seating, soundproofing) and color-coordinated, as well as technologically impressive: everything is new and state-of-the-art; there is no evidence of duct tape anywhere.

It is in this setting that we spoke at length with many and varied members of the SHS community in an effort to discover what life is like there—what problems, conflicts, and approaches to conflict are constitutive of life under the gleaming surface of this wealthy community's impressive new school.

IV. Narrative Constructions of Life at SHS

The narrative accounts of life at SHS—life as experienced by various members of subgroups within the school culture—are a valuable tool in exploring the ways in which conflicts over both community and individual identity simultaneously resist and reproduce larger cultural discourses about difference and fear. The experiences of those members of SHS, and the stories they tell about them, help to construct individual and group realties at the school and thus have material consequences for official school policy, formal and informal strategies in struggles over agency and control, and myriad subversive behaviors that occur within and across groups.

Every member of the SHS community we interviewed—students, teachers, parents, counselors, and principals—initially responded in virtually the same way, and without hesitation, to the question "What kinds of conflicts do you have here at SHS?" There appears to be a general consensus that physical violence at SHS is rare—and, even then, not "serious"—and thus not perceived as a major problem.[18] The conflicts identified by all parties as most common occur between students, and these were characterized by the interviewees as either emotional, interpersonal conflicts based on sexual or romantic relationships or as conflicts between groups and/or individuals based on perceived "differences." The latter were described most often by students and teachers alike as "harassment."

It is interesting that, despite the number of interviewees who identified heterosexual romantic relationships among students as one of the most common conflicts at SHS, very few of the interviewees had much to say about them. One teacher noted that "the most common types of conflicts are personal conflicts between the students. Boyfriend-girlfriend things are *huge,* huge. And at this age, they can be catastrophic."[19] Several students discussed "conflict" in terms of boys fighting with boys—either physically fighting or threatening to fight—over girls and of girls fighting with girls, almost exclusively verbally, over boys. Two female students mentioned in their interviews a time when they had been upset at school and had cried over fighting with a boyfriend or breaking up, but they had little else to say. Such incidents appear to be accepted by students, as well as by parents, teachers, and administrators, as a normal part of adolescent life—upsetting at the time but not indicative of a serious social issue that needs to be resolved or eradicated in some way. The seeming lack of concern over what most described as the primary type of conflict students face, and some described with words such as *catastrophic*, makes sense only when we realize that these particular conflicts are seen as "normal" within a larger cultural context of heterosexual normativity, a cultural context in which "difference" is explained in bestsellers like *Men Are from Mars, Women Are from Venus*.[20] There is nothing to fear in the kind of "difference" represented in these conflicts, because boys and girls are partnering, unpartnering, and repartnering in sanctioned heterosexual relationships. Fear and conflict are narrated in very different ways, however, when heteronormativity is used as a disciplinary agent to ensure conformity, to reproduce existing social power hierarchies, and to erase other kinds of differences among students.

V. *Conflict and Sexuality*

The most common comments made by interviewees regarding student-to-student conflicts pointed specifically to normative pressures within student culture itself and the ways in which the term *harassment* is understood by all members of the SHS community as both a crime and a near-continual occurrence within the school. "I think we have some kids who put up with a tremendous amount of harassment," noted one teacher.[21] Each time an interviewee mentioned harassment as an ongoing, serious problem at SHS, we asked what type of harassment they had observed or experienced. The students' answers were revealing, identifying harassment as a response to class difference (as evidenced by consumer consumption or the lack thereof) and perceived homosexuality:

> *Usually kids get made fun of 'cause they talk weird, talk in a different way that might sound a little gayish. . . . [A guy like that] usually has a lot of friends that are girls, for some reason, I don't know why. . . . I think the guys*

> *are pretty much jealous, cause he gets a lot of girls. . . . Sometimes you get pushed.*[22]

When asked to elaborate on what "sounding a little gayish" meant, this student identified those male students who do not sound "you know, like guys" and suggested that most of the younger boys (fourteen- or fifteen-year old freshmen) "seemed gay." This student also volunteered that the way boys sound is only one of many characteristics that might mark one as gay; he observed that those boys who are not "high maintenance"—those who do not take special care with their appearance (those who have "weird hair") and those who do not wear "cool clothes"—might also be seen as "gay."[23] The word *gay* thus comes to mean much more than actual homosexuality (issues of age and physical development in defining both masculinity and sexuality, for example, as well as class and race, are a part of this wide-ranging, even contradictory method of determining who is "gay"), while still maintaining the normative power of the tag that is arguably the most devastating in boy culture.[24]

Teacher interviews confirmed this rather bleak picture: "I hear a lot of homophobic harassment going on among straight groups . . . in that they're using homophobic language and homophobic actions toward other students." This teacher noted that, in a homophobic student culture (reflecting a wider homophobic culture outside of the school), calling someone "gay" is a powerful tool. As long as homosexual men are "the targeted, hated [group]," whatever differences are lumped under the heading *gay* are potentially controllable because of the profound power inherent in the threat of being called gay—"it's the ultimate, horrible name tag for boys."[25]

VI. *Conflict and Class*

The enormous importance placed on physical appearance by contemporary youth culture is certainly not a revelation; in that sense, SHS is undoubtedly mainstream. The widespread access of so many of its students, however, to relatively large amounts of disposable income—which is subsequently spent on fashionable clothes, jewelry, and other accessories (including, arguably, cars) and the costly maintenance of fashionable hairstyles, manicures, and so on—increases the pressure here to "look good." As a group—and this was more pronounced among the girls than the boys—students confirmed that the pressure to "keep up" with fashionable spending and appearance, and the ridicule, alienation, shame, and fear of isolation associated with either an inability or unwillingness to do so, was one of their greatest conflicts at SHS. "People don't like the way you dress, so they make fun of you, beat you up—well, not really, but like shove you around, stuff like that," remarked one student.[26] "You just get picked on," confirmed another student, shrugging. "The type of things you wear, like—if you're not high maintenance, you get made fun of. . . . Not wearing cool clothes, or your hair's weird."[27] Both male and female students agreed: "I think a lot of it is physical appearance. . . . I've never heard anybody be like, *Oh, she's so poor,* but I think it'll show by the way somebody dresses, almost like you can tell if somebody has money or not, and people get made fun of for the way they dress, like all the time."[28]

As disturbing as this wholesale acceptance and reflection of our larger culture's focus on consumerism and physical beauty is, perhaps more disturbing are the ways in which students have internalized the school's attempts at more positive messages regarding values, self-esteem, and personal goals and *twisted their meaning* to reinforce consumerist fashion as their primary value, source of self-esteem, and identity:

> *Everyone's always competing with each other to be better at something, or dress better, or just be the best at something, and so I think it's always a struggle trying to make yourself be the best person you can be. . . . I think if girls see someone else wearing something cuter, they're like, "Oh, I have to go shopping and get that too or They're wearing my shoes that I got," or, you know it's just always like a battle.*[29]

This student has conflated the notion that you should attempt to be "the best person you can be," to try to achieve your personal best, with competing with other girls to own and wear the newest, cutest clothing—and that winning that competition is where one's self-esteem properly lies.

The students at SHS—perhaps the girls, especially—embody the concept of cultural reproduction: they are at once both the products (even victims) of a consumerist culture devoted to physical beauty and sexualized images of the female body and its most avid devotees—intent upon "winning" its inherent, never-ending competition, as well as reproducing it, and even ratcheting it up by constructing it as self-improvement and goal-oriented. Many of these teenagers have the economic means to fully participate in the reproduction of materialist culture that values purchasing power and the visual image above all else—and they do. Some of the teachers at SHS spoke to this issue, but they focused less on what students' access to wealth means in terms of shallow devotion to sexual beauty and fashion and more on what such approaches to living in the world might mean in a larger context—a context where spending a lot of money on clothes is not the worst consequence of privilege and overconsumption but rather where the worst consequence is an inability to comprehend, to empathize, and to recognize human dignity and value in those who are not equally privileged. One teacher claimed that "there's a huge sense of entitlement with the kids here. They feel like they're owed."[30] Most teachers (as well as counselors and principals) agreed. Some noted that students' sense of entitlement cannot be separated from their parents', who are ultimately culpable:

> *There's among some of them a terrible sense of entitlement, so quite frankly I think a lot of them don't give a damn. . . . I think we have—and I'm speaking honestly here—we have some parents who are incredibly self-serving, that what's good for my kid is the only thing that matters. . . . we have an element—a strong element—that is very self-absorbed.*[31]

The sense of entitlement that teachers note, however, does not come without a price. The notion that these students are deserving is accompanied by pressure to *be* deserving, and the anxiety and even resulting health problems are worrisome to teachers, who see parents' unrealistic expectations of their children as a significant problem at SHS: "We're Suburbia, so every kid is above average, and will go to Harvard, and not only that, but every kid will also be a Broadway star in his or her spare time. . . . I don't know any kids that I'm teaching now who are currently allowed to be kids."[32] Such concerns, however, were briefly mentioned in the interviews, and then only by a few. Most students, and some teachers and parents, focused on harassment among students.

The harassment so often spoken of by the interviewees typically centered around the ways in which difference, as such, was most likely to be identified within this relatively homogenous group: sexuality and class. Such harassment thus most often took the form of informal social sanctions embodied in the socially devastating accusations of being gay and being poor and therefore unattractive. These normative mechanisms were used to maintain a strict definition of what the community values most in personal and group identity: being male, heterosexual, rich, and—if one is female—sexy. Being gay (read as some version of a subordinate male identity) and not being rich and therefore not fashionable are the visible markers of difference at SHS—not race, where so few of the population are nonwhite. Race was accordingly conflated by several interviewees with class, a somewhat less tangible, much more socially acceptable framework for talking about difference and for discriminating against it. One student recounted that "two kids got in a fight. I don't know what was wrong, but they got in a fight. One was my friend and he had, like, all these friends—they were black, and they came in and just started beating the other white guy up. . . . It wasn't race-related, it was, like, the ghetto people."[33] This student actively dismisses the possibility of a racial component in a fight in which "all these [black guys]" beat up "a white guy," claiming that it was a "ghetto" thing. The implication for him in using the term *ghetto* is that the black guys and their white friend were identifiable as a group because of economic class, because of where they live in town; his seeming ignorance of the layers of racial meaning in the term *ghetto*—in addition to its economic connotations—epitomizes the near erasure of race as a publicly recognizable, active social force at SHS, because of the near erasure of nonwhite bodies from the school.

This student, in conflating race and class, touches on an important point: that the categories of race and class (as well as gender) do cut one another in important ways that require attention. One teacher explicitly noted that complication, those additional layers of meaning and experience:

> *Of course, racism exists here. There's a big huge line and that line is also economic. . . . I think it's very underground, it's very subtle. We haven't had too many white-black conflicts, but there's an underlying tone. There's a place where this ethnic group goes and stands in the morning, and that's where they hang out—it's almost more isolation than . . . again, it's economic. The kids with the best economic backgrounds will be the kids that will be involved in all the after-school activities. And the kids whose parents struggle, whose parents maybe work and can't come and pick them up for an after-school activity, or the kid will end up walking home, I mean there's more economic discrepancy than you may see at first glance if you walk around the hall.*[34]

VII. *Conflict and Race*

For the most part, when asked to enumerate and discuss the types of conflicts that occur at SHS, most students did not mention race at all; in fact, students declared, as a group, that race is not really a problem here. Teachers seemed split between seeing racial conflict as nonexistent at SHS and seeing race as an ongoing source of conflict despite the relatively small nonwhite population. Among the teachers and parents, a significant number believed that racial difference itself—meaning the physical presence or proximity of nonwhites—is the cause of racial tension and conflict. A few were explicit in their view that black students themselves deliberately cause racial conflict.

One teacher we interviewed discussed race and racism—and the ways in which their pressures are experienced—in both the school and the larger community of Suburbia. This teacher is one of a very small number of nonwhite teachers in the county. He spoke of living and working in a community with so few black families and teachers:

> *So the minority population is small. I don't know all of the history behind all of this, because we weren't born and raised here, we've been here for about ten years, but I know that there's some tension and some [racial] issues at the school, and in the community—you know, it was that kind of good ol' boy network kind of thing. . . . And I don't know if they really, I mean, they give lip service to it, but I've never seen any tangible evidence of activity to say that they want otherwise. They'll all come back and say, "Well, we can't really get minorities to come here." And so, I start wondering, just how much do you really want that? You said you wanted to reflect the community, and it does not.*

The sense of this teacher's lack of advocacy in his profession and community is apparent, as are the emotional effects of this kind of racial isolation:

> *I get lonely sometimes, I mean not . . . people are nice to me. I feel respected, I feel loved. . . . I told somebody, I said, "Who knows, maybe you'll get another African-American teacher in here and we might not even like each other!" [Laughs] But boy, give me a chance to try. I don't know, there are just cultural things, sometimes, that you want to talk about, and bounce off, and share . . . so my wife and I, we just share with each other. I mean, we are*

out in the community. We're involved, very involved. My son goes here, he's very involved, but it's just, you know, just that element that's missing.[35]

Other teachers, as well as some students, talked about race when asked directly whether race was a factor in any of the conflicts at SHS. Some saw racial difference itself as racial conflict—the presence of blacks as racial conflict. One teacher noted that there is, certainly, "diversity" within the student population, "but we don't have a big minority population here, so [racial conflict] is not something that you see. . . . We've been able to control those feelings, which is a good thing."[36] A student suggested that as a merely pragmatic matter, SHS is better off with its largely white student body:

I think it [SHS's homogenous population] makes things easier, like lots of times you won't have to deal with race and whatever, 'cause there's few kids that are actually different. And, really we're just like the poster child for the white suburban community, and that just makes life easier. . . . You go to other schools, like up in inner-city schools, there'll be more conflict. I think that lots of times that is a result of diversity.[37]

The sense here is that diversity exists in the world and that diversity causes conflict. The way to avoid conflict, then, is not to conceptualize and deal with diversity in a new way but rather to isolate and separate (segregate) groups along the lines that diversity is drawn and understood (in this case, along racial lines) and to remove difference from the sight and experience of those who belong to the dominant group—that is, the unmarked group, the default, the norm without which we cannot even conceptualize difference or Other.

Others we interviewed took this notion of difference, or of diversity itself as the problem, a step further by suggesting that any racial tensions or conflicts at SHS are at least in part caused by blacks themselves—either because black students have developed an understandable paranoia, a defensiveness because racism exists and affects them, or because they have internalized a victim mentality and prefer to complain rather than work. Some interviewees believe that racial conflicts are caused by black students' insistence that all conflicts they are involved in are about race, when in fact they are about something else altogether—in other words, black students play "the race card." One teacher, who seemed saddened by the lack of progress made in addressing racial conflict, observed that over the thirty-six years she has taught in Suburbia County, black students have become "more and more alienated" from what she calls the "center" of the school. She claims that "they don't buy into us at all; they don't buy into us academically, they don't buy into us in terms of sports, in terms of music . . . and it seems to me that there's almost a paranoia, a self-defense mechanism that sets up among the black kids, and if I were black I think I would probably be part of that, too."[38]

One black teacher at SHS talked about his own experience as a boy growing up in the South and the ways in which he was taught the importance of education, especially for a black child: "I grew up with this understanding that education is a way out, a way of success, a way forward, it's something once you get can't anybody take it away from you, you know, that kind of thing, and I think we've lost that."[39] His bootstrap narrative reflects a larger Horatio Alger, American Dream myth about hard work and meritocracy that has proved useful in denying systemic discrimination and in placing the responsibility for poverty and community despair squarely on the shoulders of those individuals and communities most affected by racism. This does not mean that individual stories of hard work and reward or instances of social equity and class mobility are untrue or do not happen; what it does mean is that the inductive leap from observable moments of individual success to a general statement that a system of meritocracy is in place and functioning properly is far too great to be persuasive.

The bootstrap narrative serves an important role, however, in constructing a partial explanation for why this particular black teacher is working at SHS:

> *And so they [black students] continue to get in this excuse-making mode, and you know, if you look hard enough, you'll find prejudices. They're there. But I don't run around looking. I really don't. If it comes up, we deal with it, we try to move on, but I don't go around looking for it, I don't play this race card: "Well, you know the reason why this happened to me is because I'm black." And I know here in the last two–three years I heard a lot of that from the small minority population we have. As a matter of fact, I was called prejudiced against black students by black students. Because I didn't want to take any mess, I'm about business; I love to help, but I don't have time for that kind of nonsense. Get a life! Let's do what you need to do and move on. You don't like it here, then do some positive things, change it, and help somebody else, and let's move on. And they would just rather sit and com-*

plain, and you know, kids do it, it doesn't matter what race—but blame-shift, there's always this finger pointing there, and I don't have time for that. If you make a grade in my class, I give it to you. If you don't make the grade, I give it to you. I have lots of tissues, I'll cry with you, but you got the grade. That's what you get. And so, the few black students I had, some passed and some didn't . . . but they said I was prejudiced against the black kids, and the white kids said I was prejudiced against the white kids, so I said, "I guess I don't like anybody, do I?" And you know what? I'm OK with sometimes having to stand by myself. I'm OK with it.[40]

This teacher is in an untenable position: the fact of his race isolates him to some degree within his community, and the professional and personal attitudes he holds regarding race, work, and merit make him acceptable—even desirable—to school officials and the larger community, while alienating him from those who might argue that sometimes things *do* happen to you just because you're black.[41]

One parent appeared to try very hard in her interview to never use any form of the word *race* while conveying her opinion that racial problems at SHS are caused by black students playing the race card:

We do have some African-American students. They oftentimes—I don't want to say start things more than the other students—sometimes they like to see things that way, if you know what I mean. You know, they'll make something out of it that may not necessarily have that meaning because there might be an African-American student involved in a conflict, whether it be with a staff member, or with another student, or what not, when it may not really be that.[42]

Another parent explicitly identified the ways in which racial tensions, conflicts, and discrimination in the larger culture outside of schools necessarily become a part of what happens inside schools. Her job, she said, is to visit high school music programs in the area when they are ready to begin a fund-raising program that the school has purchased from the company she works for. The program she sells offers a product—such as candy—that the students in the music program sell at school and in the community, and the company and the music program split the proceeds. She told us, however, that schools with large black student populations are treated differently by her company: "I do notice that the company seems to have a different policy for urban schools that have a lot of black students. . . . The suburban white schools can do their fund-raisers, sell all the product, and give the company the money at the end. The black schools have to buy the product up front." After telling us this, she seemed to recognize the implications of her story and half-heartedly commented that the policy difference "could be because the company had had real problems in collecting money afterwards from black schools"—the policy, in other words, if based on something "real," like a late payment or nonpayment from a black school, may be understood as nonracist when applied to any black school.[43] The assumption here is that blacks are held accountable as a group for an individual member's behavior and that accountability is not a form of racism.

VIII. Approaches to Conflict

Official Strategies: Tensions between Therapy and Punishment

In the course of the more than thirty interviews we conducted at SHS, it became clear that some programs for conflict prevention and resolution do exist but that there is more than a little confusion as to what programs exist, which ones used to exist but are now defunct, how those programs are utilized, and what role teachers and administrators are supposed to play in helping students to take advantage of those programs. There was also some cynicism—on the part of both students and adults—regarding the effectiveness of such programs: "We have had some peer mediation programs that I think have had some success, although again, it's generally the kids who handle conflict well that get involved in those programs."[44]

Most teachers understood the administration's disciplinary policies to reflect—when deemed appropriate—a dialogic, respectful approach to conflict and rule breaking. One teacher noted that while

> *some teachers probably think they [administrators] need to be gorillas, you know, that come down hard . . . for the most part they're not. They sit and they talk to kids, and they talk to parents. . . . we don't issue a lot of out-of-school suspensions, because that's just self-defeating. How do you get a kid involved in a school if you say, "You're not allowed to come here"?*[45]

This approach was commonly reflected in teachers' descriptions of the ways in which they try to prevent and resolve conflicts in their classrooms, but teachers did not always agree that the administration took such an approach in practice—or, indeed, any approach: "In my classroom, it's more of a creation of an environment that's safe, and open, and understanding. But school-wide, I see only reaction, I see no prevention." This teacher considered the administration's efforts to maintain order and reduce conflicts as largely ineffective, primarily because "the perpetrator is not being taught any differently, it's just an outright consequence, either an after-school detention or an in-school suspension. Those are effective consequences *only* if there's some teaching involved. . . . So I don't see those as very effective, but that's what's used."[46]

Another teacher had a unique perspective on the relatively few disciplinary problems that SHS deals with: "I think it's luck," she said. "I don't really think that we're such great people-managers that we could take this staff or the administration and go into an inner-city school and have it be like this." She went on to describe the kinds of problems the students had to deal with at the urban school where she used to teach and contrasted those problems with the security and comfort of SHS students' lives:

> *Our kids, if they want to eat breakfast, they can eat breakfast. If it's cold out, they can put warm clothes on. The majority do not have the problems that I think would provoke serious, serious conflicts in school. . . . When I subbed inner-city, those kids had problems. I had a girl that came in that prostituted herself to take care of her siblings, in Columbus. I mean, that's a problem, that's a kid that's going to come to school, and if they don't have their homework done, they could care less. Kids here, 95 percent of the kids at this school, have no idea that things like that exist—they may know, but they really don't know.*[47]

The tensions between a gentle, dialogic approach to conflict and rule breaking and a more traditional, disciplinary approach within SHS became more apparent with each successive interview of teachers and administrators. "We try to say things we think make them feel good when that's not what they need. I don't think kids have a problem with feeling good about themselves. I think sometimes they think more of themselves than they ought to."[48] This teacher's sense that coddling students by attending to their self-esteem is unnecessary and ineffective was echoed by one of the House principals, who argued that "what many schools are doing that is not effective are these character lessons, usually in elementary school. Respect, integrity . . . the kids aren't picking it up. . . . it's supposed to be the age of tolerance, but it's not. It's really the age of intolerance. I think what we're doing is ineffective and there's got to be a better way."[49]

Some teachers focused on what they see as the ineffectiveness of a punishment approach to discipline: "There's a ton of in-schools," observed one teacher. "Some are conflicts with teachers and students. Some are student-to-student conflicts. Some are just being late to class or truancy, stuff like that. I don't see it helping."[50] Most students appear to agree. One student observed that, when students fight and counselors or principals instruct them to do or say specific things in an attempt to resolve the issue, it doesn't really work:

> *You don't feel like anything's, like, changed, or better, so you still have like the same internal things. . . . And then, like, giving students suspension or in-school suspensions, or ASDs [after school detention], or whatever, doesn't resolve anything—yeah, sure, it punishes us for that, which is what needs to happen, but it doesn't resolve anything; they're gonna have even more anger after that 'cause they got punished for it.*[51]

Even though this student has accepted that punishment "needs to happen," he does not believe that punishment resolves the conflict. Others, however, believe such tactics do work: "I think they work. I think they put fear in kids' minds, not to really mess around here at school. If they're gonna do it, do it somewhere else. You know, a lot of kids won't really start things in school because of that, 'cause they're afraid of the repercussions."[52]

Some attempts have been made to integrate these two approaches. Several teachers told us that the House guidance counselors organize and facilitate support groups for students who might need help—both as a therapeutic service and as a way to prevent and resolve conflicts. Among those groups are a women's group that focuses on stress-related problems, drug and alcohol abuse groups, a trauma-support group, and an anger-management group. The groups are voluntary but are sometimes bundled together with a (reduced) punishment on condition of attendance. One teacher told us that she didn't think voluntary attendance was very good. She said she distributed the flier that describes the groups, asking students to check those groups they might be interested in. "I gave it to my first-period class and they all checked the box that said None' and handed them back to me," she said. "I think the kids think that if they go to one of those groups that they'll end up with a bunch of burn-outs. Or kids who, you know, do bad things. Like it's cool to have pressure and to talk about how much *pressure* you're under, but it's not cool to acknowledge that it's governing your life so much that you need to do something about it."[53]

Official strategies aimed at helping students prevent and resolve the problems they face are often seen from a different perspective by students than administrators might expect.[54] For example, sincere attempts to construct an open and inviting atmosphere in the office, so that students will feel comfortable approaching teachers, counselors, and administrators for help, are not so easily accomplished:

> *I really don't like when teachers and administrators say that their door is always open, it's completely confidential, because it can't be confidential. If somebody else knows your problem, they will pass judgment—they can't just keep it all to themselves, they will have to tell somebody. Eventually you know people will find out about your secrets if you tell somebody. The best way to keep a secret between three people is if two of them are dead, you know? If you tell one person, like a teacher or a counselor, they're gonna tell somebody else.*[55]

This student's concerns with confidentiality were powerfully validated in an interview with a parent who also happens to be an office employee at SHS. In her discussion of the House Concept at SHS, this parent confided her desire to help, if the opportunity ever presented itself, by passing on information that she might have inadvertently received about a student whom she would determine was "troubled":

> *You know some students are troubled and they don't ever speak up, and those are the ones that you worry about, you know, how do you reach them? But if you get to know people, it's more likely that you'll catch some. If I would hear something or get word of something I can share it with them [administrators], or, you know a student may say something to my daughter, and she would pass it on to me and I would try to see if there's anything that I can do, being an employee here, if I can help in any way, and I think a lot of us feel that way.*[56]

Despite her good intentions, this woman's very language (hoping to "catch" some of the kids who have opted not to share their problems with school officials) serves to confirm students' fears that teachers, counselors, principals, and other adult school workers may not understand or agree with students about the nature of the conflicts they experience or what the best course of action may be. And while a student may not have broken any rules, he is clearly always a potential disciplinary object, always under surveillance, without even the autonomy to define and gauge the severity of the conflicts he faces or whom to approach and when, should he decide to go to a school official.

One student noted that, while the school no doubt means well, its efforts to get students "thinking" as a way to prevent conflicts often fall flat. "I guess they *try* to do stuff to help kids deal with conflict," she conceded. "I remember a couple of weeks ago we had an officer come in and talk about school violence and stuff, but if somebody wanted to hurt somebody they would go through with it if they really wanted to. . . . they probably won't change it a whole lot by, you know, having another speaker come in."[57] "We did have Peace Week," another student said. Students received "stars" if they were observed performing a "good deed," and at the end of the week the stars were put into a hat, and a few were drawn randomly for prizes. Every day there was "a different fact about peace, like about road rage, or whatever," she recalled. "I don't know if students took it seriously, though, you know, they were just like *Oh, Peace Week.* It could have been, like, anything-week. I don't think they really thought '*Peace.*' They're just like, *Oh, Peace Week* [Laughs]."[58] One parent, when asked what strategies the school employs to prevent or resolve conflicts, drew a blank for a moment. Then something occurred to her: "I see signs around saying *No Bullying Zones,* and stuff like that, so I guess that's what they're doing."[59]

Extracurriculars—officially sanctioned and supported activities outside of academic and other for-credit courses—are a part of the informal structure that SHS employs to maximize student investment in the school and to minimize conflict. The kind of group identity and sense of belonging that extracurricular activities can foster is seen across groups as almost exclusively positive. Some teachers expressed concern, as discussed earlier, that these activities were not as accessible to all students as they should be, and this resulted in negative consequences for particular groups of students. One teacher noted,

> *We have some kids to whom school is everything, I mean, you know, that's where their self-worth is—they run, they're in honors classes, they're in the choir, they buy into it a hundred percent. But then we have a whole bunch of kids who haven't bought into anything, and I think that we need to get them to buy into something, find some things that are meaningful for them here.*[60]

All of the parents interviewed felt that extracurricular activities were an unambiguously effective way to keep students busy, productive, and out of trouble. Students had mixed reactions; one student thought that it depended on which club or activity one was involved in: "If you're, like, in *chess* club or something, you'll most likely get made fun of. . . . Those people are kind of on the weird side."[61]

Informal Strategies: Subgroups and Subversion

Our interviews revealed that teachers often subvert officially sanctioned policies and strategies for dealing with students, rule breaking, and discipline. One teacher told us that "there was a movement three or four years ago where we were all supposed to be in the hall . . . *you should be walking the halls between classes, we're taking the halls back,* you know, *the kids aren't going to be doing whatever they want in the halls,* and it was this *huge* deal." Without voicing any objections—even, for the most part, to each other—the teachers simply let some time pass, and things calmed down, and the teachers never increased the amount of time they were already spending policing the halls or altered their behavior regarding surveillance of the students.[62] Instances of teachers quietly doing what they believe is right, defensible, and effective in direct opposition to official school policy appear to be common. As one teacher told us,

> *I decided twenty-five years ago I will never give a detention. I think a detention is an absolutely stupid thing. I say to you, "You're late to my class, here's a detention, now sit down and be positive." . . . You know, we'll give a kid two hundred detentions, and it's not working, and at some point you say, Hm, if you've tried it two hundred times and it hasn't worked, what makes you think that two hundred and one will work?*[63]

Other teachers choose to devote class time to issues that they feel transcend the lesson plan of the day in terms of importance—and they see such moments as crucial to students' educations: "When things are not respectful, I expect a conversation or some sort of context to be created for a conversation about why things are not being respectful," declared one teacher. "So it takes class time, but I think that's important class time in the long run."[64]

Some teachers refuse to accept the role of disciplinarian and insist, by just quietly doing it, that their job is to teach their subject—period. One woman claims she rarely sees students behaving badly or breaking school rules. "I don't see much of that," she said. "I mean, I'm sure it happens around me, but I don't see it. I guess I try and make a point not to see the kids in a situation where that might occur, which I guess is kind of a cowardly thing to do, but after five years of cafeteria duty and seeing kids at their *ugliest,* and seeing them at their best in my classroom, I shouldn't have to see them in that way."[65] She has refused to include in her professional identity the roles of police officer, truant officer, or disciplinary authority; she has decided that she is a teacher, and teach is all she does at SHS. Other teachers object to additional duties on other grounds. One man told us that before the new building was complete, teachers—who are generally resigned to working in cramped spaces and don't mind "sharing a lot of stuff"—reached a point where they had "made due" for too long, and their "collective response to any administrative request was, *You know what? You're asking me to do more. I don't have any more I can do. I've done all I can do.*"[66]

Students—not surprisingly—are also at work within the school, variously supporting and undercutting school policy and strategy. Sometimes this is done in an attempt to construct and maintain some autonomy, some agency, and to find pleasure and satisfaction in those things they deem valuable; other times such subversion is enacted simply because school adult-officials do not understand that what they are asking students to do is impossible or ill-advised within students' social codes.[67] To tell is to support—even escalate—the increasingly punitive school culture within which students must operate. The most common example offered by students we interviewed was that while teachers, counselors, and principals all encouraged and expected students to tell the adults when they were experiencing any sort of conflict with another student, all students were reluctant, at best, to do so. Some of the administrators and teachers understood this, but all seemed at a loss as to how they might circumvent it. "The kids don't want to tell on each other. And they don't want to get in trouble by all the rest of their friends, they don't want it to escalate to even worse because they did go to an adult, they don't want to take all the BS from their friends that they ran and told somebody," one guidance counselor acknowledged.[68] Students confirmed her suspicions: "They could be seen as a tattletale or something like that, and that would create more conflict," agreed one teen.[69]

One teacher noted, "We have some terrible issues of hazing," and "that kind of stuff tends not to get into the adult realm."[70] "The psychological is not reported. . . . But any time it goes physical, that's when someone will talk to me, or when someone will report to any other adult," noted another.[71] Parents seemed to agree. One woman thought that students might seek out an adult for help only if it was a situation in which "somebody would really be hurt." She thought that students were more likely to talk to their friends at school if the problem was "just a relationship issue."[72] This parent's take on the relative importance of different kinds of conflicts and problems students experience may explain why students are unlikely to go to adults over any issues that do not involve the immediate threat of violence and physical harm: clearly, at least some adults see "relationship" issues as unimportant, conflicts where no one "would really be hurt." In addition to potentially being faced with an adult who thinks the problem you've come to her with is trivial, some students are likely intimidated by the power and authority embodied by school administrators. A guidance counselor admitted, "You know as an adult when I get called to the principal's office—and this is somebody that I work with every day—I still get nervous and my hands are sweating! It takes a lot for a kid to go to an office and tell somebody there's something wrong."[73] When kids opt not to go to adults to mediate their conflicts, they opt to go to others or to resolve them themselves, according to some teachers: "I'll tell you the real way that kids mediate their own conflicts: they go to a place called The Park and they beat the crap out of each other. That's what they do, and the conflict is somehow resolved—I don't think it's a good way, but I think a lot more conflicts than we think get resolved that way."[74]

It is worth considering here that not only is there a disconnect between how school officials and students define conflict and how these groups and various subgroups believe conflicts should be approached, but it is also likely that students don't always want to prevent or resolve conflicts—that they enjoy them, derive pleasure from them, and look forward to them. One student declared, "I don't think kids *care* about preventing them. I don't know if they thrive on it, but it just creates, like, controversy, so it's interesting, it's not the same-old same-old, you know."[75] Another student said that SHS was not a bad school, and in fact he kind of liked it. "I feel it's a nice environment," he said. "It's alright to get up to everyday just to see what's going on."[76] Most students felt that conflicts—particularly the physically violent ones—serve as events, as entertainment: "[Fights] happen, and you'll hear about it, like, *Oh, are you gonna go to the fight today*? Because it's like one of those things you go to, and you watch kids fight, and so you'll try not to let adults or teachers hear about it, because sometimes they do and they'll send police there and break it up."[77]

Some informal strategies that students adopt to organize their own social structure and to construct their identities relative to others actually mirror both the intent and the manifestation of official school strategies, policies, and organization. For example, while sanctioned extracurricular activities like sports teams, performance groups, and special interest clubs may be intended to satisfy multiple goals, such as fitness, skills enhancement, practical experience, and community service, they are also identifiable as a unified strategy recognized by the administration, teachers, and parents as serving primarily to invite student investment in the school and to create and support student identity through affiliation and commitment. Arguably, extracurricular groups often accomplish those goals. Some students, however, form and maintain their own groups for exactly the same purposes. These groups are viewed with suspicion and fear and in some contexts are understood as gangs. One student told this story:

> *There's different kinds of groups, there's like the punks, and then there's the preps, and you know the jocks, and just different things like that. There's this one that I think is almost like a gang, called the Elf-Gang, because they all have this one stupid T-shirt with a picture of elf on it. They all stick together—like if something happens to one of them, it'll happen to all of them and they'll go right after you. . . . they're kind of weird. They're kind of like punks, and . . . when they hear there's like an open house or a party or something, they'll go and they'll trash it. . . . they're really crazy. . . . And there's guys and girls in that group . . . just older kids, like eleventh and twelfth graders. . . . they get in fights and stuff, and they do really creepy stuff—do you know what sissy bridge is? Well, it's this bridge that's supposed to have this like haunted theme to it or whatever, I don't know. Well, my friend is in it [the Elf-Gang] and he jumped off it, and you can die, because underneath it is, like, a road! They do crazy, insane things like that, for the thrill I guess, I don't know.*[78]

Certainly, the behavior described by this student is not what any of us would wish for—the destruction of property and dangerous stunts performed for "thrills" are illegal and potentially deadly, respectively. But it is not difficult to imagine this same story being told—in fact, hundreds of versions of it have been told—in which the "Elf-Gang" is instead a group of high school football players. They have a uniform, and they stick together, and they party, and sometimes they do crazy physical things that could hurt them, and sometimes they trash people's stuff, and they find strength and power and confidence in numbers, and sometimes they are brutally violent. Not only is the formation and purpose of the unofficial groups the same as officially sanctioned school groups, but many of the social activities and consequences of the groups are the same as well. The football team, however—or the Chess Club—is probably not characterized by most as "crazy" or a "gang."

An examination of those formal and informal strategies within SHS culture reveals the tensions between a therapeutic and a disciplinary approach to order, and those tensions are exacerbated by proponents of both approaches, who believe that students, individual teachers, and the school itself are ill-served by the other approach. This results, as we have seen, in subversive attempts by both students and teachers to undercut administrative attempts to maintain order, to coerce students to self-revelation, to control teachers' movements and professional work, to define and categorize student conflicts, and to construct a unified identity for the student population that defines "different" as deviant, ensuring that what is unfamiliar will instill fear.

IX. Fear

The one constant in every interview, across populations at SHS, is fear—fear of the students inside the school building for one reason or another. Certainly, members of each subgroup at times expressed fears or concerns that overlapped with those of other groups, but each group (students, parents, teachers, and administrators) tended to focus primarily on a specific version of fear of the students themselves. Students fear their peers' social power, which, if directed at them, may result in ridicule, alienation, loneliness, and, ultimately, failure to achieve and maintain enough social status to make school life bearable, let alone happy. Parents are primarily afraid of drugs—not often articulated in the interviews as either "drug use," "drug dealing," or even the broader fear that the presence of drugs in their child's school might eventually lead to their own child becoming involved with drugs. Parents simply referred to "drugs" as a vague and amorphous fear of the existence of drugs themselves, in general, in the world and in all schools as a form of unacceptable power beyond their control. Teachers were markedly similar in their concerns about unknown, anonymous students who might turn SHS into another Columbine—and their related fear that those potentially violent students are unrecognizable, making prevention and accountability a virtual impossibility.

As students expressed their fear of their classmates, several things became clear. First, these young adults can be cruel, and their cruelties are deeply felt by those whom they hurt. Second, they are quite savvy in their ability to avoid either detection or a provable offense. One student described an ongoing problem with several other girls in the school who had been harassing her for several weeks with relentless phone calls.

> *I was getting anonymous phone calls from a private number—I can't prove who did it, even though I know. And of course they don't say "I'm going to kill you," which they could really get in trouble for. They say, "Why don't you go kill yourself" instead, because it's not a threat.*[79]

She went on to explain that her mother had hired a private tutor for the following semester and that she would not be returning to SHS after the winter break. "I'm actually leaving this school because of it. . . . I don't feel comfortable being here. . . . it affects the way that I work at school, it affects my concentration. I don't feel comfortable here."[80] Although no other students we interviewed spoke of leaving the school because they were afraid or were made so "uncomfortable" that they couldn't concentrate, every student confirmed the general cruelty of the student culture. One student said she doesn't think the adults have any idea "in general how *mean* people are to each other."[81]

Some parents seem vaguely aware of the problem but are essentially at a loss as to how to address it—particularly since they appear to understand it as a larger cultural phenomenon that is not unique to SHS. "I see it as a lot of bullying," remarked one student's mother. "I see the girls are sometimes just catty. Some are immature. And cruelty—it always surprises me how cruel they can be to one another."[82] Another parent noted that the "verbal abuse" in junior high consisted of comments like "*you're too skinny or too fat,* that kind of thing," but at the high school level "it's like, *I hate you and I'm gonna kill you* type thing—and that, to me, is just unbelievable."[83] She did not mention SHS specifically, instead referring to this as a "high school" problem. Other parents, when asked what they thought students might be afraid of, turned the question around and spoke about what they feared *for* their kids. One parent supposed that some kids might be afraid and supported her supposition with a thirdhand account of "other schools [where] kids won't even go to the bathroom" for fear of encountering students doing drugs, because those students will retaliate if they get caught, assuming they were reported by the unsuspecting kid who walked in on them in the bathroom. "So there are kids who don't even go to the bathroom all day. [Laughs] I don't think it's that bad at our school."[84] Her story was told in the manner of a ghost story that is entertaining because everyone knows it can't really happen.

The preoccupation with drugs was repeated in some form by more than half of the parents we interviewed at SHS. Their collective sense is that the teachers and administrators are well aware of the presence of drugs in the building and are either unable or unwilling to do anything about it. Their absolute conviction that this is a rampant problem appears to be based not on actual SHS data or confiscated drugs on campus but on rumor and a wider mass-mediated cultural fear about drugs and the necessity for waging war on them.[85] In a high school setting, educators and education administrators are held responsible for the war on drugs. "I don't really see them doing anything, to tell you the truth," said one boy's mother:

> *They pick the kids that aren't in real big trouble and make a big thing about them when they don't do hardly anything. And yet, these kids that do drugs and stuff . . . they don't do anything to them, so it's not exactly a deterrent for kids not to do it again. They need to be more strict, especially when it comes to illegal drugs, you know . . . they just look the other way.*[86]

The subtext here, of course, is that this parent feels that some students are given preferential treatment—presumably not her child—while others are unfairly targeted for surveillance and discipline. She makes that point explicit later in the interview:

> *Sometimes the kids that dress preppy and all that, they kind of think they're like better than the kids that are into the more skater, the T-shirts and the jeans—because this community is like . . . if you dress a little different, then they're like all over you, you know, and yet the other kids—some of the preppier kids—are more into drugs and more into stuff than the other kids could ever be. But they've got the look, you know, and I think the school . . . I don't know what it is about this school, but they're really that way, they're not looking at the people, they look at your clothes.*[87]

This woman has concerns about the ways in which class differences play out in ways that privilege some and punish others in the larger community of Suburbia and the ways in which those inequities are echoed in the high school. Her fear, in effect, is that the high school students who occupy a lower social and economic position in the SHS social hierarchy are being treated exactly the way she understands (or experiences) that the adults who occupy a lower social and economic position are treated in the community. Her belief is that the most serious and most commonly committed crime in the high school is drug related and that the "preppy" kids—the wealthy kids—are the likely culprits rather than the working-class kids who are targeted most often by teachers and administrators as potential rule breakers and criminals. In Suburbia, the poor kids are the blacks of the school—and so class and race are once again fluid, permeable categories moving around and through one another.

Teachers, too, expressed grave concerns over issues of social justice within the school—but only in terms of students' social conflicts with peers, which occupy a separate category than school violence and were usually not expressed as fear. Teachers' anxieties were almost exclusively centered on students in the school whom they do not know; they are afraid of students who might have "a screw loose," as one woman phrased it.[88] Teachers as a group drifted in their conversation, time and again, to references of the school shootings at Columbine, toward the similarities they saw between SHS and Columbine High School. They spoke of their fears about not only the potential violence that some SHS student might be capable of inflicting but also of their inability to visually pick out a potentially violent student in time.

One teacher confided in his interview that he walks around the hallway thinking to himself, "OK, there's a camera here, a camera here, a camera there, so, if someone was planning something like this, where are they going to come in that avoids cameras or avoids detection?"[89] Another teacher observed wryly, "Oh, it's a beautiful school, and we have all these things—but it is a total false sense of security. . . . anybody could bring anything in here."[90] And while these teachers case the building, trying to anticipate how a student intent on violence might case the building, other teachers observe the students themselves, trying to imagine what combination of stress, alienation, and mental illness might set someone off: "There are some kids that you just know are going to explode, you just know it."[91] One teacher noted,

> *Overall the school is pretty calm, but you never know. You never know. I worry about the kids that we don't reach; I worry about the kids that are lost in the crowd. They're not A students, they may not be B students; I worry about the C students that may not be involved in a lot of stuff, maybe they can't be involved in a lot of stuff because they're not financially able or they have no transportation. I worry about those kids. And I worry about racial problems here . . . because I think that's where you just never know what's gonna happen.*[92]

This teacher has located her anxiety about school violence, about dangerous young adults, in those students who are academically average or below average and who are not involved in many—or any—school-sponsored extracurricular activities. Statistically, the students she has described, as a group, imply particular racial and class categories, despite the profile of the school shooters she likens them to and the makeup of the majority of Suburbia's student population: white, middle to upper middle class, successful in school, and engaged in extracurricular activities.

One parent told us that a teacher had been concerned that the year before the Columbine shootings Columbine High School administrators had come to SHS to give a talk, because their school was so similar in population and building organization to their own: "And the teacher said, *Oh that's great, why's he telling the kids that?!* [Laughs] You don't want to, you know?"[93] This particular teacher's fear illustrates the complete lack of agency—of any control over their own and students' safety—that SHS teachers feel when they consider the potential for random, inexplicable violence that students might be capable of: if we tell students our school is like Columbine, one of our students might decide to shoot us too.

The old school building was overcrowded, in need of repair, and less than ideal for maintaining order among so many teenagers. The problems were numerous, and the list of needs that the new school would address was long. As we listened to our interviewees talk about the problems they faced, both in the old building and in the new, the ways in which they approached those problems, and their hopes for a safer, more effective educational setting for students, it became clear that the physical structure of the school itself had become the locus for the community's anxieties, fears, and hopes. The House Concept is an organized attempt to eliminate one source of fear that teachers expressed:

the fear of anonymous students and the inability of the administration to target them, to keep them under surveillance, and by doing so to subvert any potential violence before it could be realized. But teachers don't seem to feel that it's working:

> *I walk in the school everyday and I see a student I've never seen before. . . . I think this is a really big school, and we're too big. There are lots of lost kids out there. Even with the houses, we're still too big. My kids come to class, they don't know three-fourths of the kids in their class. Because they're constantly changing.*[94]

Concerns about stranger-students were expressed over and over again by the teachers we interviewed—and it's a concern about the sheer size of the student population, something the new building accommodates but does not alleviate. "When I first started teaching, I literally knew the name of every kid in the building. Now, every day, I see a kid I've never seen before," said another teacher.[95] Parents, too, are fearful of the"unknown student." One parent not only noted her and other parents' fears but commented on the difficulty of trying to identify potentially violent students while not succumbing to the urge to profile:

> *Sometimes we see a student and we think, you know if anybody's going to do it it'll be someone like that, but then we have to think back and say but wait a minute, [the teachers or neighbors always say] I never would have expected it from that one, so you can't really, you know, stereotype people, or appearances, or whatever.*[96]

Generalized fears about the number of students in the building and the fear of potential violence are addressed, interestingly enough, by particular design features in the new building that allow the administration to section off the school and lock it down—nobody gets in or out. The publicly articulated rationale for that design and the codification of a lockdown procedure is, as one student put it, to make students "feel that it is a lot safer in here," although fears of administrators, teachers, parents, and the community are clearly focused on students inside the building. Entrance and exit doors are regularly locked during school hours, security cameras are active, and parking lots are patrolled—in the name of greater safety. The same student cited the unannounced lockdowns as a protective measure "in case somebody breaks in," even though the school only locks down to accommodate the K-9 narcotics units that periodically sweep the school and its students for illegal drugs.[97]

Some members of the SHS community prefer freedom to an increased sense—or claim—of safety. One student confessed that he liked the old, crowded building better "because you could probably get away with more things." The teachers and administrators are more strict in the new building, he claims. "Probably things just changed after Columbine," he figures, but he can't quite make the connection between that particular tragedy and what feel like the countless new rules and regulations—and all of the new ways that he can find himself in trouble. "It's kind of ridiculous, like, a dress code, and you get sent to the office. I don't really see the point in that." As for fear, he agrees—there's plenty of fear to go around, but it's not what we might think, he tells us. He's not afraid of somebody going crazy and shooting him or his classmates. It's the "way they run the school, there's like so many cameras I'm sure like everyone's afraid, all these—even though you're not doing anything—all these cameras."[98]

X. *Conclusion*

The subtitle of Barry Glassner's 1999 book, *The Culture of Fear,* is crucially important to our project: *Why Americans Are Afraid of the Wrong Things.* In our study of Ohio schooling and the larger political and cultural context in which SHS and other schools operate, we ask this question, among others, and attempt in part to answer it, revealing in the process the increasingly punishing nature of public schooling in both affluent suburban and poor urban locations. Careful analysis of the stories that students, teachers, and administrators tell of life at SHS reveals the ongoing construction and reconstruction of group and individual identities and the ways in which a dominant narrative about who the community is and, by extension, who occupies the school works to control those who teach and learn at SHS.

It is no overstatement to suggest that we can observe similar tensions between fears for our safety and the maintenance of personal freedoms and individual rights in the schools and in the wider culture in which schools operate; the issues we address here, related to one suburban high school, have broader implications. One parent told us this:

> *My husband and I were talking about our country, that we seem to be losing some of our freedoms in the name of security, and it's the same thing*

> *here. In trying to make it [SHS] a more secure place, they do have cameras in some of the hallways, at some of the entrances. . . . And they have beefed up the rules, you know, not permitting coats—some of them have the long trench coats. We've seen problems at other schools with that type of attire and so they try to eliminate that factor. We have one security guard here, and during the school day he does patrol the parking lot. And that is not only to prevent people from coming in that don't belong, it's also to prevent kids from leaving that shouldn't be leaving. They also watch the cars. I think obviously we could be another Columbine, anybody could be. . . . And so it definitely could happen, and I think that I feel that the things the administration has put into place, certainly it could feel like an invasion to have the security and the surveillance, and on the other hand I would hope it would make some of them feel safer. Our security cameras have been used to find a student who has stolen something out of someone's locker, so you know if that was your property that was stolen, you're probably thankful for the fact that there was a camera that was in your hallway where your locker is. For the other person, probably not that thankful. [Laughs]*[99]

Law-abiding kids, in other words, will be thankful for surveillance; only rule breakers will object. The articulated rationale is that the overabundance of surveillance at SHS will protect students, teachers, and the community against SHS's becoming another Columbine; yet the surveillance is used to catch students skipping class, a student stealing from a locker, and other such problems. Fears about random violence have been amplified and responded to with policies and procedures that purport to be about student safety, when they operate, quite literally, as erosions of privacy and tools of law enforcement.

The conflicts students experience at SHS are interpersonal and manifest primarily as verbal harassment, despite the fears of concerned adults that center around fears of random stranger violence and drug use associated with black, urban, poor settings. And yet it is the fears of those adults that command the development and implementation of new and increasingly zero tolerance policies rather than the more immediate and pervasive problems that students actually face. We can make sense of this seeming disconnect between problem and policy by placing SHS within its larger context of schooling and the political and economic struggles that construct that context, including the punishing attention schools receive from state and national leaders. The ongoing production and voracious cultural consumption of mass-mediated nostalgia for the small town and fear of the urban ghetto encourage SHS to distance itself as much as possible from the markers of diversity and chaos, *whatever form they might take.* Thus this resource-rich school deliberately constructs itself as vigilant, disciplined, and disciplining, armed and ready to protect students and the community; in so doing, SHS also constructs students as either potential victims in need of protection or criminals in need of punishment. Importantly, either option is predicated on a lack of agency.

In the next chapter we will explore the ways in which popular culture texts help to produce and maintain particular fears of youth and echo calls for school policies that contain and control youth and punish *all* members of public schools and their communities. We will examine the ways in which zero tolerance approaches to crime have extended into the school and expanded to include preemption, in addition to response, causing both a more decisive movement in schools toward prison-like settings, organization, surveillance, and culture and an unassailable policy trajectory whose rationale appears independent of outcomes for its continued existence. In fact, by definition, zero tolerance prevention policies are their own rationale, in which an ever-increasing number of unannounced lockdowns and drug searches are in themselves considered successful strategies in the war on drugs and in the community's efforts to keep their neighborhoods, schools, and children safe.

Chapter 3

Popular Culture and Public Pedagogy
Fear and Identity in Suburbia and Pleasantville

Popular culture is one of the sites where the struggle for and against a culture of the powerful is engaged. . . . It is the arena of consent and resistance. It is partly where hegemony arises, and where it is secured. . . . That is why popular culture matters.

—Stuart Hall (1981)

Films . . . become important as public pedagogies because they play a powerful role in mobilizing meaning, pleasures, and identifications. They produce and reflect important considerations of how human beings should live, engage with others, define themselves, and address how a society should take up questions fundamental to its survival.

—Henry Giroux (2003b)

I. *Introduction*

In the previous chapter we explored the ways in which one suburban high school community experiences and responds to the fears of parents, teachers, and students—fears that appear to center around the students themselves. Asking questions about why we fear young people, why we fear some young people more than others, and what the broader contexts are in which such fears are generated and reproduced are crucially important if we are to increase our understanding of the ways in which our public schools are punished, the ways in which schools punish their members, and the effect of these actions.[1] We begin this portion of our analysis by turning to popular culture and, in particular, the role that filmic representations of youth play in both supporting and producing a larger culture of fear in which schools operate, on our children as well as on our imaginations and democratic aspirations.[2] Images and stories of educating youth; urban and suburban sites as dangerous or safe, respectively; teenagers as an essential threat to social-sexual order; and race as inextricably bound in a causal relationship to crime, poverty, and a war on drugs both produce and support our fears—fears *for* our children and, simultaneously, fears *of* our children.

Such fears, we argue, lend themselves to the implementation and broad acceptance of school policies characterized by containment and zero tolerance,[3] further blurring the boundaries between the school and the prison and providing evidence of the movement toward "education as enforcement."[4] The well-documented "white flight" from cities and city schools is more than just the physical removal of both white bodies and white wealth from urban schools and school districts; suburban schools and communities are actively engaged in a careful construction and preservation of identities that attempt to put as much distance as possible between themselves and the mass-mediated identity markers of *black, urban,* and *poor* and the material consequences of such markers.[5] The result of these official policies, as well as the formal and informal social codes that help to create that distance, is twofold: the further abandonment of those schools and communities already most vulnerable to the escalating failure of the state to fulfill its obligations to effectively educate *all* of its young citizens and the increasing isolation of the most powerful schools and communities whose privilege depends upon naturalizing and maintaining the status quo.

II. Culture, Identity, and the Pedagogy of the Popular

Exploring the ways in which power is both reinforced and undercut in the symbolic forms of cultural texts is an important component of cultural studies work.[6] Analyses of the narrative structures and images found in print texts, television, and film, for example, help to illuminate the co-constitutive relationships between such texts and the broader cultural context within which they are produced and received. As Henry Giroux (2003b) points out, the study of popular culture acknowledges and explores the "multiple dimensions of oppression and how such antagonisms expand the meaning and nature of pedagogical, political, and democratic struggles." It is equally important, he goes on to say, to "understand how agency, identities, and subject positions are constructed through the pedagogical force of culture and what this suggests for engaging and struggling over and within those institutions and public spheres that articulate between everyday life and material formations of power" (18). Popular cultural texts, in other words, offer specific and limited subject positions for individuals and groups to occupy, through the re-presentation of *particular* ideological frameworks that promote some values, identities, practices, and histories and undermine or erase others.

Cultural representations, which are selected and repeated, allow and encourage us to define ourselves in ways that coincide with the dominant culture and its explanation for unequal distributions of power and resources. And, as Stuart Hall (1981) argues, while such representations do not find in us a *tabula rasa,* neither are they ineffectual. Rather, there exists an ongoing "dialectic of cultural struggle," in which the dominant culture attempts "constantly to disorganize and reorganize popular culture; to enclose and confine its definitions and forms within a more inclusive range of dominant forms." Importantly, however, popular cultural texts exhibit this dialectic of cultural struggle in the gaps and inconsistencies in their structures, narratives, and images, revealing both resistance to and complicity in dominant culture and existing power relations. In the age of mass media, such struggles are continual, cultural forms and images variously reinscribing and contradicting one another through "complex lines of resistance and acceptance, refusal and capitulation, which make the field of culture a sort of constant battlefield . . . where there are always strategic positions to be won and lost" (228).

Commercial popular culture texts are both manipulative and transparent in terms of the experiences and attitudes presented to audiences—and thus in the subject positions offered by the text. The danger lies, as Hall (1981) argues, in thinking of cultural texts as either only corrupt or only authentic.[7] In fact, cultural texts are "deeply contradictory; they play on contradictions, especially when they function in the domain of the 'popular,'" and, importantly, what constitutes the popular is continuously in flux (229). Certain cultural forms will be understood as an elite cultural text or activity, while others will be deemed popular; over time those forms will shift, however, in terms of their perceived cultural value; some will lose prestige and find themselves in the category of the "popular," while others will increase in cultural value and move to the category of elite forms. "The structuring principle does not consist of the contents of each category," Hall insists, but "will alter from one period to another" in such a way that the "categories remain, though the inventories change. What is more, a whole set of institutions and institutional processes are required to sustain each—and to continually mark the difference between them." Social power relations, he explains, are "constantly punctuating and dividing the domain of culture into its preferred and its residual categories" (230).

Exploring "the popular," then, must proceed from an understanding of popular culture as it relates to the dominant culture in terms of tension, influence, antagonism, and the contingent nature of its content. Understanding the essential instability of the contents of the category of the popular allows us to locate political and pedagogical meaning in cultural symbols that once were understood as radical, for example, and to trace their movement and more recent effect as objects of nostalgia in service to the status quo—effective, in some cases, *precisely because* they carry traces of their earlier radical, subversive meanings.[8] In an editorial published in the *LA Weekly*, John Powers (2004) reminds us of the role popular culture plays in the public discourses that construct and define complex issues and identities: "More and more, Americans address huge social issues not on news shows, op-ed pages or the campaign trail, but through popular culture." He notes that we both legitimize certain issues and attempt to resolve them through cultural texts. For example, we "use Michael Jackson and Eminem to explore racial identity, Martha Stewart and Buffy to examine changing ideas of womanhood."[9] Americans, he contends, struggle over identity—and the power that is always at stake in such contestations—in part by talking about movies.

What Powers does not address is how films function as "teaching machines" within the broader culture—what Henry Giroux calls "public pedagogies." Giroux (2003b) argues that popular films function pedagogically in that they operate as "public discourses that address or at least resonate with broader issues in the historical and sociopolitical context in which they are situated" (75). In order to effectively read films as, among other things, dominant cultural articulations of fear, he adds, "they have to be understood within a broader network of cultural spheres and institutional formations rather than as isolated texts. The pedagogical and political character of . . . films resides in the ways in which they align with broader social, sexual, economic, class, and institutional configurations" (78). In this chapter, we examine the alignment between one popular film and public schooling. Film helps us to understand when and how some meanings and fears are constructed as legitimate and useful, while others are not—a pedagogy with political consequences, reflected in the ways some fears are amplified and others muted—in films as in schools.

In an effort to shed critical light on how popular films, among other cultural texts, work to highlight some fears and veil others in order to construct citizen identities consistent with punishing schools, we examine in the following section the 1999 New Line Cinema film *Pleasantville.*[10] We begin by analyzing the narrative structure of the film, exploring the gaps and contradictions in its politics of representation, which reveal simultaneously a critique of the oppression of sexual curiosity in young people and a depiction of sexually active young women as promiscuous and, therefore, in need of containment and punishment. The film also simultaneously critiques a xenophobic, anti-intellectual model of education while celebrating knowledge as tourism and social philosophy as authored exclusively by white, Western, twentieth-century male authors. Further, the film's narrative simultaneously deplores gender and racial segregation, while situating the struggle for agency, equality, and sexual choice in a world that is eerily devoid of history, class, and homosexuality. *Pleasantville* embodies a politics of representation that includes profoundly conservative views of education, sexuality, race, and political empowerment; while applauding particular social struggles, *Pleasantville,* through an overemphasis on individual self-help, encourages audiences to understand that the outcome of such struggles is dependent upon the relative strength or weakness of personal conviction and individual will. These representations work with and through the American bootstrap myth exemplified in countless cultural narratives of the righteous individual conquering evil against all odds—a metanarrative of extreme individualism where individuals have wives at home, meritocracy where only individual effort counts, and moral certitude where democratic deliberation becomes a source of conflict.[11] Any oppression we might experience or observe in our daily lives, such narratives assure us, is due to the failure of individual victims, not to any systemic inequities or institutionalized discrimination that is always already at work producing both social injustice and our consent.[12]

By analyzing *Pleasantville* as both political and pedagogical, we attempt to illuminate the dominant cultural assumptions upon which it rests and to explore both how as a text it "works" in the culture and how that work might be challenged. In addition, we connect the public pedagogy of *Pleasantville* to the previous chapter's reading of Suburbia's individual, school, and community narratives, reading them with and against each other in order to better understand a wider set of cultural associations and meanings that shift the discourse of fear from questions of the state's obligation to invest in social welfare and public goods and of the systematic abandonment of the poor and the non-white to an uncritical celebration of individualism and a liberal discourse of diversity that remains complicit in defining youth as dangerous and in absolving the state of its social responsibilities.

III. Going Back to School: The Pedagogy of Pleasantville

Pleasantville's writer, director, and producer, Gary Ross, tells the fantastic story of teenaged siblings, David and Jennifer, who are magically transported from their shallow, 1990s suburban existence, where traditional family values appear to be all but dead, into the idealized family and small-town life of the 1950s TV sitcom *Pleasantville,* which David loves. In their "real" lives, David is a soft-spoken, unpopular high school student who cannot summon the courage to ask a girl out on a date and who escapes from the emptiness and pain of his parents' antagonistic divorce, and his mother's subsequently visible sexuality, into the predictable and happy life found in Pleasantville, where neither divorce nor sex ever happens. Jennifer, on the other hand, pours her considerable energies into securing a popular position within the high school social hierarchy, which ranks students as consumers and sexual objects and produces in them an affected attitude of cool disinterest and cynicism about their own lives. Once David and Jennifer are transported to Pleasantville, they set in motion a series of changes within the small-town community that supposedly alter the very nature of education, as well as gender and racial power politics. On its face, *Pleasantville* depicts a collision of 1990s and 1950s social and sexual order, and both are deemed better off for the encounter.

The film recognizes and pokes fun at our collective penchant for sentimentalized notions of 1950s life in suburban America; the initial depictions of David and Jennifer's TV mother, Betty—with coiffed hair, high heels, and full makeup, serving her weight in pork products and carbohydrates each morning for breakfast—are both fun and funny. Jennifer's comment that her 1950s bra, which lifts, pads, and points her breasts in an alarming manner, could "hurt somebody" indicates to audiences that this film will not be merely a stroll down memory lane: the 1950s *have* been improved upon, Ross hastens to reassure us. But consider the degree of import and the negative aspects of such progress—yes, underwear can signal progress—in the context of the film's initial scene, where David stands in the open, paved courtyard of his late 1990s suburban, Southern California high school, talking to someone outside of the camera's view. There is nothing green in sight; there is a sense of space, open sky, and a few concrete-gray institutional buildings on the periphery of the courtyard, where young people walk alone or mingle in small groups. A quick succession of close-ups of these high school students reveals excessive black eye makeup, cigarettes poised between fingers heavy with gothic jewelry, pierced tongues, black clothing, and slouchy postures; everyone looks tough, experienced, sexualized. It seems quite probable that many of the students will eat a salad for lunch and that the girls are wearing less structured and constricting underwear: progress has been made. But the school feels both crowded and barren, a visual metaphor for contemporary social life in which anonymity, overpopulation, and loneliness coexist as the norm. Even with advances in foundational garments technology, are these children better off, the film asks us to consider?

David faces the camera in this scene, haltingly asking a girl out, but when the camera angle shifts to his perspective, we see that the girl he has been addressing is fifty feet away and, in reality, talking to another boy. She doesn't even know he exists. David is clearly not a social-sexual powerhouse at his high school; the sudden shift of viewpoint creates the effect for viewers of David's desire for communication and contact and the literal and metaphoric gulf that separates him from the possibility of meaningful human relationships. After lingering a moment on David's resigned acceptance of his own inadequacy in taking that crucial first step—a conversation—the scene changes quickly from one classroom to the next, where a succession of teachers, who appear either completely uninterested or shell-shocked by the information they are conveying, paint a bleak future for the students sitting in their classrooms. Even if they go to college, one teacher tells them, their chances of getting a job and earning a living wage will be less than they are right now; it's a "competitive world," he drones. HIV is on the rise, warns another teacher, giving students the frightening news that drug-addicted homosexuals are not the demographic whose rate of infection is on the rise; it is, according to the teacher, heterosexuals in the students' own age group who are now most at risk.[13] *Pleasantville* argues that this is David and Jennifer's world—this is the world of all American high school students in the late 1990s: devoid of intimacy, dangerous, confusing, and hopeless when compared to a no-conflict view of life in the 1950s. But in the film, Ross reveals a 1950s with plenty of conflict.

At lunch, David informs his friend that a *Pleasantville* marathon begins that night and will be followed by a trivia contest he intends to win; *nobody* knows as much about *Pleasantville* as David does.[14] The black-and-white 1950s sitcom centers on the Parker family, whose members interact continuously; problems are uncomplicated and easily resolved, and everyone's place in the family and community is unchanging and unquestioned. The problems faced by the characters in *Pleasantville* are indicated by the episode titles that will be shown during the marathon: "Trouble at the Barbershop"; "Fireman for a Day"; "Bud Gets a Job." When David's friend suggests that one of the show's characters is homeless because "they never show where he lives," David responds with absolute authority that "nobody's homeless in Pleasantville—because that's just not what it's like."[15]

At home, while David lounges on the sofa in the living room, watching TV and waiting for the marathon to begin, we hear his mother on the phone with her ex-husband, David and Jennifer's father. She is arguing with him about who is supposed to watch the kids for the weekend. We see David's face during the argument, which is heard but takes place off-camera. David's expression does not change; he watches the television screen, remote in hand. The TV announcer describes *Pleasantville* as "chock full of pure family values," while David's mother, nearly shouting now and clearly upset, tells her ex-husband that she is going to a spa for the weekend and that if she wants to "take a mud bath" with her new boyfriend, she will. David's expression remains passive, and his gaze never leaves the TV, but he points the remote at the screen and turns up the volume, drowning out his mother's pain, his father's absence, and the sexual and emotional chaos that we are made to understand is his home life. In case we haven't gotten the point yet, Ross cuts this painful scene of contemporary family life with the TV screen David is watching, where we see a commercial for the upcoming marathon featuring the main characters of *Pleasantville* in their homey living room. George Parker, the family patriarch, walks in the front door, calling, "Honey! I'm home!" and is immediately greeted by Betty Parker, his wife, who enters bearing a martini, which he takes from her hand.[16] George tells her that he might be getting a promotion, and Betty is joyful in her support of his triumph; the children enter, and Betty both praises and corrects her son, Bud, while Mary Sue says nothing but beams adorably at everyone. The contrast is pointed, and, while we know (and Ross underscores) that the TV sitcom version of 1950s family life does not reflect the reality of either families or the wider culture of the 1950s, like David, we are constructed as the film's audience to find it attractive—especially as it contrasts with the impoverished family and school scenes from "real" life that we have just witnessed. This image of the past in the present—the past as the antipresent—effectively masks reality as the TV announcer simply asserts that what must be achieved already *is:* traditional family values. In the end, no new mechanisms for achieving those "values" are proffered, just a new assertion of dominant hegemonic discourse, offered as an individual choice for the taking.

When their mother leaves for the weekend, David and Jennifer, who has a date with a boy coming over to watch a concert on MTV, both prepare for the evenings they have planned. At six o'clock—when the marathon begins and when Jennifer's date is scheduled to arrive—they both enter the living room and reach for the remote at the same time. A tussle over the remote ensues, they drop it, and it is smashed into pieces that scatter across the floor. At that very moment the doorbell rings and a TV repairman, complete with coveralls and a work van parked outside, tells them he is there to fix their broken TV.[17] He gives them a replacement remote control, talks to David for a few minutes about *Pleasantville*—a show the repairman says he loves—and leaves. David tries out the remote, and it works; the *Pleasantville* marathon is just beginning. Jennifer grabs the remote as well, they struggle over it, and when one of the buttons is inadvertently pushed, a strange light emanates from the device. The scene of David and Jennifer grappling over the remote is mirrored in the TV screen, where Bud and Mary Sue Parker are struggling over a transistor radio. Suddenly, David and Jennifer disappear from their living room and appear on the TV screen—in black-and-white, in Bud and Mary Sue's 1950s clothes, and, clearly, in Pleasantville.

David and Jennifer find themselves standing inexplicably in the Parkers' living room. It becomes clear immediately that it is morning, they are Bud and Mary Sue, and George and Betty are their parents. The two play along, with differing degrees of enthusiasm, and head off to school when they are told to do so. At the high school in Pleasantville we find the curriculum a caricature of cold war isolationism and xenophobia: there is literally nothing outside of Pleasantville. When Jennifer raises her hand in what appears to be a geography class and asks what is at the end of Main Street, the teacher is confused; finally, she tells the class that Jennifer's question is "silly" because, as they all know, the end of Main Street is the beginning of Main Street. She points to the line drawing on the chalkboard, which depicts Main Street and two cross streets—all of which simply end in nothing; with her explanation to Jennifer, she draws a line that circles around, connecting one end of Main Street to the other. Everyone looks relieved. Ross appears in this scene to offer a critique of teaching and learning that occurs without a historical or wider cultural context. In fact, he extends that critique in Jennifer's later discovery that all the books in the library have blank pages, clearly targeting attempts by various contemporary groups to censure high school literature curricula by naming *The Adventures of Huckleberry Finn, The Catcher in the Rye,* and the works of D. H. Lawrence—texts that are frequently targeted by various groups for removal from high school reading lists.[18] The covers have titles and authors but remain blank until David and Jennifer begin to talk about life "outside" of Pleasantville and to answer their peers' subsequent questions about what they know, what they've seen, and the books they've read—at which point the pages magically fill in. Young people need to learn about the wider world, Ross's film argues, but his nostalgic construction of a past created in the present as an argument for what the present should and could look like does not allow for contestation or discomfort. The pages of books fill in—a beautiful and natural occurrence, like teenagers making out and raindrops falling—but the authorship and content of those books, those knowledges, those representations, remain unchallenged, and Ross's no-conflict view of the world is ironically preserved in a film that purports to critique that very view.

The narrative progresses as David's and Jennifer's presence, their actions and their words, begin to create a chain of events that radically alters desire and power and, thus, social relationships in Pleasantville. Jennifer introduces sexuality to Pleasantville by having sex with Skip, the captain of the high school basketball team, who details his adventure for his teammates; suddenly, the team who could not miss a shot and has never lost a game is incomprehensibly inept. Kids start spending all their time at Lovers' Lane, having sex in cars and making out on blankets spread upon the grass; suddenly, young people are walking around in color—a disturbing development that causes concern among parents and local politicians. Jennifer explains sex to Betty, who sadly admits that George "would never do anything like that," and Jennifer responds by telling her that she can do it herself; she does not, in fact, need George. When Betty masturbates that night and her orgasm causes the tree in their front yard to burst into flames—the first fire that has ever burned in Pleasantville—the consequences of female sexual desire and initiative have progressed from the purely comical (the basketball players' shots won't drop) to the potentially dangerous. It is one thing to cripple the high school basketball team and disappoint the men in town who eagerly follow their games; it is quite another to risk harm to property and life to the unexpected, uncontrollable, engulfing flames of unchecked female sexuality. The residents of Pleasantville are no longer in the garden: sexual knowledge and female sexual desire have crept in, and all of the male residents of Pleasantville are going to have to learn how to put out fires.[19]

David, too, is having an effect in Pleasantville, albeit not a sexual one. In encouraging the owner of the soda shop to show some initiative and break up his dull routine and to extend such independent thinking to an exploration of his latent artistic abilities, David becomes the catalyst for an artistic and intellectual movement that intersects with the sexual revolution to bring Pleasantville to a moment of crisis. David himself begins to change, as he increasingly takes on a leadership role: he talks to the other teenagers, recounting the narratives of the books he has read; the missing words appear, and suddenly all the kids are reading and talking about what they're reading. Bill, the soda shop artist, pours over a modern art book and begins to paint colorful, abstract works in his shop window that the still predominantly black-and-white town finds disturbing. The consequences of sexual, artistic awakening are not just colorful—beautiful—they are also dangerous. Most of the film locates the danger in others' responses to art, sexuality, and freedom of expression, in a critique of a puritan censorship, a repressive, officially sanctioned set of acceptable sexual practices, acceptable texts, and acceptable topics for public representation, education, discussion, and desire. As individuals begin to take charge of their own lives, make unsanctioned decisions and personal discoveries, they change from black-and-white to full color. Sexual awakening causes this transformation for some, intellectual activity or art for others.

This revolution—sexual, intellectual, artistic—is not without the political and social resistance, in both public and private spheres, of patriarchal power and privilege, however. In one of the funniest scenes in the film, George walks home, briefcase in hand, along with all the other men in suits and hats. He enters the dark house, hangs his hat on the coatrack, and sets his briefcase down, calling, "Honey, I'm home!" Thunder rolls and lightening flashes in the window—an unprecedented meteorological event in Pleasantville. George repeats his call.

Still no answer, but more thunder and lightening. "Honey, I'm *home*," he says with emphasis, clearly confused and uneasy. He walks toward the kitchen muttering, "Where's my *dinner*?" He opens the oven, lifts the top off a pot on the stove, but doesn't turn on a light; everything is dark, empty, and cold, in a parody of the 1990s home where women are no longer required to meet their husbands at the door, martini in hand, while dinner bubbles happily in the warm, well-lit kitchen—dark days, indeed. Seemingly barely able to function, George leaves the house in what has become a downpour with no hat, no coat, and no umbrella.

The scene cuts to the bowling alley, where the mayor and dozens of other men are bowling perfect strikes and spares. The mayor and his cronies are shocked when they see George, who stumbles in, stricken, soaking wet, and needing to be helped to a seat. He is clearly traumatized as he tells his story: "No wife. No lights. No dinner." There are audible gasps from his audience; clearly, there is a crisis at hand. The mayor takes charge, assuring him that "It's going to be fine, George. You're with us. We're safe for now—thank God we're in a bowling alley." He turns to the others and sounds a warning for their way of life, his voice no longer reassuring: "But if George doesn't get his dinner, any one of us could be next. Something is happening to our town. And I think we can all see where it's coming from," he concludes with a knowing look around. He commands one of the men to stand up, remove his jacket, and turn around so they can all see the iron-shaped burn on the back of his shirt. The men gasp and recoil in horror, and the mayor says with quiet emphasis as he looks at each of them in turn, "He asked her what she was doing. She said 'nothing.' She was 'just thinking.'" And then, with renewed determination, striding back and forth in front of them, the mayor says, "It's not about George's dinner or Roy's shirt. It's a question of values. It's a question of whether we want to hold onto those values that made this place great." Ross's characterization of male dominance runs along a continuum, from George, who is likeable, to the mayor, whose power and privilege are linked to his male relationships and his greater understanding that their "way of life" is dependent on maintaining the status quo, to Whitey, the angry young man who has become a violent sexual predator because of his inability to control female sexuality.

The mayor calls for a meeting, and notices are put up around town stating that all "true citizens" are expected to attend—making the connection between citizenship, privilege, and officially sanctioned fears explicit. True citizens fear change because what *is* is natural and therefore right; true citizens share a "no-conflict" view that conflates their fear of change with a fear of others, because even the possibility of seeing the choices that others make as anything but morally bankrupt would reveal the constructedness of their own position—give the lie to their own lives and choices as "natural" and open the way for conflict, deliberation, negotiation: change. Betty tells George she will not go—she is openly in color to him inside their home and says, "That meeting's not for me." George reassures her that "it will go away," but she insists through clenched teeth that she doesn't "*want* it to go away." Exasperated—terrified by what he cannot control—George says, "Now you listen to me. You're going to put on some makeup and you're going to go to that meeting. You're going to be home every night at 6 o'clock and you're going to have dinner ready." "No," she says gently and immovably, "I'm not, Sweetie." She gets up and explains that she has made some food for the next few days and gives him instructions for the kitchen appliances. "I'm going to go now," she tells him. As she walks out, he shouts at her, "They'll see you!" Betty has successfully skirted what in another context (the mayor or Whitey, for example) might easily be construed as a menacing conversation and leaves the protection of her husband and the private, domestic sphere for the unknown public world, where, as a mobile woman whose sexuality is *visibly apparent* to anyone who looks at her, she is in danger and, importantly, has become dangerous herself.

At the meeting, the townspeople are in an uproar—"Roy Campbell's got a blue front door!" cries one woman, pointing her finger at someone across the room. The mayor interjects, trying to calm everyone. "Things have always been pleasant—recently, some unpleasant things have been happening. Seems to me what we have to do is separate out the things that are pleasant from the things that are unpleasant." The next day, new store signs are posted around town that say, "No Coloreds"; the absence of visible markers of difference—racial difference, sexual difference and desire, gender inequities—must be eradicated in order for things to remain "pleasant," the same, for those who enjoy privilege within the current power relations. The townspeople discover that Bill has painted an abstract reclining nude of Betty Parker in his shop window. They are incensed and become an unruly, dangerous mob seeking the violent sanctification of their particular vision of propriety, community, and identity, breaking Bill's window and destroying the painting. A gang of still black-and-white teenaged boys see Betty walking on the street and accost her; these young men without color are frightening, because as genuine thugs, their lack of color puts them outside of Betty's community, and without community constraints, any kind of violence in this scene becomes imaginable. In this context, Betty's newfound freedom and independence are transformed into a desperate dependence on new male heroes. David saves Betty, so the contradiction is resolved in the narrative of a hero's coming-of-age. David has remained in black-and-white until he is able to stand up to this mob, led by Whitey, that is threatening Betty with physical, possibly sexual, violence because of the painting and her color, which indicates her sexual, and thus unprotected, status. The mob destroys the soda shop completely and begins emptying the library and burning books, while black-and-white boys chase full-color girls and women through the streets as they run for safety. The mayor calls for calm and suggests a code of conduct "we can all agree to live by." The new rules include Courtesy and a Pleasant Manner; the Indefinite Closure of Lovers' Lane and the Library; only a few select Songs of a Temperate or Pleasant Nature are permitted; No Umbrellas or Preparations for Inclement Weather may be sold; No Big Beds; No Paint Colors but the White-Gray-Black palette; and the School Curriculum will teach the Non-Changeist View of History, emphasizing Continuity over Alteration.

David solidifies his leadership role at this point by encouraging the teenagers to listen to whatever music they want to and by helping Bill paint a new mural on a brick wall on Main Street—a mural that depicts recent events: Pleasantville's sexually active teenagers, the book-burning mob, young people dancing like savages, the bowling alley as center of political power, the destruction of art and the artist's soda shop, the thunder and lightening and rain in all their chaotic upheaval. The mural is much more than a visual representation of recent events; it depicts and *names* the typically invisible power of dominant culture in Pleasantville—power that resides in fearmongering, cronyism, and the unarticulated but always present threat of physical force. David and Bill use every prohibited paint color; they are arrested, and everyone in town attends the hearing—black-and-whites in the main courthouse gallery, coloreds up in the balcony seats. David argues that he understands they want things to be pleasant but that "there are other things that are so much better—like silly, sexy, dangerous, brief." All of these, he claims, are in us all, all of the time, and we must have the "guts" to let them out; he argues, in effect, that the strength of individual will can overcome dominant forms of cultural power. "This behavior must stop at once!" shouts the mayor, banging his gavel. "But see, that's just the point, it can't stop at once because it's in you and you can't stop something that's inside you!" shouts David, angering the mayor so much that even he turns colored—the last one to do so; official, white patriarchal power of the state is the last to come around but eventually does so through the moral conviction of the righteous individual. The entire town spills out on the street, and amid the celebration David looks over at the TV and radio store and finds that the television sets in the store window are moving from channel to channel in full, glorious color, depicting various locations all over the world: the Eiffel Tower in Paris, the pyramids and the Great Sphinx in Egypt, natives surfing and racing dugout canoes off of some Pacific island. Suddenly, there are street signs indicating how many miles it is to the next town over—indicating that there *is* a next town over. Pleasantville has a context; the individual has defeated the state, which turns out to have merely been the man behind the curtain and not really powerful after all; life is good *because there is no conflict.*

The scene cuts to David saying good-bye to Jennifer at the bus stop in Pleasantville. She is off to college—in the 1950s—suitcase in hand. "You sure you don't want to come home?" he asks, referring to the 1990s. "Yeah, I gotta do this," she replies. "Besides, you think I even have a *chance* of getting into college back there? I did the slut thing, David. Got kind of old." They look at each other for a moment. "I'll come back and check on you soon," he promises. They hug, and she tells him he's turned into a "pretty cool guy"; she gets on the bus and is gone. Back at the Parker house, David says good-bye to Margaret, his love interest, and Betty, who have each packed him a brown-bag lunch to take on his "trip." Margaret begs him not to forget her, and Betty cries, hugs him, and tells him she loves him and is proud of him. The women lock hands and stand aside—David actually tells them they should "step back"—while he uses the remote and returns to the 1990s.

Back at David's house, the TV repairman is sitting in his truck with a knowing, contented smile; his work done, he starts the van and drives away—everything broken has been repaired, apparently, with the sexual young woman put back in the 1950s where she belongs and the young white male a more powerful, more traditionally masculine leader capable now of using persuasive public discourse, winning political battles, and taking care of his women. The TV is still on, and only one hour of the *Pleasantville* marathon has passed. David hears his mother crying in the kitchen. He goes to her, and she says her weekend was ruined—her young boyfriend, she says, doesn't make her feel younger but instead old. "Everything's just so fucked up," she sobs, her jarring word choice emphasizing that we are back in the 1990s, where life really is not as pleasant. "I'm forty years old; it's not supposed to be like this," she laughs through her tears. "It's not supposed to be like anything," David tells her. Then Ross presents a slow-motion series of shots—all in the 1950s, all pleasant—of the Parkers' neighbor watering his green lawn on a gorgeous sunny day; Skip, Jennifer's high school lover, eating a popsicle and appearing none the worse for wear; a little boy crossing the street, holding his mother's hand; and Jennifer at college, sitting on the steps of a campus building on a warm day and talking with a young man while holding an open book on her lap. In the final scene we find Betty, wearing hat and gloves and lightly clutching her handbag in her lap, sitting on a park bench next to George. They look straight ahead, not at each other. Then a close-up of George, where he says, "What's going to happen now?" is replaced by a close-up of Betty, who replies, with some wonder, "I don't know—do you know?" "No," says George, shaking his head, as they both laugh softly. The camera shifts again to Betty, as she laughs, and when the angle swings back once more to show George, we find that Bill is sitting beside her. "I guess I don't either," he says, smiling pleasantly.

IV. **Pleasantville** *and the Fear and Celebration of Youth*

As a mainstream, highly successful Hollywood film, *Pleasantville,* in its representations of high school students and the critically important roles they play in the broader social-sexual order, helps to illuminate the often contradictory fears of and for youth that play out in the policies that form the teaching, learning, and social landscapes of schools. *Pleasantville* offers a critique of our cultural nostalgia for the 1950s, in which we imagine or remember the family, high school, and the larger community as a racially homogenous or at least harmonious space, a safe and wholesome place, with images of a gendered social and educational model based on cold war xenophobia, isolationism, and repression. The quiet and orderly town of Pleasantville is only pleasant, we find, as long as no one questions or threatens the status quo; sexual desire, racial difference, history, critical thinking, and messy, democratic forms of public debate, dissent, and civil disobedience both challenge and, eventually, alter life in Pleasantville—as civil rights and the feminist movement altered the laws and social relations in towns and cities across the United States between the 1950s and the 1990s—and those changes were both unavoidable and *good,* the film implies.

As we have seen, the narrative structure of the film offers a critique of sexual repression, as well as gender and racial oppression; it critiques a "banking" form of education in which information is merely deposited in students by the authority of the teacher-state and whose curriculum is determined by a literal politics of privilege and ideology in the wider community.[20] These critiques acknowledge and support a post–civil rights, liberal politics that conditionally celebrates human sexuality, racial and cultural difference, and a secular-humanist approach to education. At the same time, however, the film undercuts what it presents as an argument for social change by *simultaneously* defining sexually active young women as promiscuous and as literally having no future; depicting family and domestic partner choices as exclusively heterosexual and monogamous (at least serially); celebrating knowledge as tourism and white, Western, male-authored literature from the previous century as the quintessence of radical social thought and movement; situating the struggle for agency and equality in a world in which history and class have been obscured; and erasing difference and conflict in a we're-all-the-same-inside argument that also, inexplicably, supports some of the worst and most destructive racial stereotypes. *Pleasantville,* as a political and pedagogical text, urges audiences to understand that conflict is merely episodic, bad behavior and that the outcome of social struggle is largely dependent on the relative strength or weakness of personal conviction and individual will, while it minimizes the presence and erases the reproductive power of oppressive institutions—an erasure that serves to support those institutional structures. Finally, the filmic construction of youth at risk in the contemporary family and school supports and reproduces those cultural fears of our children and for our children that lead to the criminalization of youth and the subsequent preventive or perpetual war on youth culture, as well as the increasingly desperate and contradictory desire that youth will produce heroes to save us. The cultural fears of the potentially disruptive and destructive power of youth upon which this film rests resonate with current policies of containment and zero tolerance in our schools and the experiences narrated by parents, teachers, and students at SHS.

Ross's film argues that, when simple means ignorant and when being pleasant requires both repression and oppression, we create problems rather than avoid them. But Ross's critique of our collective cultural nostalgia for the idealized 1950s family—a nostalgia that understands the patriarchal, heterosexual nuclear family as the heart of social-sexual morality and the foundation of progress and economic strength—is undercut by the film's simultaneous insistence on both grief and fear for what it portrays as an unambiguous *loss* associated with contemporary youth and family life. That loss is predicated on a conservative notion of traditional family values that requires the suppression of young female sexuality and the wholesale, uncritical acceptance by young (white) men of their right and responsibility to lead us toward propriety and stability and to frame our freedoms within appropriate and acceptable parameters that do not acknowledge the complex relationships among race, class, education, and opportunity. In its limited understanding of cultural struggle and its no-conflict approach to social problem solving, *Pleasantville* depicts education as capable of resolving gender and racial inequities by enforcing gender and racial stereotypes within an unexamined caricature of liberal tolerance.[21] The representations of racial conflict in *Pleasantville,* however, are situated within a context where the brutality of U.S. racial history and current racial inequities have been completely erased, and gender oppression and its handmaiden—domestic violence—have been reduced to questions of equitable divisions of labor and sexual satisfaction within middle-class white homes.[22]

Equally disturbing is Ross's authorial and directorial treatment of female sexuality, which boils down to an assertion that *renunciation* by young women of both their own sexuality and the second wave of feminist movement is necessary for the *redemption* of the family, the school, the community, and the culture. This process of renunciation and redemption is illustrated by the strongest character in the film, the sexually powerful Jennifer, who literally chooses to inhabit the 1950s—and that choice is understood within the film, astonishingly, as one of liberation and empowerment.

While *Pleasantville* appears to address such problems in a critical way, it also succeeds in reproducing them. Understanding the film as a form of public pedagogy, however, creates an opportunity to examine and analyze this popular text as a part of a larger cultural politics of representation that produces, confirms, and relies on a culture of fear in which young people figure prominently and in which their futures are literally at stake. For example, the film's treatment of female sexual desire is located squarely in the high school, in youth culture, and in uncontrolled or uncontrollable teenaged girls. Jennifer remains in black-and-white through her sexual activities in Pleasantville, as well as through her discovery of literature, her ability to see the "potential" in her classmates whom she initially saw as hopelessly beneath her social consideration, her gentle and candid discussion of sex with Betty, and so on; she grows and strengthens in multiple ways throughout the film, but the visible marker of these changes—the transformation of black-and-white into color—eludes her through all of them. She comes into color only when she *chooses not to have sex* because she would rather do her homework. Jennifer, reading D. H. Lawrence, opts to do her homework instead of Skip.[23]

We can read Jennifer's choice here in several ways. The narrative structure of the film encourages audiences to understand Jennifer's insistence that she will choose when and with whom she has sex, and her refusal (at least at this point in the film) to buy into a good girl–bad girl sexual dichotomy, as evidence of the film's support of strong, independent young women making their own (sexual) choices; we can read her refusal of Skip on this occasion as a choice freely made, despite an attempt by Skip to control her body and her choices for his pleasure, and applaud it as such. We can also, however, understand her choice to do her homework as a foreshadowing of her later choice, which is far more difficult to applaud, despite Ross's efforts to frame that choice as empowering. Later, when Jennifer chooses to remain in the 1950s because, ostensibly, at the played out age of seventeen or eighteen she has *a brighter future in the 1950s than she could possibly have in the 1990s,* audiences are compelled to see her choice as a pragmatic one. The film attempts to disguise the far more powerful interpretation that this is a *moral* decision made within the framework of the film's relatively conservative social-sexual value system. Jennifer has chosen to inhabit the 1950s, to embody the 1950s young woman as an act of renunciation—"I did the slut thing"—and as a sacrifice aimed at 1990s cultural redemption that can only be achieved by containing youth and refusing to tolerate the dangerous acts that undisciplined young people are likely to commit. Her decision does not appear to be based on her intellectual abilities nor on the late 1990s economy, or disease, or any of the other dire messages her teachers delivered in the opening scene, but *because she was sexually promiscuous there.* When Jennifer says, "I did the slut thing," she names her own sexuality and her choices as immoral, a negative interpretation by her that is unsupported by anything her character has done or said throughout the film, whether in the 1990s or the

1950s. This is a key moment in the film, where the dangers of female sexuality and unchecked youth materialize in failed education and a dismal future for young people—thus, *containing* and *controlling* some youth, rather than educating and empowering them, is constructed as for their own good (a good indicated by Jennifer freely choosing her own containment and characterizing it as liberation), and a zero tolerance approach to an increasingly criminalized youth becomes *prevention* and *care* extended to young people by the community.

David's choices and subsequent transformation also speak to conservative notions of the responsibility and ability of individuals to solve collective social problems; David's "awakening," however, while certainly gendered, is not explicitly sexual. As a young white male, David must learn leadership skills, to acknowledge his power in the public sphere, and to exercise control—in the form of protecting the women in his family—over the private. In the 1990s, the family is in ruins and society is increasingly fraught with danger. The pedagogical power of this film's narrative instructs audiences through its conclusion that it is the young white male—David—who can strengthen our institutions. He has learned how to do this by literally going back to the 1950s, by determining what from that era—whether real or a political by-product of nostalgia—is worth salvaging and how to work for social change by observing the lessons of the past. Jennifer's role as the Woman of the Future is to simultaneously provide the sexual catalyst for social change based on an acknowledgment of women's sexuality and sex as amoral and then to opt to live in the past for her own and the social good; her agency is found in self-sacrifice and controlling her sexual self. David's role as the Man of the Future is to increase his self-confidence, to accept the mantle of leadership that is naturally, rightfully his, and to make the world—whatever the decade—a better place for everyone; his agency is found in controlling others. David inexplicably retains the ability to move back and forth between the 1950s and the 1990s at will, we learn, as he promises to come back soon and "check on" Jennifer, while Jennifer has been immobilized, her destructive sexual power rendered harmless by quite literally removing it from the contemporary world (she exists now, remember, in a TV show)—she and her sexual power/promiscuity have ceased to exist. David has been empowered and has gained greater freedom of movement and control, while the remaining women in his life—his real mother, Margaret, and Betty—are brought into their proper places in the private, domestic sphere.

David's real mother is depicted as weak and emotionally fragile; she is the adult version of 1990s Jennifer, giving in to shallow sexual desire and consumerism and discovering that happiness does not lie there—this, the film warns viewers, is what our world, what family life, will look like if we don't contain and control certain weaker, in this case female, youth who are incapable of self-discipline. *This* is the morality tale of *Pleasantville.* She sees her extramarital sexual choice, and her related absence from the family home, as destructive in the end—thanks to the support and insight of David, to whom she has returned in her rightful role: the mother, at home and available to her children. Margaret is told to "step back" into the 1950s and away from David as he leaves to do the important work of men in the troubled society of the 1990s, but not until she has made him some food and begged him never to forget her. Betty discovers sexual desire and pleasure and connects her unfulfilled sex life with George to her unfulfilling life as his wife in general. Once her sexual awakening is complete—or at least on its way—she decides to leave George, leave their home, and leave her homemaking duties, including her duties as Bud and Mary Sue's mother. In the end she is left by the narrative without closure; yet, the linear progression of the final scene depicts Betty with George and then Betty with Bill—a suggestion, perhaps, that in a fairly conventional way Betty leaves George for Bill and an arguably more satisfying, but still mostly conservative, sexual domestic relationship.

Pleasantville argues that women are sexual beings—not exactly a radical point. It argues, even, that sexual curiosity and experimentation are natural and, to a point, healthy. It also contends that women—at least women who have fulfilled their childbearing and child-rearing responsibilities—have the right to pursue sexual satisfaction and a fulfilling, monogamous, heterosexual partnership. Young women may be sexual—the film tells us that they may find D. H. Lawrence sexy—and they may even look sexually attractive in tight red sweaters for the visual delight of old white men feigning disapproval; but they may not engage in sex too often—or with too many partners—without *damaging themselves, the family, and the community.* The sexual ideology of the film is made visible in these contradictions; audiences are encouraged to understand Jennifer's decision not to return to the 1990s—and the conflated mother-figures of Betty and Margaret preparing food and then "stepping back"—as properly locating women in a 1950s context for the greater good of society. Youth has learned to put away childish things and to forge ahead with a more pragmatic project than sexual satisfaction—education—which serves the individual as well as the wider culture, *Pleasantville* assures us. Midway through the film, the teenagers continue to head in droves for Lovers' Lane, but it is no longer a scene of illicit groping. Lovers' Lane has become an idyllic Greek *gymnasium* where small groups of boys and girls in various stages of repose sit on the grass by the lake or recline under trees, holding books and conversing. Sex, the movie tells us, is a fine thing in that we are all sexual beings. But while we don't want to subscribe to the (conservative) notion that sex is bad, an overemphasis on sex as pleasure is a distraction that young people are unlikely able to resist on their own, not because sex is immoral but because some youth, by definition, are undisciplined. Ross makes a powerfully effective move in relocating sex from the immoral to the amoral—naturalizing sex and locating its greatest danger in young people, who are depicted as a kind of noble savage.[24] But as a practical matter, unrestrained sex has consequences, and containment of youth is thus deemed necessary for their own—and the community's—greater good; Ross attempts to skirt the issue of self-sacrifice by having his youthful characters make such choices on their own, without coercion—again, hiding conflict in the appearance of consent. Such inconsistencies are often found in texts that depict the power and freedom of the individual and the (a)morality of individual desire but that simultaneously reveal the need for individual sacrifice for the greater social good.

Sex and gender are central to the question of family, understood within the film as a contested site where struggles over the power to determine its structure, as well as its moral, economic, and educational function, take place among children, parents, the school, the larger community, and the state. At her 1990s school in the film's opening scene, we see Jennifer making a date for sex, and later she tells David that he can't spoil her date because she "even bought new underwear." Her actions here are meaningful only in the context of a cultural conviction that a seventeen-year-old girl who is sexually powerful will become a somewhat "monstrous" creature, the antithesis of nostalgic, sexist representations of youthful, female, sexual innocence: the experienced, jaded, consumerist, cynical, teenaged slut, the 1990s Jennifer. The ground has been laid for Jennifer to learn the error of her ways, to renounce and repent, and to encourage audiences to learn the lesson along with her.

Both female sexuality and the structural integrity of the traditional family impinge on the central question of power in Pleasantville—male power and its reliance on maintaining order and gaining the consent of those less powerful. As dissent begins to bubble up in various ways, however, gaining consent begins to appear less likely, and those in power *mobilize fear* to gain the consent of the governed in an attempt to crush perceived threats to order and stability, through threats of physical harm and actual mob violence and, eventually, by adjusting laws to criminalize difference itself and turn young people *as a group* into suspects, some more suspected than others. The fear of youth and any social practice that might call into question the existing structural order is located by the men in the bodies of their wives and children; as a group, the men appear to feel shame and emasculation at what they all agree is their increasing inability to control the women and children—the proper role of men. The film does not question this assumption of male power and control; in fact, it reinforces such a view by having David learn how to take control of both the public and private spheres—his social vision is a more contemporary liberal one than the Pleasantville establishment would have liked, *but the underlying premise is the same:* men are in charge of protecting and containing women and of ordering the social world as a world without conflict; women are in charge of caring for children and of the safekeeping of community morality through their own sexual repression.

Masculinity thus is defined as the power that properly orders and controls both public and private spheres, and individualism becomes the thread that brings the film together as it celebrates difference (within an all-white cast[e]) and reinscribes the notion that power resides with a few individuals, not through institutionalized structures, and that individuals are really free to do as they like. The people in Pleasantville turn colored when they discover their individual power, what is "in all of us, all the time," and recognize desire—certain desires—as natural and good in moderation. And moderation is the key: some things need to be changed, but only some things and only to a certain point. The mayor, who embodies the state, patriarchal oppression, misogyny, and repressed sexuality, stays black-and-white longer than any other character because these things he embodies belong to dominant culture and privilege. But David—literally the hope for the future—is *also* defined by his power in both the public and the domestic realms, his superior knowledge, his willingness to engage in violence, and his role as protector of women's sexuality against other men who would assault them *simply because they are walking around in public,* because their public presence exposes dominance and subordination.

His violence is necessary and good *only* if we accept a logic of male aggression and sexual predation. David does not come into color when he successfully dates and, presumably, has sex with a girl;[25] when he encourages civil disobedience in the form of artistic expression; when he comforts Betty with gentleness and understanding. He only comes into color through violence in service of male protection of the female body, a rationale for containment and control with a long historical precedent.

Similarly, Ross's attempt to portray the violence of racial discrimination, segregation, and mob violence of the 1950s in *Pleasantville* is remarkable in its conflations and contradictions. He begins by confusing the racial labels of "black" and "white" by making Pleasantville and its inhabitants, at least initially, black-and-white, and when individuals change from black-and-white to color, they are understood in Pleasantville as racially "colored." This is a potentially interesting move, but as soon as actual color begins to appear, any potential relevance to racial discrimination, violence, and its devastating material effects is erased from the film's political and pedagogical project. The impact of racial discrimination and violence on real people with visible racial markers is alluded to in the film; signs begin to appear that read "No Coloreds"; a teenaged, still black-and-white boy makes a sneering sexual comment to David about his "colored girlfriend"; and a violent gang of black-and-white young men attempt to attack Betty on the street after her nude portrait has been destroyed, with one of the youths suggesting they "see if she's the same color underneath her dress." But these indicators of a film grappling with real race issues lose all their power as we see the "color" applied to fruit, flowers, cars, and bubble gum as well as hair, skin, and eyes. Being "colored" is thus, in the underlying ideology of *Pleasantville,* both naturalized and excised from its cultural construction and lived history. Being colored in the 1950s, in Ross's no-conflict approach to difference, is not a problem once everyone "sees" that we're all the same—and he appears to mean this quite literally: the entire cast of *Pleasantville* is white; their features are unmistakably Caucasian, and whether in black-and-white or in color, the contrast of skin tone to everything surrounding it makes each character indisputably white and still the unmarked racial norm.

Another gap in the racial narrative of *Pleasantville* is the disturbing support of several racial stereotypes: that being "colored" is *rightly perceived* as being unusually sexually active and unable to restrain oneself from satisfying one's desires. Ross allows these stereotypes to stand because he attempts to frame both characteristics as "natural," and thus as good, but as a point in a larger narrative of progress. In depicting those in color as healthy and natural for having thrown off their repressive social chains and embracing desire and pleasure, and then *moving* them, through their own choice, to moderation and discipline and self-sacrifice, Ross tells a secular morality tale of maturation that conflates the racial Other, the sexually active young woman, and youth itself as immature and in need of containment and control in order to ensure the growth and prosperity of the larger culture. As they mature, Pleasantville's teenagers move past sexual to intellectual curiosity, education, and knowledge—where everyone is now in color, so difference no longer exists and everyone is, incidentally, actually white. It is astonishing that Ross attempts to argue that, in the end, racial diversity, freedom, and self-expression have won by depicting an all-white town without class, racial history, or conflict—in the end, the film insists that we are all the same.

The inherent danger to the stability of the family, school, community, and state that resides in youthful bodies and desires is apparent in the initial treatment in the film by parents and doctors of kids turning colored; the town doctor tells a concerned mother that the explicitly sexual, lush red lips, tongue, and mouth of her otherwise black-and-white daughter will "clear up on its own" and that the girl should stay away from chocolate and fried foods. This amusing reference to the advice doctors gave in the 1950s to teenaged patients who presented with acne suggests that we understand our racist and sexually repressive culture as having no more evil intent than exhibited by the kindly old family physician who is innocently working from what we now know to be faulty assumptions and inaccurate information. *Pleasantville* does offer a critique of sexual repression, racial discrimination, and gender oppression in its depiction of the generative possibilities of youth and the dangers they both face and present to themselves and their communities. But the film articulates a particular political and pedagogical agenda in making invisible the conditions and consequences of diminishing social investment, the privatization of public goods, crippling poverty, and systemic violence central to these issues.

Audiences are made to understand through the public pedagogy of *Pleasantville* that contemporary youth is at risk, both from outside forces and their own actions—actions that are taken because they either don't know any better or are unable to exercise self-control. Importantly, in Pleasantville *youth are not held responsible for either,* and thus a rationale is provided for prevention and response policies designed to contain and control the threat that young people pose to themselves and their communities. The political utility of *individual* and *structural* becomes more complex and more explicit here: oppressive gender roles are understood within the film as nonchangist structures (male dominance culminates in political office and the law) but rather easily made safe by individual (male) leadership. Further, while the film critiques such structures as unjust and solely about privilege, regardless of attempts by the privileged to "naturalize" the benefits they receive by linking them to a priori values, within the same narrative the power of male individuals is a given, unquestioned and unexamined. Conflict is rooted in bad individual behavior in the 1950s, while individual male leadership is depicted as the solution to the resulting injustice and structures are given and nonchangist in both worlds: family values and patriarchy. Injustice in the 1990s, however, is construed as an overwhelming cultural abandonment of an ideology of individual sacrifice for the greater good—particularly on the part of women—and the solution is individual choice to go back to the 1950s as a liberatory move. Ross's dilemma is one of contradiction that he does not resolve: in his nostalgic view of the 1950s, the structural power of white patriarchy successfully constructs some individuals and their lifestyle choices as a threat to social-sexual order; in his dire predictions of social-sexual decay already at work in the 1990s, Ross constructs some individuals and their lifestyle choices as dangerous and encourages a return to, or a reinvigoration of, white patriarchy, in the form of David, to make us safe once again. The seeming ineffectiveness of schooling to improve opportunities for youth in a dangerous world and to succeed in engaging them in their own educations is contextualized within a larger culture of anonymity and despair predicated on the disintegration of the family. Late 1990s schools and classrooms are understood within the politics of this film as devoid of both discipline and love, echoing its critique of the contemporary American family. This depiction of society's failure of its children, which results in those children facing a more dangerous world and, importantly, *becoming dangerous themselves,* resonates with and through other cultural texts, including the narratives of students, teachers, and parents, in ways that reproduce fear, construct particular identities, and result in punishing schools.

V. Zero Tolerance Policy: Prevention, Response, and the Rhetoric of Success

By focusing on the complex mobilizations of fear in the narratives of both *Pleasantville* and SHS, it becomes clear that even schools built in our most affluent suburban areas become punishing schools—by constructing particular notions of individual identity and agency around an empirically unjustified, but politically powerful, image of youth as both dangerous and in danger. As Giroux (2003b) argues, "the criminalization of social policy has now become a part of everyday culture and provides a common reference point that extends from governing prisons and regulating urban culture to running schools" (39), including affluent suburban schools. "Rather than attempting to work with youth and making an investment in their psychological, economic, and social well-being," he continues, "a growing number of cities are passing sweeping laws—curfews and bans against loitering and cruising—designed not only to keep youth off the streets but to make it easier to criminalize their behavior" (43).

> Fueled by moral panics about the war on drugs and images of urban youth of color as ultra violent, drug pushing gangbangers, *a national mood of fear* provided a legitimacy for zero tolerance policies in the schools as both an ideology of disdain and a policy of punishment. (47)

The criminalization of youth and its lack of empirical justification are highlighted by the contradictory notions of what constitutes "success" in both prevention and response policies. One young man at SHS said, referring to the lockdowns, that he thinks "the whole thing" is stupid. "It doesn't work," he said. "Plain and simple. The cops come in and they must feel really stupid because it's such a failure; they leave with nothing or very little in terms of catching anybody." He claimed, and others in class nodded in agreement, that people "have shit" in their cars, their lockers, and their backpacks, and they don't get tagged. "People know how to hide it on their bodies if they bring it to school, but most don't. If you want to get high you get high before school, and when school's out you can go get high, it's everywhere and you can get it in a second, so you just wait till after school. So it's pointless," he argued.[26] This student's conclusion that the drug searches are a failure whether they tag something or not is in sharp contrast to a comment made immediately after a lockdown by one of the principals: "I consider it a success if we find something in a lockdown. And I consider it a success if we don't find something. If we don't, that's a day in Suburbia there weren't any drugs here. If we do, we got it out of the school and somebody will pay the consequences."[27]

The policy of lockdowns and surprise drug searches is made unassailable in the administration's view, *regardless of the outcome,* in this logic of surveillance-itself-as-effective. The absence of drugs becomes evidence that the lockdowns are effective; the logic extends to a rationale for an ever increasing number of lockdowns or searches, since it is the searches themselves that constitute success rather than a confiscation of illegal substances and successful prosecution of and/or treatment for students found in possession of such substances.[28] But the logic is faulty only if we assume that its purpose is to address the actual problem of drugs on campus, since the evidence appears inconclusive both that there is a drug problem on campus that would merit such a response and, if there is, that the response is effectively addressing it. We should expand our understanding of the purpose of the lockdown and drug search policy, however, to include an ongoing and deliberate attempt to construct the kind of identity that renounces agency for the residents of Suburbia, and a wider citizen and political culture of SHS as a suburban white school that is safe and crime free, and using its considerable resources making sure they stay that way.

Not surprisingly, students' views about lockdowns and other zero tolerance surveillance strategies, in which all students are equally suspect, appear to have no impact on school policy formation and implementation. The fears and the beliefs about drugs held by administrators, teachers, parents, and other adults in the community shape school policy, as we see in the disjuncture between students' perceptions of the need for, and the success of, the lockdowns and the administration's perception. During a fourth-period seniors-only class we were observing, one of the House principals joined our discussion about the lockdown that had just ended moments earlier. We asked him how many lockdowns they had the previous year, and he said one; in that search, they caught one person with marijuana in his possession—an adult construction worker laboring on the new school building.[29] The principal told us later that SHS expected to have four or five lockdowns this year—an increase of 500 percent in the number of lockdowns annually, an increase based on the apprehension of one adult nonstudent in possession of an illegal substance on school property.

The benefits of the identity SHS constructs for itself as a school may be seen in the school's ability to contract for expensive surveillance equipment and police searches; community partnerships that make the school a hub of activity for the neighborhood; and its impressive school facility, exceptional teachers, and the relatively high test scores and graduation rates of its students. But what are the costs, to students, teachers, and the community, of the zero tolerance atmosphere deemed necessary to construct and maintain the identities patronized by community leaders? One fairly obvious result is the further erosion of the distinction between the prison and the school.[30] For example, the visual impact of the lockdown we experienced was made possible only because we weren't stopped from walking around while it was taking place. Consequently, we spotted things from far away, saw things happening in different places; we were able to more fully understand the entire exercise that was taking place. But neither the students, parents, nor teachers have that mobile vantage point; they no doubt are aware *in the abstract* of what happens during a lockdown, but they cannot *experience* the procedure because *everyone present is immobilized* and subjected to a centralized, aggressive, and unaccountable gaze. As soon as the lockdown is announced, no one moves.

One SHS parent commented, "It appears that the school moves quickly to—I don't want to use the word 'squash' . . . [but our son] will talk about one or two people getting in trouble and how it was very swift and very quick, it's like [snaps fingers quickly] they did something wrong, and Bang! They were gone."[31] Not unlike the principal's surveillance-itself-as-success approach to policy, this parent appears to assume that if only a few people are caught doing anything wrong, the hard-line approach and perpetual prevention and surveillance must be working—instead of assuming that if only a few people are caught, perhaps only a few people are doing anything wrong, undermining the crime prevention justification for such expenditures and leaving only the expressive and symbolic justifications.

The broad assumption by parents that drugs are "everywhere" in the school is not borne out by the results of the lockdowns, and yet the school building is designed, implemented, equipped, staffed and surveilled in order to deliberately and specifically guard some students (this is the claim) against the threat of other students (drug users or potential killers). Like Pleasantville, fear is mobilized to gain the consent of the "Whiteys" to punish—formally and informally—other individuals in color as a visible sign of their lack of self-control, despite the audience's knowledge that the meaning of being in color in Pleasantville is more complex. It means active citizen agency in search of living a full life—in search of the American Dream—as much as being a nonconformist and as much as being labeled a frightening individual threat. But with this prison approach at SHS comes real incarceration; one teacher, when asked if he sees a lot of fighting, said, "I haven't seen a fight. I've heard of kids saying . . . but not that I see. Of course I'm trapped here in the building . . . [laughs]."[32] Teachers feel imprisoned. Students feel imprisoned. Another teacher noted,

> *A lot of kids think that school—here, especially—is like a jail. Like they come here, and they have to do everything by the rules, and I think they don't really—they feel like they don't have any freedom. . . . It's really hard, if you want to control the kids, not to be strict. Because I think that if the administration wasn't strict, there'd be a lot of kids roaming the place and not being found. I mean the administration really walks around and checks every nook and cranny, all the time. And I think that really discourages kids, which is kind of a bummer. That brings . . . bad attitudes toward school itself. . . . I guarantee you could find at least half the kids here would say they don't like SHS.*[33]

Constant surveillance, every move regulated—the overwhelming impression the students receive is that the adults are waiting for them to break the rules; the adults have the impression that chaos and violence could come from any quarter at any moment. Everyone is fearful. They are all offered a palatial prison in a high-tech, expensive setting, but the disciplinary vigilance and punitive consequences reveal the prison mentality at work.

According to one teacher's description of in-school suspensions, the kids are sent to a particular room upstairs. "They're in one room," he said. "They can't move. They can't move from room to room. They're allowed to go to the bathroom. I think that's the only time they're allowed to leave. They eat their lunch in there, everything in there. They're not allowed to talk, not allowed to sleep."[34] As one parent put it, "they've decided the problem is in the building," and the administration has consequently put its energies in "crowd control, crowd management."[35] The school's strategy, according to one student, is "just pure adult supervision, because when something happens in the cafeteria one day, the next day there's like twice as many teachers there. Just to prevent it from happening again."[36]

SHS is busy producing Foucault's docile bodies, where the students have internalized the surveillance and discipline themselves.[37] One parent noted with startling enthusiasm that the "security people are in control, and the kids don't even know they're in control. And that's good! And the kids now are helping control because they're comfortable with the [security] people in the crowd."[38] At some point, the students begin to discipline themselves. Already, according to one guidance counselor, "90 percent of the cameras do not work because they haven't gotten them to put them in yet," and "most of the kids are unaware of this." There are no cameras in most of the wells, she told us, but while she knows that, the students do not, and "it's the perception" that counts. Tellingly, this counselor moved directly from talking about the *perception* of surveillance having the same effect as surveillance itself to commenting on another perception: "It appears," she said, "they're still student-centered, but there's definitely a lot more of a They-are-in-charge" attitude at SHS. "Even as an employee here, I'm told what to do a lot."[39]

The rhetoric of success employed by administrators and teachers at SHS to not only support the lockdowns as a policy but to *increase* the frequency of lockdowns enables such policies to stand immune from scrutiny or any empirical justification for their use. Such a reliance on fear-without-evidence creates fertile ground to expand a policy of response to a policy of preemption and thus to create a culture—a zero tolerance culture—that encourages naturalizing existing social relations and making power less visible, creating obstacles to critical scrutiny and democratic deliberation. Such a culture becomes the frame within which SHS and the wider community of Suburbia operate and the lens through which students, parents, teachers, and administrators—citizens—understand others and order the social world.

VI. Zero Tolerance Culture: Fear, Identity, and the Logic of Absence

The public pedagogy of *Pleasantville,* when read with and against Suburbia's individual, school, and community narratives, helps us to better understand a wider set of cultural associations and meanings that shift public discourse from a fear of diminishing social investment that disproportionately affects youth, the poor, and the nonwhite to fear of increasing decay of asserted values placed beyond critical scrutiny and safety, disproportionately targeting youth, the poor, and the nonwhite. The zero tolerance policies increasingly implemented in schools is part of a broader, growing zero tolerance culture that is a collective response to the latter, to those fears that are amplified rather than muted. These are broader cultural fears that have been mobilized by spending priorities that emphasize the need for *protection* and *punishment* over the need for *innovation* and *investment.* Zero tolerance responses to rule breaking—zero tolerance policies—define deviance as crime; a zero tolerance culture extends this thinking from response to *preemption,* where difference is culturally constructed as dangerous; where surveillance and lockdowns are successful as spectacles of official power, regardless of results; and where the shrinking distance between the school and the prison, adolescence and criminality, and the tensions between containment and control, on the one hand, and individual rights and democratic processes designed to build and maintain a participatory public sphere, on the other, remain largely unarticulatable in mainstream public discourse.

The unarticulated relationships and disappeared bodies in *Pleasantville* and the narratives of SHS are critically important to understanding the ways in which these texts help to construct and maintain a zero tolerance culture within which punishing schools increasingly operate. The absence of people of color in popular textual representations like *Pleasantville,* in affluent communities like Suburbia, and in the hallways of their high schools is remarkable. While *Pleasantville* purports to highlight issues of race, our analysis here demonstrates that to the degree that it does this it is premised on traditional gender subordination and an extremely thin understanding of racial discrimination that relies on the notion that *racial difference exists but doesn't matter.* In this liberal humanist rhetorical move, racial difference itself is disappeared in the name of equality, gaining the consent of self-identified nonracists for deliberately obliterating discursive resources for examining the consequences of racism. It feels like a good thing to say, "We're all the same; race shouldn't matter," but when we do we effectively dismiss racially based struggles over representation, access, economic parity, and bodily harm that mark the lives of millions of American citizens. The insistence by students, parents, and some teachers that racial "issues" do not exist at SHS, because actual nonwhite bodies are absent from most aspects of community life and are missing from the interpersonal interactions of the overwhelmingly white student body, reveals to some degree the logic of erasure in problem solving that informs the pedagogical and political projects of these texts.

Making explicit the implicit erasure of black bodies in narratives and experiences articulated through a discourse of tolerance and diversity serves to illuminate muted fears of the consequences of being black and poor—of even being associated with black and poor: economic divestment, social abandonment, fear, loathing, and imprisonment. At SHS, where most parents have some economic and political capital, the "muted" fears of the community are those fears that are discouraged, and thus remain unarticulated, because they disrupt the dominant, no-conflict identities so carefully constructed there. Analysis of *Pleasantville* and SHS narratives reveal a nonchangist, rugged individualist view of citizen identity and agency where individuals are explicitly understood as white, Christian, heterosexual males who will likely have a wife at home some day. In the context of SHS, the limitations of these identities remain invisible, and therefore are never addressed, revealing a powerful political utility based on a logic of absence and erasure and resulting in punishing schools and the punitive zero tolerance culture they reflect and reproduce.

The erasure of black bodies, ironically ever present in narratives that reveal a fear of the black other, a fear of difference, and a fear of powerlessness—a fear, in other words, of becoming the Other—suggests that the physical absence and geographic distance from inner-city black communities is, at least in part, constitutive of the fortress community emerging around SHS, and parallels the muting of black fears through the amplification of white fears that focus on (disembodied) young black males. Our analysis suggests only a few of the many ways in which cultural forms and myriad media images of youth construct and reproduce *particular* fears about young people, difference, and change, and collective conclusions about the proper role of the school in addressing and resolving those fears, and is consistent with analyses of other media that help to construct these fears as well.[40] In *The Culture of Fear,* Barry Glassner (1999) notes that, after a school shooting in Arkansas in March 1998, news media across the country characterized—and continued to characterize—such violence as a growing trend of inexplicable, deadly violence by teenagers *despite* the fact that months went by and the trend of "killer kids" heralded by the media never materialized. The news media, however, "[i]n stories on topics such as school safety and childhood trauma," told and retold the "gory details of the killings" with the result that, months later, when a deadly school shooting did occur in Oregon, "the event felt like a continuation of a 'disturbing trend'" (xv).[41]

> Punishment and policing have come to at least compete with, if not replace, teaching as the dominant mode of socialization. But the very real violence of a few schools concentrated in zones of hardened poverty and social disadvantage provides a "truth" of school crime that circulates across whole school systems. Once we start talking about the governance of schools, we are confronted with the security response that is clearly far more widespread than crime, governs more people and more situations. The degree of the response varies greatly from school district to school district, but to an amazing degree it has become nationalized with similar experts, strategies, and practices showing up in urban, suburban, and rural schools in all sections of the country. (Simon 2006, chap. 7, 9–10)

The examination of this one punishing school in one affluent American suburb—SHS—serves to illuminate these troubling transformations in education as a mechanism for socialization that reflects national educational reform in response to the challenges faced by other schools, inner-city schools (Simon 2005). We argue that the observed absence of black bodies and the fear of association with mass-mediated images of the consequences of being black, urban, and poor, articulated throughout the SHS narratives about conflict and conflict management, combine to reveal a punishing school animated by politically potent and incomplete notions of nostalgia, premised upon forms of citizen identity that are disempowering to SHS, and reinforce a politics of dependency that supports less accountable forms of state agency that more aggressively punish distant, black, inner-city schools.

Like *Pleasantville*'s limited and unchallenged notion of progressive change that is driven by heroic white men with women at home, the student and parent identities constructed at SHS are represented as progressive and emancipatory. But both are premised upon critical rhetorical and material exclusions insulated from deliberation by their placement in contexts where fears of difference and change are amplified and fears of official misconduct or concentrated disadvantage are muted. This serves to punish those most victimized communities and to patronize suburban constituencies in ways that actually *disempower* them. Within *Pleasantville*'s no-conflict ideology, frightening images of female bodies in blazing technicolor, a threat to community and to women themselves, made Jennifer's otherwise incomprehensible decision to return to the 1950s ordinary and pragmatic—a given. In Suburbia, frightening mass-mediated images of distant black male bodies, a threat to community and to children, are both physically absent *and* present, written into collective imaginations driven by a fear of the inner-city chaos they represent, making the repetition of these disembodied images a defense of a nostalgic community that defends privileged identities like David's by repeatedly and symbolically rejecting other identities in ever increasing punishments, including the exile of Jennifers to chaste and subservient identities and inner-city students to the hyperghetto (Wacquant 2000).

In Suburbia, students are present primarily as objects of suspicion and concern; they are strikingly absent from any attempt to help define goals, common values, and priorities—especially in a context of extensive public rhetoric about community partnerships and unity. And when we consider that, even with the community's participation in the facilities and events at this "hub" school, the students themselves are still imagined to be the primary beneficiaries, indeed the reason for the very existence of the school, this erasure of their presence and any attempt to include their voices in its conception and daily (cultural) structure reinforces the notion (and students' experience) that schooling is something that is done *to* them rather than something in which they participate or something that constructs for and with them citizen identities consistent with effective democratic agency. We might recognize or remember that schools, not unlike other public spaces, are "produced as a set of rights and interests backed by the force of law" (Docuyanan 2000, 111). In the case of SHS, the interpretations, rights, and interests of adults account for the conception, physical structure, curriculum, range of activities, and daily rules and regulations that construct and govern students' lives. Youth as a population is deemed in need of containment and control, and a pervasive intolerance of difference, because difference itself is understood as a threat to authority and order, results in a no-conflict approach to identity that relies on a particular construction of nostalgia.

VII. *The Good Old Days: Nostalgia, Community, and the Fear of Association*

Our collective fears about youth and schools are inextricably bound to concerns about social order and stability and, as such, reflect an ongoing struggle over identity. The unequal treatment of communities, schools, and students constitutes one means of identifying who has power and who does not; whose fears are heard and whose are not; whose children will find support in the wider culture and whose will not; which young people are more likely to end up in prison and which in graduate school. Examining fear is one way to illuminate these inequities; examining various community responses to those fears, and the ways in which identity production is an integral part of such responses, is another. In Suburbia, the community and the school work together to construct identities in which the neighborhood culture is an unambiguous benefit to the school and its students.[42]

SHS is doing understandable things for its children: working hard to provide them with excellent facilities and technologies, the best teachers and curriculums, extracurricular programs and wide community support, and a safe environment in which learning might take place. And yet, the removal of white social and economic power from urban centers removes white agency, political and economic capital, from the cities, leaving urban, nonwhite schools weaker and more vulnerable. By separating themselves, and thus defining themselves as white, innocent, safe, rich, and effective, suburban schools and communities define their necessary, always present Other as black, criminal, dangerous, poor, and ineffective, contributing in material and discursive ways to the decimation of those schools.[43] Such identities do not operate solely within the bounds of individual communities; they resonate within larger social formations and serve broader ideological functions. The identities of white suburban communities constructed in the narratives of Suburbia and *Pleasantville* help to shift the focus of fear onto the young, the poor, and the nonwhite and away from a state that, as Giroux and others have argued, is rapidly abandoning all of its social functions but that of policing, to the detriment of all our communities. The schools, as state institutions, are mirroring that model, and this is having a *disastrous* effect on today's youth.[44]

We can see all of this at work at SHS, where random school lockdowns with K-9 narcotics units occur regularly. Lockdowns are an expensive, time-consuming school effort to prevent illegal drug possession, use, and sales and their harmful effects on youth and the community. The inconsistencies in these two identities—SHS as white and thus not black, rich and thus not poor, suburban and thus not urban, as opposed to SHS as safe but in ever increasing need of security, having good kids but in ever increasing need of surveillance—reveal the fear of association with black, poor and urban from which SHS operates, and its responses that seem inexplicably irrational become thus rational because they are about muted fears and identity-as-disassociation.[45] In our examination of these school narratives, within a context of the criminalization of youth culture that is widely supported by popular culture and media, we can see that the zero tolerance culture of punishing schools is less about protecting students from drugs and violence and more about the disassociation of more powerful schools and communities from those schools and communities whose markers (black, poor, urban) are most likely to result in punishment by the state. Lockdowns *perform a particular identity* that is an expressive and symbolic marking of one community as power-rich, responsive to officially sanctioned fears, and intolerant of poor blacks—a position articulated as socially acceptable by virtue of its fit within a zero tolerance culture.

The ongoing struggle in Suburbia for a particular community and school identity relies on its opposite—that which it is *not:* SHS is not an urban school; it is not a black school; it is not a poor school. Suburbia's attempts to construct and maintain both an impressive building and an impressive education for its children are made with good intentions—and have in many ways accomplished positive results. But school policies that govern student movement and behavior reflect, upon close examination, fears that are unsubstantiated by data of student-related rule breaking.[46] Instead, the fears that motor policy appear to be related to a fear that if difference—in the form of racial difference, sexual difference, even consumer difference—thrives here, their school will degenerate into "those other" schools, no longer excellent in the ways they've identified as desirable. The *associative* understanding of "those other" schools—urban schools—makes (racial, sexual, and class) difference about instability, crime, and drugs.

In Pleasantville and SHS, the insistence on the power and moral stature of heroic (economically powerful, white, male, heterosexual) individuals provides a means for both supporting socially progressive objectives and *simultaneously* disassociating from those most likely to experience the punishing force of disenfranchisement: youth, the poor, the nonwhite. The nostalgia in both texts for traditional communities is premised on excluding difference and exalting citizen identities premised on denying citizen agency. Nostalgia and the fear of association create insular, isolationist living in privileged communities, which leads to the naturalization of the social order—no democratic deliberation—and, eventually, to an inattentiveness to power, education as reproduction of passive bodies, and the disengagement of youth from public spheres and democratic processes.

VIII. Cultivating Inattentiveness: Agency, Education, and Disengagement

A zero tolerance approach to crime, as it has expanded even to wealthy suburban schools, has become an official intolerance for disorder, misbehavior, and noncomformity as well and remains largely insulated from public scrutiny and justification. The critical public scrutiny constitutive of democratic deliberation in public spheres is constructed as a luxury that schools on the brink cannot afford and is viewed as another aspect of the frightening dis-orders threatening our children. Parents who complain are viewed as troublemakers, even as schools actively seek more parental involvement. Students who resist the prescribed identity of passive consumers of education are not leaders but rebels. Teachers increasingly forced to reduce teaching and learning to standardized tests and accountability measures enforce and cultivate an *inattentiveness to power* in which mentoring young citizens is transformed into encouraging passivity in the face of adult authority, understood increasingly as the authority of law enforcement. Such mentoring invites students to voluntarily embrace passive acquiescence as an identity without agency, much as Jennifer does when she opts to remain in 1950s Pleasantville. What is common to these constructions of student, teacher, and parent identities is their remarkable deference to state agency, even when official actions cannot be empirically justified. At SHS this includes lockdowns that are recognized as a success regardless of whether any illegal drugs are found; search procedures that include tactics that adult authorities insist do not occur because they are dangerous and possibly illegal but that students and teachers readily acknowledge are commonplace; surveillance cameras of which 90 percent do not work; and rules that make no sense but are enforced with enthusiasm.

This cultivated inattention to empirical reality and the best available data is not unique to SHS or to schools. Simon (2006) argues that in our most recent national efforts to reform education President George W. Bush relied heavily on inaccurate statistics to provide a frightening foundation for reforms that are insulated from scrutiny and that displace education with enforcement, despite overwhelming data that shows "schools are among the safest places for school aged children to be." Simon contends that the president's "gross exaggeration" makes political sense because "crime's relevance to the discussion of school reform is not dependent on its actual prevalence as a threat in schools but rests instead on crime's success as a rationale for recasting governance." With recasting governance as the goal, then, the mobilization of fear—even empirically unjustified fear—has enormous political utility. Thus, despite the relative safety of our schools, hysterical efforts to redefine education as enforcement, based on the unjustified but often repeated assertion that our schools (and youth) are dangerous and in danger, are doubly harmful and serve to both punish schools and create punishing schools. First, they demonstrate to our children that persuasion is a matter of simply saturating communication with statements amplifying familiar, if inaccurate, fears—a function of power. This provides a distorted view of democratic deliberation, making the public sphere appear unreasonable and undesirable, and undermines the efforts of educators to teach children the importance of defending claims with evidence. Second, these efforts colonize educational reform with a prison-industrial vision of limited governance where state agency becomes the only imaginable form of public agency, and, in this context, the only legitimate form for an active public agency is coercive force expressed as punitive approaches to conflict management: education as enforcement. The war on drugs and war on terror creep into a war on youth and a war on schools.

> Today, the merging of school and penal system has resulted . . . in speeding the collapse of the progressive project of education and tilted the administration of schools toward a highly authoritarian and mechanistic model. At its core, the implicit fallacy dominating schools today consists of collapsing all the vulnerabilities of youth into variations of the problems of criminal violence on the one hand and criminalizing their own failures in the name of "accountability," "zero tolerance," and "norm shaping" on the other. (Simon 2006, chap. 7, 3–4)

The student, teacher, and parent identities constructed in punishing schools reveal rhetorical efforts to support teachers, improve student learning, and increase parental participation to be limited to those forms of parental involvement, teaching, and learning that do not challenge the particular vision of state agency and limited government constituted by the forms of citizen agency identified here: a penal-industrial complex. Even in SHS, education as a value itself worthy of investment remains a secondary consequence of community partnerships privileging economic development and private property.[47] As we move closer to an acceptance of schooling as a mechanism for the production of docile bodies, passive citizens reinforcing less accountable state agency, we move further from more democratic and traditionally American approaches to education as the process through which we enable active, informed, and innovative citizen identities that can provide the cultural foundation for democratic deliberation and economic prosperity. Instead, punishing schools increasingly embrace a zero tolerance culture,[48] encouraging students, teachers, and parents to occupy subject positions defined by their dependence on impersonal and punitive forms of state agency, and redirect educational energies away from the active and open inquiry that teaches students the skills they need to become productive democratic citizens and toward enforcement of increasingly severe punishments for an enlarging menu of offenses, from bringing weapons to school to sending threatening e-mails, from wearing unapproved clothing to being late for class or exhibiting behavior that is willfully read as questioning authority.

The effect may be found in part in the criminalization of youth and difference at every level. At SHS, one teacher complimented students, claiming they are "pretty good" because "If a serious incident happens, I mean even something as stupid as somebody pulls a fire alarm, we nearly always find out who it is, because there's nearly always somebody who realizes that that's over the line, that there's a line there and if kids step over it, somebody needs to tell."[49] How do we reconcile the recognition by this teacher that some infractions are "stupid," in this context meaning "unimportant," with her characterization of these student-citizens as "good" for properly recognizing that even unimportant infractions are "over the line" and need to be reported? The underlying message for students is that *all* infractions, all differences, regardless of their nature or severity, are "over the line." When every infraction is equally punishable and the school, like the prison, is a space where inmates are under constant surveillance, the result is the docile bodies Foucault speaks of, not the active, critical citizen-participants of Dewey's model educational sites.[50]

And yet, that criminalization is discursively constructed by teachers, administrators, and parents as investing in students and providing the very best for Suburbia's kids. When one of the SHS principals was talking to a class we were observing about the K-9 drug task force from East Cleveland—not, he assured us, the local Suburbia police—he clearly understood himself to be providing information that would exhibit the care of their young people that Suburbia is committed to: he understood the information to be impressive; he was very proud of the credentials of the cops, and we were struck by this continuing vibe in Suburbia, that *there is nothing too good for our kids,* even in this: that we get the very best narcotic squad for *our* kids. But criminalizing youth, governing through fear, and the resultant zero tolerance culture train students to be inattentive yet entitled, passive, and cynical: "Seems like, you know, everything's so negative," one student glumly confided. "There's never really anything that's good. . . . you do something, and there's consequences—detentions, whatever. First thing every day, on the announcements, it's all about the punishment you'll get."[51]

Simon (2006, chap. 1, 4–5) notes that governing through crime provides a "focus [for] interventions of power," displacing fear of an unregulated market or fear of racially segregated schools with fear of crime as "our paradigm social problem." This displacement serves to dissipate public energies on fears that draw attention from failed leadership and focus it instead on difference and undisciplined youth. Rather than debates about how to maximize participation and balance rights and regulation, punishing schools assert what must be achieved, reducing the available identities to victim or offender—and at the high school level, these two options support rationales for containment and control, both as preemption and response, because *all* youth are either victim or offender. These become the only politically recognized roles dependent citizens can play, roles that narrow the options for effective agency to plugging into the system as a frightened victim or a frightening threat.

Even the architecture of the school encourages passive identities willing to defer to state agency. Leder (1993) argues that "Architecture helps determine the individual sense of autonomy. . . . architecture is crucial in determining the possibility of social interactions because, after all, as an individual, you only have so much freedom or power unless you associate with others and form communities to accomplish things in the world." This is seen nowhere more clearly than in the fact that in Suburbia the new high school was *designed to be locked down.* The ability to separate spaces, to separate bodies, and to immobilize "inmates" at SHS is based on prison architecture, which is "designed for control, to be able to separate one part of the prison from another part . . . without interfering with other operations in the jail" (31).

As we have seen, the perception on the part of students of constant surveillance is understood by administrators as effectively keeping at least some students from breaking the rules. Not breaking the rules—any rule, however insignificant—becomes the sense of agency central to the identities constructed in a punishing school. Passive acquiescence as what citizens can aspire to reduces the likelihood that students might see cultivating attentiveness to power as either possible or empowering. In education, this means a failure to teach children about power, conflict, and the social foundations and citizen skills essential for a stable, participatory, democratic order.

At SHS, like all punishing schools, it is not only the students who are made visible, and thus docile, by the disciplining gaze. The identities of teachers, administrators, and parents are also constructed as more subject than citizen. Leder (1993) similarly notes that, in a "panopticon, not only are the prisoners under surveillance but somebody might be watching the guards as well, all the employees of the institution" (33). At SHS after the lockdown, we asked approximately fifty students, two principals, and four teachers whether the dogs search or sniff the students or just the lockers and the backpacks (everyone was asked after we had already witnessed them doing so, with their noses anywhere from two to three inches from the students' bodies or in actual physical contact with students). We got different answers from each group.

One principal answered authoritatively that the dogs are not allowed to go near the students; when we said we had seen them search students, she said that she'd "look into it." The students, on the other hand, all agreed that the dogs regularly search or sniff them. "Oh, yeah," said one girl. "Definitely, the dogs do search the students—not everybody, but when the cops decide, 'Let's sniff out *these* students,' then they do." "I've been sniffed," said first one student, then others added, "I've been sniffed too" and "I know somebody who was sniffed!" until about half the class had admitted to firsthand experience with being searched by a dog; the majority of the others either offered secondhand confirmation of the practice or nodded in agreement.[52] The students, through experience, know that the dogs sniff the students regardless of the school's policy or the adults' belief that the legal limits of the policy are being upheld. We asked another principal if the dogs ever searched the students, and he responded that they *definitely* did not: "That would be dangerous," he said. "When they find something, they scratch and they bark and they growl, they jump up on whatever it is, a car or locker or whatever. They don't go near the students."[53] None of the students chose to disabuse him of that belief. Even the administrators are not exempt from the discipline of punishing schools or the coercion to passively accept—or turn a blind eye to—the undeniably militaristic power of the state they have partnered with, in the name of protecting "our children." Foucault argues that this is all the same structure of discipline: examination, which results in everyone inside the structure becoming visible, operating under surveillance, and thus moving toward self-discipline and docility.

It appears possible—perhaps probable—that some illegal procedures take place during the lockdowns at SHS. What is remarkable about the school community's official and unofficial views of those procedures, however, is the disjuncture between protecting students and stripping them of their rights. The day we witnessed the lockdown at SHS and spoke to so many students about it, it became impossible to imagine any student responding to an order to put her backpack in a pile on the floor, back up against the wall, and allow a dog to sniff her body by saying, "Excuse me, but I think my rights are being violated." *Impossible.* We asked one class explicitly, "What would it take for you to refuse?" They were incredulous. "I'm not going to say 'No' to the police!" said one boy. "Of course I'm going to do whatever the police tell me to do!" said another. When we attempted to draw gentle parallels to historical events where rights were eroded as a precursor to systemic violence, the students were unwavering in their insistence that they would follow orders. We persisted: "You're Jewish," we said, "and you've been ordered from your home and told to get on the train. Would you?" "Yeah, I'd do that if the police told me, I'd get on the train," said one girl. "Of course." "At what point would you draw the line?" we asked. "When somebody starts shooting at me," answered a thin young man. "That's when they've gone too far." Indeed. But that's also when it's likely too late.[54]

The slow hemorrhage of freedoms—like mobility and privacy, just cause and representation, made in the name of safety and in response to the mobilization of particular fears—and the construction of schools as prisons, where students are suspect and learning occurs under surveillance, contribute to a decreasing sense in privileged communities of oneself as intimately concerned with issues of individual rights and a growing inattentiveness to power that reduces education to disengaged, passive acquiescence. The "increasing fortress quality of American schools—which are marked by the foreboding presence of hired armed guards in the corridors, patrolled cafeterias, locked doors, video surveillance cameras, electronic badges, police dogs, and routine drug searchers" (Giroux 2003b, 49)—marks, in part, the transformation of schools from sites of democratic education to sites of social control and punishment. Further, as Giroux (2003b) argues in reference to the increasing number of gated communities also found in wealthy white suburbs, as these fortress-schools "abandon their role as democratic public spheres and are literally 'fenced off' from the communities that surround them, they lose their ability to become anything other than spaces of containment and control" (49–50).

Giroux (2003b) insists that "children should be understood as a crucial social resource who present for any healthy society important ethical and political considerations about the quality of public life, the allocation of social provisions, and the role of the state as a guardian of public interests" rather than as "a private consideration." He argues that the "backlash against children" evident in cultural representations of them—particularly adolescent African-American males—is symptomatic of "an attack on public life itself," as evidenced by the ways in which "particular groups, such as youth, are being abstracted from the language of justice, reciprocity, and compassion; and how the institutional and collective structures that once protected such groups are also being privatized, displaced, and defined almost entirely through the logic of the market." The "language of the public" is being "emptied of its social considerations," he argues (33–34).

> Most insidiously, zero tolerance laws, while a threat to all youth and any viable notion of democratic public education, reinforce in the public imagination the image of students of color as a source of public fear and a threat to public school safety. Zero tolerance policies and laws appear to be well-tailored to mobilizing racialized codes and race-based moral panics that portray black and brown urban youth as a new and frighteningly violent threat to the safety of "decent" Americans. (49)

The work of identity in suburban schools serves to *punish.* It punishes those in the community and school by seriously impeding their ability to move around, their rights to privacy and freedom from surveillance and scrutiny, their right to an adolescence that has not been already criminalized, and their ability to explore identities and perspectives that might enrich their lives and that of the larger community in a move away from fear. Further, urban schools are punished in that they are further impoverished by the withdrawal of potential allies in the increasingly brutal battle to keep public education alive as both a public good and an effective measure of freedom and opportunity in this country, so that in effect those most vulnerable to the failure by the state to meet its obligations to its young citizens are left in the crosshairs, standing alone, those with the least ability to change their situation. And, importantly, the culture loses in the identity work done in punishing schools because the structuring of identity as nonblack, nonurban, nonpoor, noncriminal has as its necessary opposite the reinforcement of systemic racism and racially coded acceptance of "those people" as criminals and as impoverished city dwellers, despite the articulated—and no doubt sincere—attempts by the community, school administrators, and teachers to work against racism and its devastating effects.

Chapter 4

Punitive Politics and Punishing Schools

Indeed, in Ohio, education is seldom mentioned in the same breath with investment. Rather, the state's appropriation for higher education is called an "instructional subsidy"—a gross misnomer suggesting an obligatory gesture no different than the many entitlements in the state budget.

This subsidy syndrome about education appears to have deep roots. Back in 1960, for example, a widely circulated study by Dr. George Thatcher, the former chairman of economics at Miami University of Ohio, turned up some disturbing facts about Ohio's dismissive attitude toward education. Although the state's personal income ranked 5th in the nation, its per capita support of higher education ranked near the bottom. Today, the figures are hardly more encouraging: Ohio is still near the bottom in per capita support for higher education, and, predictably, it has dropped to 22nd in personal income! Clearly, Ohio's subsidy mentality has had time to work its course during the last 40 years, and apparently for the worse. Thus, there should be little doubt that this idea of subsidy in educational spending is one that must change dramatically, and quickly, if our campuses are to serve as Ohio's most powerful engine for economic development.

—President of Central City University[1]

I. *Introduction*

This statement from the president of a local state university represents the politically anemic progressive flank in the education debates taking place in Ohio. The prevailing position in these education debates at least since the end of World War II, and as the state has dropped from fifth to twenty-second in highest income in the nation, has been dismissive in three ways that have been harmful to the state. First, state public and private leaders dismissing the value of public education have failed to invest in communities resilient enough to adapt to changes in employment opportunities. Second, leaders dismissing the importance of intellectual inquiry have encouraged an anti-intellectual culture based on a blue-collar job base that exists only as nostalgia. And third, leaders dismissing investment in the public sphere have left Ohioans today with a legacy of public impoverishment through a uniquely right-utopian combination of tax breaks for companies that still left the area and a public school system so seriously neglected that the only viable response to unsafe buildings was for the state legislature to exempt schools from building code requirements.[2]

State-level support for education has ranged from scarce to stingy. But the battle has been waged at many different levels, from neighborhood struggles to reverse a district decision to close a nearby elementary school, to electoral contests where local judges battle to be the toughest on youth violence, to extralegal enactment of vouchers and charter school reforms, to urban renewal efforts that fracture inner-city communities and leave their high school with the pejorative title of a school without a neighborhood, to a decadelong series of state supreme court decisions ruling that the state's system for funding public education was unconstitutional. And these ongoing struggles—political and economic, statewide and neighborhood—provide the context for our examination of efforts to better manage conflict at one inner-city high school located in the downtown section of one of the largest cities in the state: Urban High School. We will call this city Central City.

A History of the Present in Central City

Central City was first settled in the early nineteenth century at the intersection of critical commercial waterways that provided the foundation for the manufacturing facilities that settled in and around this city from its founding until the 1960s, when the capital flight associated with deindustrialization turned Central City, and the entire region, into part of the Rust Belt. One of the first two New England families to come to the area settled in the section of downtown where UHS was built in the late nineteenth century, the first high school in the city. This neighborhood was powerful enough at that time to remain independent when Central City was incorporated as a village, but it was annexed when Central City became a city thirty years later. The area was home to blue-collar working families, some of the city's most prominent families, a college established by a local church and named after a prominent local industrialist, manufacturing facilities, and UHS. And these connections were not simply a geographic coincidence. One of the early philanthropists to support UHS lived in the neighborhood, the owner of a farm machine manufacturing facility.

A graduate of UHS, writing to celebrate its fiftieth anniversary and quoting from the city newspaper's coverage of its opening, provides a wonderfully complex portrait of the disorder that reigned in the 1880s and the 1930s and the importance of this larger context for understanding the early prominence and later decline of UHS.[3]

> It was a period of adjustment between labor and rapidly expanding industry and of social conflict generally. Only two days after school opened, for instance, "nearly 1000 people prevented the Valley Railroad from laying switch across Ash Street this afternoon. . . . Lewis Miller, Jr. was pushed over, an Italian got a black eye and several citizens received slight bruises. . . ." Within a week of the opening of the school were recorded all sorts of strikes of packing house employees, railroad brakemen and coal miners; infanticide; tar and feathering; crude swindles; killings at local option riots; horrible deaths by hydrophobia, etc. (Alumni 1936, 4)

After describing the chaotic beginnings of UHS, this alum outlines an early focus on academics, music, and debating; the introduction of athletics by the "rowdy elements" of the student body in 1892; a "loss of innocence" marked by anti-Chinese yellow peril rhetoric in the school paper, *Forging Steel;* and the emergence of support for gender equality as manifest in a slogan advertised by the women's debate society. According to this author (1936, 7), "By 1897 the Woman Question in all its aspects began to burst American Society asunder. The [Philomathean Society's] contributions were numerous and practical, viz., 'Learn to say NO; and it will be of more use to you than to be able to read.'" The bicycle craze of the 1890s gave way to the Roaring Twenties, creating 122 local millionaires in three years and resulting in the construction of a new UHS gymnasium (still standing today) with Lincoln's words carved in stone: "I will study and get ready and perhaps some day my chance will come." Much of this account focuses on athletic achievements, noting, however, that the "Rooters Council" evolved into the school's student council sometime after the new gym was built (8–15). This author concludes his account as he began, with a sober assessment of the complex and challenging political and economic contexts within which UHS students prepared for adult living.

> Urban High's history began in troubled times. Again today the world is wrestling with one of the greatest problems it has even struggled with in its history. . . . US poverty dogs the footsteps of the 20,000,000 on relief, and menaces millions of others. . . . Decay has set in. UHS, once the pride of the finest residential section of the opulent '80s, battered and grimy, rests amid the remnants of that glory. In houses once the property of early founding families, but now housing many teeming thousands in their high-ceilinged rooms, live many of the dispossessed of Central City. (Alumni 1936, 21)

UHS was forged and grew during periods of great social conflict in a city and region experiencing rapid increases in population, prosperity, and poverty. Industrialization was disrupting farming families and community life, bringing together laboring families with different religious and ethnic backgrounds, but since the boom-and-bust cycle came with a generally expanding pool of jobs (until the 1960s), the numerous conflicts the alum describes—conflicts that ignite outrage, legislative action, and culture wars today—did not create the kind of moral panics, the struggles over the meaning of law and community, that characterized similarly conflicted communities in a context of steady job loss and economic insecurity.[4]

In chapters 2 and 3 we argued that the key conflicts for Suburban High School were internal, and we analyzed these to highlight the ways in which even in our most affluent suburbs schools are becoming more like penal institutions. In chapter 5 we will present similarly rich narrative data on an inner-city school in a district adjacent to SHS and argue that the students, teachers, and parents there also share a common discursive construction of the central conflicts and approaches to conflict management constitutive of their school culture, but the consensus at UHS focuses on tracing the roots of their inner-city school conflicts to the neighborhoods their students live in. This reveals a second aspect of punishing schools. While SHS students and teachers experience their palatial building as a prison, the students, teachers, and parents of UHS experience their school as a target for punishment from state and (to a lesser extent) local leaders, who punish their school for the challenges their students (and by extension their teachers) face.

Before we turn to that narrative data on UHS, however, this chapter provides a critical examination of the larger political, economic, and cultural contexts within which UHS and, to a lesser extent, SHS have been constituted as punishing schools. We highlight several aspects of that context to argue that the current controversies within and surrounding UHS are not simply the story of one school gone bad but are the foreseeable consequences of a series of choices made by public and private leaders at the national, state, and local levels—choices that reflect and challenge what we call in our final chapter America's zero tolerance electoral coalition and its associated zero tolerance culture. For reasons we will examine here, state leaders in Ohio, a state that has been dominated by conservative leadership for the entire postwar period, have consistently chosen to starve public education in favor of a vision of limited government that begins with an ideological unwillingness to collect sufficient tax revenue to avoid impoverishing public infrastructures, while imprudently increasing public investments in prison construction and probusiness subsidies even as manufacturing firms have left the state in droves over the last three decades, resulting in the steady loss of the previously high-paying blue-collar job base, including the loss of over 150,000 jobs in the last three years alone.

The failure to invest in education in Ohio is manifest in low higher education funding, low state-level funding for primary and secondary education, state-level redirection of lottery funds intended for education to other purposes, only reluctant investment in education when forced to provide local matches for lucrative federal urban renewal grants that generally funded preexisting industrial development needs to the detriment of schools like UHS, rapidly expanding vouchers and charter school movements that shift public education funds to either subsidize existing (and declining) religious school enrollments or to support for-profit educational management organizations (EMO) building schools with less innovative curriculums and much lower proficiency test scores, and choosing to ignore four separate state supreme court mandates to repair the school funding formula over a period of ten years.

The data provided in this chapter are presented to argue that, given this state (and national) context, leaders are punishing our inner-city schools for the challenges they face, as if their decaying buildings, decades of disinvestment, disappearing residential neighborhoods, and status as power-poor communities stand as evidence of parental neglect and uncontrollable youth. We argue that the evidence does not support this claim. Instead, we are persuaded that this approach to conflict management, to teaching and learning, in the inner city reflects a perspective on limited government that Ira Katznelson (1976, 220) calls one that encourages "a politics of dependency," where governance is limited to amplifying the largely punitive efforts to "manage the consequences of their inability to solve urban problems"; one that Mike Davis (1998) argues is based on an ecology of fear; and one that Jonathan Simon (1997) persuasively contends is best understood as an effort to govern through crime control.[5]

Our objective will be to clarify the political utility of amplifying and ignoring, mobilizing and redirecting, the often competing fears of inner-city and suburban parents. And the contextual data provided in this chapter are the first step in this process, making it clear that the leadership decisions that have constituted UHS as a problem building were also choices that favored responding to the (often politically amplified) fears of white suburban parents and muting the fears of black inner-city parents. Thus, this chapter examines the social foundations for what we call punishing schools, the current approaches to school conflict that exclude some communities and include others in ways that disempower both.

Cities cannot control deindustrialization, suburbanization, or federal government decisions to create additional burdens for urban areas in programs to eliminate welfare as we know it or compel local resources to be allocated to enormous unfunded mandates like No Child Left Behind. Yet, cities, unlike state or federal government agencies, also cannot find solace in simply symbolic or expressive approaches to the social control problems that result (Lyons and Scheingold 2000). As a result, city efforts to "manage the consequences of their inability to solve urban problems" (Katznelson 1976, 220) provide the final context we will examine here for understanding conflict management in our schools. Yet, while local leadership has certainly been more ambivalent about simply expressive and extremely punitive approaches to conflict, even their efforts have more to do with containing political conflicts and insulating this management strategy from critical public scrutiny than with providing a "thorough and efficient system of common schools" as required by the Ohio state constitution.

Industrial Development, Reluctant Educators

The growth of education in Central City, and particularly the downtown neighborhood where UHS and the state university are located, has been somewhat reluctantly supported by Central City residents. Educational investment after 1886 was stingy except when it was driven by state or federal funding opportunities. Even according to one prominent civic booster, the geographical expansion of the city limits from six thousand acres to over six times that number just before the Great Depression was driven by an intersection of industrial and developer interests. "First Steel Production had run out of space in east Central City and was ready to expand outside the city limits to the southwest. Fortunately, Central City's industries needed the structure of a city to supply basic services. So did developers and residents in areas of potential growth. That, combined with Central City's need for revenue from property taxes, made annexation an easy choice" (Booster 1996, 151). Later, when basic services were no longer linked to being located within city limits, joint economic development districts replaced annexation as the preferred strategy for developers and with it eliminated the indirect support for schools that was a secondary consequence of urban annexation.

In what can only be described as an incredibly loving portrait of Central City, this booster (1996, 160–62) argues that industrial interests drove development in a variety of ways beyond the pre-Depression era preference for annexation. It also meant that the kind of maintenance of public and private housing stocks characteristic of resilient communities was overlooked by local leadership—public and private. Parkland, for instance, was not put aside because private developers did not prioritize parks until the coming together of a combination of legal changes (development rules that required adequate park space and the creation of the Central City Metropolitan Park District), WPA work projects for building a network of paths and shelters with federal funds, a series of enormous land grants from local industrialists, and the designation of these together as the largest park in the area.

Even though parkland did eventually get set aside, entire inner-city neighborhoods were left to deteriorate "so that nothing but clearance was available for some neighborhoods by the 1960s" (Booster 1996, 158), because the decision to patronize industrialists with an annexation strategy that punished inner-city neighborhoods left enough open space available that the condition of existing housing stocks could be ignored in a sort of neighborhood-to-neighborhood inner-urban capital flight. This trend was accentuated by federal law. Home Owner's Load Corporation (HOLC) surveys ranked neighborhoods in ways that even this booster concludes mobilized shocking amounts of racial and ethnic bias, concentrating "undesirable populations" in clusters of poorly maintained homes with absentee or simply inhumane property owners[6] and without access to the same credit more desirable homeowners used to maintain their property until the 1977 passage of the Community Reinvestment Act (160–62).

> The conclusion is unavoidable that the rush of the boom period construction had *created* some poor housing in Central City. The Depression *created* something worse . . . Hoovervilles. . . . The tragedy is that, along with the shacks and the "jerry-built" housing identified across the country by the HOLC surveys, *many good houses well worth preserving and some good, stable neighborhoods headed downhill* under the burden of low grades [in the surveys]. Just as surely, and altogether unjustly, *many suitable borrowers were denied loans* or discouraged from seeking them. (Booster 1996, 161–62; emphasis added)

This civic booster describes the historical support for the local state university in terms that again suggest tepid enthusiasm for education. "The Church reasonably counted on local contributions to keep the college going, but the community was more inclined to be grateful than generous. . . . money was not flowing in" until outside funds were made available. Even then it still took the city three years to raise the matching funds. "For operating funds, the college lived on the edge of indignity, despite tuition increases and salary cuts" (1996, 166–67). Neither leaders nor laborers in Central City were particularly interested in investing in public education during this period. Their record was mixed at best, perhaps in part because economic success for working and industrialist families in Central City at this time was intimately tied to manufacturing. In their lived experiences, getting an education was at best only remotely associated with financial security, family values, or resilient communities. Just as for women "learning to say NO" might have been seen as more important than learning to read, men were arguably better off taking a factory job than pursing an education in schools that taxpayers only reluctantly supported.

In this context, a powerful union was born when workers in Central City factories successfully struck against First Steel Production Company in the early twentieth century, winning legal recognition of their right to bargain collectively. Progressive politics were channeled through unions, and success was measured in the terms of the contracts negotiated, leaving party politics and state governance to industrialists inclined to see contract concessions as the costs of doing business in Ohio and increasingly leaving education and other public (dis)investments as corporate externalities without citizen or community constituencies. In this period, World War II defense contracts played a major role in sustaining this unstable and anti-intellectual class compromise, supporting manufacturing in the area as local firms produced gas masks, anti-aircraft guns, tail assemblies for military aircraft, and other naval aircraft and parts, and wages rose in working-class neighborhoods populated with prosperous working families. But when defense contracts dried up after the war, other sources of support had to be found, a search that still consumes Central City leadership today and remains dependent on military contracts, federal funding, and a right-utopian view of the free market that first pretends that earlier prosperity and current revival efforts were not, in large part, a result of government involvement in the private sector and then asserts that a free market requires less government, lower taxes, malign neglect of schools, and public subsidies for corporations with far more shallow roots in the local communities than the children and families subjected to punishing schools.

Following World War I, employment in Central City fell more than 60 percent, and one of the most prominent industrial families in town lost control of the family manufacturing company he had started with his brother (a company that remains today an internationally known manufacturer, with no production facilities in Central City). By 1950, when bread cost twelve cents a loaf and milk forty-eight cents a gallon, manufacturing employment was growing fast again. There were six large firms with headquarters and production located in the city, which drove a powerful economic expansion that made Central City known around the world for manufacturing. Employment in the metropolitan area peaked in 1960. According to one scholar who studied Central City (1949, 4) there was "considerable Federal and War Housing residence construction" in Central City after the war, but the map he refers to shows none of this housing to be located in or near downtown. Instead, populations were being directed into what would become racially and class divided school districts by federal housing policy, leaving the poor and minority residents in the inner city to await forced relocation through urban renewal.

Three of the major industrial employers provided more than 50 percent of the jobs, and there were several smaller manufacturing facilities in town at this time. Wartime experience created a foundation for postwar production and catalyzed other diversifications—from ordinance production to metalworks, anti-aircraft guns to all-welded, stainless-steel containers. While there was some fear that this decentralization would hurt the city, it proved beneficial, when all of these manufacturing firms left the region in the 1970s and 1980s, that the city had already started to move from the company town structure (Scholar 1949, 7). While the early twentieth century was marked by industrial development, population growth, and a mixed legacy of support for education continuing through the post–World War II period, it was in the 1960s that this political and economic legacy, mobilized as an unstable anti-intellectual class compromise that fragmented community power, was transformed into a statewide, taken-for-granted, right-utopian view of the free market that relentlessly focused voter fear on taxes, including prominently a tradition of antitax fearmongering assaults on one of the foundations for sustained economic prosperity, vibrant democratic institutions, and resilient community life: public education.

II. State Leadership and Education on the Edge of Indignity

In 1960 the fortunes of the region, the state, and Central City—particularly the downtown neighborhood where we find UHS—began to change for the worse. Deindustrialization hit hard, turning the thriving blue-collar town into a collection of boarded up business districts with deteriorating neighborhood schools and residents lacking the education (or even the respect for education) that might have provided the resilience needed for community revitalization. Between 1960 and 1990 all of the manufacturing firms that had been the backbone of the city's employment closed their production facilities and moved out of the state. First Steel Production closed Plant 1 in the early 1970s, eliminating 1,300 of Central City's best jobs. In the late 1970s, it fended off a hostile takeover by firing hundreds more and selling off the divisions they worked in to other companies, leaving no production facilities and only their corporate headquarters to remind residents of better days. Two decades later they announced the layoff of 350 white-collar workers and 200 salaried jobs at the headquarters.[7] One respected Ohio historian, George Knepper, described the decline in these terms.

> Before the end of the sixties, ominous clouds already shadowed in some sectors of Ohio's economy, and in the seventies and eighties the state lost a considerable part of its industrial base. . . . Unemployment skyrocketed as industries moved out of state or succumbed to the streamlining of their new owners; around 300,000 of the world's best

> industrial jobs were lost. Ohio's unemployment rate exceeded the national average until the nineties. (Knepper 1994, 13)

A Tradition of Antitax Fearmongering at the State Level

According to many, these changes were both foreseeable and manageable, perhaps even avoidable. Political scientist John Gargan argues that the devastating impact of deindustrialization on Ohio communities ought not to be seen as simply a market phenomenon, an invisible hand beyond the control of local, state, or national leadership.

> The loss of well-paying jobs has drastically transformed many communities and increased the need for state-financed social services. And these economic changes have significantly altered Ohio's fiscal patterns. Decreasing manufacturing has shrunk the income, real property, tangible personal property, and corporate franchise tax bases available to the state and local governments. The fiscal bind has been compounded by decreased assistance from the federal government. . . . One analyst estimates that from 1980 to 1990, controlling for inflation and excluding welfare grants, per capita federal aid to Ohio state government fell 15.8%, aid to Ohio local governments fell 51.5%. (Gargan 1994, 280)

From the end of World War II until the collapse of the local manufacturing economy, according to Tom Diemer, "Ohio politicians in Washington were behind the curve." As he describes it, "under the watchful eye of the sixth-largest delegation on Capitol Hill, Lake Erie nearly died, industry fled to lower-cost sunbelt locations, and defense contracts were lost to coastal states" (Diemer 1994, 231). Gargan concludes that the inability to raise enough revenue to fund education and other essential government services is a manifestation of "Ohio's political culture"—a right-utopian political culture where nearly thirty-five years of conservative leadership in the Lausche-Rhodes era (1945–83) is best characterized as one filled with the "recurrent campaign and governing themes of . . . 'no new taxes' and the positive benefits of low taxes and a limited number of state employees" (Gargan 1994, 280).[8]

The political culture described by Gargan is one where those governors who did respond to budget deficits and crumbling schools were consistently pilloried in the press by conservative opponents willing to frighten voters with doomsday scenarios about how taxes—not capital flight driven by deindustrialization or the long-term disinvestment in public education—will destroy the Ohio economy. Not only were they wrong, since the economy tanked even with more than three decades of leaders running on antitax, corporate welfare platforms that led to consistently underfunding public education; their mistakes have weakened the possibility of a democratic political culture by dividing the public in ways that "dissipated their power by putting it to trivial uses" (Schattschneider 1975, 136–38) as they mobilized electoral support with fearmongering antitax pledges to unseat leaders who tried to fund education and other essential services.[9]

A brief look at Democratic governor Michael DiSalle—who was attacked for raising taxes—reveals what the later collapse of the Ohio economy and crippling of the Ohio school system proved: that the modest increases in taxes proposed (and vehemently criticized) are, in retrospect, best understood as efforts to ensure sufficient investment in essential public infrastructures *and* to balance the state budget—that is, to move toward greater, not less, fiscal responsibility at the state level.[10] When Governor DiSalle came to office in 1960 the state's conservative leadership had been spending only $106.20 per capita (more than $30 below the national average) and ranked seventh in spending on education among the twelve Great Lakes and Plains states. This same leadership, according to a study by the Legislative Service Commission, had also been increasing spending 9 percent annually from 1947 to 1958, while revenue increased only 4.3 percent, demonstrating that low investment in education was not part of a larger commitment to fiscal responsibility but rather characteristic of a right-utopian fear of the public sector articulated as antitaxes and antieducation by Ohio leaders during this period. Governor DiSalle called for two-cent increases in the gasoline and cigarette taxes; small increases in the horse racing tax, the corporate franchise tax, and the sales tax; and an alcohol tax (Curtin 1994, 50–53). These efforts turned him into a one-term governor, defeated by leaders willing to amplify public fears about even modest tax increases and to mute fears about the long-term deleterious effects of punishing schools: undermining secure employment.

Another short-lived initiative for fiscal responsibility and educational funding was put forth under one-term governor Jack Gilligan (1971–75). Described as "one of the few quick-witted, genuinely intellectual governors in recent Ohio history," by the political columnist Hugh McDiarmid, Governor Gilligan succeeded in passing the "first-ever corporate and personal income tax" legislation in Ohio. As a result, this one-term liberal democrat "faced near-continuous, knee-jerk resistance from conservative, largely rural, mostly Republican naysayers . . . which had ruled local and state government since the mid-1940s."

> The irony, of course, was that Gilligan—and, yes, the controversial income taxes that took him nearly a year to push through a hostile, suspicious legislature—were the key factors that enabled relatively affluent Ohio to begin escaping the low-tax, low-service stigma that had settled on the state following the post-World War II boom, a stigma more commonly associated with states such as Arkansas or Mississippi. (McDiarmid 1994, 85)

How were these efforts to fund education and to balance existing fiscal needs with tax revenues greeted?[11] Both leaders were attacked by gubernatorial candidate James Rhodes as "tax and spend" liberals, though neither the media nor the public seemed concerned enough to point out that the attacks were coming from "don't tax yet still spend" conservatives who had been running the state since World War II (and running it into the ground, though that would not become crystal clear until just after Governor Rhodes left office for the last time). According to McDiarmid, this fearmongering was not unique; rather, it was "vintage Rhodes hyperbole . . . [and] Ohioans had bought it in the 1960s and, shortly, would do so again at Gilligan's expense" (1994, 85).

> Both DiSalle and Gilligan were defeated after single terms by Rhodes, who, in campaigning against Gilligan, attacked the incumbent for taxing "everything in Ohio that walks, crawls, or flies." The politics of taxation shaped state politics. (Gargan 1994, 280)

The devastating economic decline ushered in by thirty years of anti-tax leadership with little to offer other than an opposition to funding government services, including education, also had a large negative impact on the political power of the state as a whole. "Ohio, the seventh largest state after the 1990 census, had lost 250,000 manufacturing jobs during the previous two decades; another 70,000 evaporated during the 1991–92 recession as the state faced an extended period of flat growth. After the 1990 census, Ohio claimed only 21 electoral votes, compared to Florida's 25, New York's 33, and California's 54. In 1936, the state had 26 electoral votes to California's 22" (Diemer 1994, 231). After the 2000 census this measure of the political power of Ohio dropped again to twenty electoral votes, while California increased to fifty-five. And the trends outlined here have become an enduring legacy in the state, a legacy of unemployment and tax giveaways to businesses, a legacy that has consistently supported funding for prisons in place of funding for education.

In addition to the data given previously for the period 1947–58, state data show that the funding choices made by Ohio leaders from 1976 to 2002, with the exception of one year, have been for the state to increase spending on education an average of 6 percent per year and to increase investment in corrections at a rate of 11 percent a year (not in the criminal justice system, just prisons). Investment in education, measured as a percentage of the state budget, dropped slightly (0.1 percent) over this period, while investment in corrections alone more than doubled.[12] But it is not only that funds for education have been low and are getting lower as funding for prisons explode. In a state where leaders are consistently frightening voters into defending the free market by opposing taxes to fund schools or other public infrastructures, tax funds are consistently raised for punishment and to support the "free market" with generous corporate subsidies. And subsidy patterns compound school funding biases.

According to Mark Cassell (2003) of Policy Matters Ohio, Ohio's Enterprise Zone Program provides high-income school districts with more than twice the number of new jobs and nearly five times as much property investment as very low-income school districts in the state (see table 1). According to three studies conducted by a second researcher at Policy Matters Ohio, Zach Schiller, corporate subsidies in the state are enormously costly in terms of tax dollars, quality of service delivery, and program accountability. Ohio has promised the largest company in America (Wal-Mart) $10 million in various types of corporate subsidies, including job creation tax credits that the state approved months *after* construction had already started on a new food warehouse, raising questions of "whether such help was needed to secure these positions" (Schiller 2002c). Businesses in Ohio are paying a shrinking share of state costs, as seen in the decline in Ohio's franchise tax from 16 percent of general revenue in the 1970s to 4.6 percent in 2002 (Schiller 2002a). And, in the past ten years, state leaders have more than doubled spending to contract for services with private outside vendors (Schiller 2002b).

TABLE 1. Enterprise Zone Investment of Tax Dollars, per 1,000 Residents, 2001

	Lowest Income School Districts	Highest Income School Districts
New Jobs	14.98	29.2
New Investment	$658,466	$1,774,436

Source: Data from Cassell 2003.

Privatization—spending public funds for services provided by private firms that were formerly provided by state employees, often at lower costs—does not reduce taxes but does reduce public oversight of how taxes are spent, and if the current efforts to review outsourcing practices remain focused simply on saving money (rather then cost-benefit calculations for each), it also provides a convenient first step toward service termination. Outsourcing in state educational expenditures includes "$5,000 a piece for a Columbus marketing firm to research and write six newspaper columns for its superintendent," continuing the larger political trend toward investing in public relations to persuade citizens that government agencies are doing a good job rather than investing in doing a better job. Educational outsourcing also includes more than $10 million annually on proficiency tests (Schiller 2002b).

This larger context—the right-utopian-, and antitax-driven, military-penal contract-financed, development strategy subscribed to at the state level—did provide several decades of high-paying manufacturing jobs in Central City, but it also established a statewide legacy of shifting the burden to local communities expected to pick up the slack for absent state investment (framed as "educational subsidies" in the state) in the public sector. Nowhere is this legacy—and the extralegal nature of it—more clearly manifest than in the decadelong legal battle over school funding that surrounds *DeRolph v. State of Ohio.*

Leaders Compound Inner-City Burdens: The DeRolph *Controversy*

In 1991 a coalition of 550 Ohio school districts filed suit in Perry County, arguing that the state funding formula for education was unequal and unconstitutional. In 1997 the Ohio Supreme Court agreed, ruling that the state's educational funding formula was unconstitutional because it "permitted vast wealth-based disparities . . . [and] worked to the substantial benefit of wealthier districts." In the majority opinion the court stated plainly that "the current system fails to provide a thorough and efficient system of common schools" as required by the state constitution.[13] In 2000 the court again ruled that the state funding formula was unconstitutional. In 2001 the court ruled a third time that "horrible funding inequities persist between school districts," and, unlike the two previous cases, this time the court retained jurisdiction in order to compel state leaders to respect what they had ignored since 1997: state law.[14] In 2002, after elections changed the composition of the court, it again ruled that the funding mechanism was unconstitutional but no longer retained jurisdiction, referring the case back to county court for enforcement. In 2003, reflecting electoral efforts by state leaders, the new Ohio Supreme Court blocked that same county judge from holding any further hearings on the case, in effect changing the law to accommodate what had been six years of elite-led, extralegal violence against the already most victimized students in the state, further concentrating disadvantage in inner-city communities.

Metro News ran a special series analyzing the funding imbalances that were challenged by the plaintiffs in the *DeRolph* case and the initial, arguably extralegal, response to these challenges from state leaders.

> From 1984–1994, 112 of Ohio's 611 school districts went bankrupt. . . . 104 had fewer dollars per pupil than ten years earlier. Voters in 89 of those districts agreed to pay higher property taxes, but spending per pupil in those districts still dropped. . . . Statewide opinion surveys have consistently shown that Ohio voters place a high priority on education. . . . Voinovich, who billed himself as the "education governor," promised in his 1990 campaign that education would be "No.1 on the issue agenda" for his administration. . . . He said he would raise education's share of the state general fund back to above 30 percent. . . . Instead, it has fallen from 27 percent at the time of his election in 1990 to less than 25 percent in 1995. . . . The response from state leaders to 1989 findings that school buildings were unsafe and crumbling was simple. The legislature passed and Governor Voinovich signed a law exempting schools from state building code requirements.[15]

The *Metro News* reporter outlined the dramatic funding disparities that drove school districts, starting with Perry County schools, to sue the state. The suit started in Perry County, which received 85 percent of its ($165,028) operating revenues locally, 14 percent from the state, and 1 percent from the federal government. The inequalities generated by the state funding formula become apparent when numbers like these are compared to other districts in the state. Medina received 63 percent of its ($61,580) operating revenues locally, 35 percent from the state, and 2 percent from the federal government. Central City received 41 percent of its ($58,046) operating revenues locally, 51 percent from the state, and 8 percent from the federal government. And the poorest district in the state received 27 percent of its ($42,284) operating revenues locally, 69 percent from the state, and 4 percent from the federal government.[16]

The *DeRolph* case demonstrates that not everyone in the state supports the tradition of antitax fearmongering to underfund education. The willingness of local communities to continue to pass school levies in response to state stinginess is additional evidence, but it also contributes to the gross inequalities in educational funding that exist when suburban schools are compared to inner-city or rural schools. "Central City is one of those districts where voters have increased property taxes, but per-pupil revenues still have declined. After factoring out inflation, Central City has $417 less to spend per pupil than it did 10 years ago—a reduction in 8 percent." Ohio Senate president Stanley Aronoff (R-Cincinnati) in support of the governor is quoted by *Metro News* as asserting that the state's hands have been tied by state and federal entitlement programs, saying that "schools have become the victim of the increasingly big human services part of the budget, a good part of which is mandated from Washington."[17] But state data do not support this assertion (see table 2).[18]

This controversy is instructive in a number of ways. First, the court rulings constructed a history of Ohio that exaggerated support at the state level for education, noting without a basis in fact in 2001 that there was agreement between judicial and legislative branches on the importance of "a thorough and efficient system of common schools" as the constitution requires and disagreement only on which branch had the ultimate authority to determine when this standard had been achieved

TABLE 2. Expenditures as a Percentage of Total State Budget

	1976	2001
Primary and Secondary Education	41.8	38.0
Higher Education	16.9	13.6
Human Services	27.5	24.7
Corrections	3.6	8.5

and whether the means were appropriate (constitutional). Second, even if we accept the courts' rosy portrayal in 2001 of past legislative support for education, the reaction of state leaders to the court's ruling tells a very different story. Rather than respond by fixing the funding formula and repairing decades of neglect, state leaders responded with a "carefully planned" two-year, $4 million campaign run by a group linked to the Ohio Chamber of Commerce called Citizens for a Strong Ohio to defeat state supreme court justice Alice Resnick, repeatedly characterizing her support for a constitutional school funding formula as a frightening effort to raise taxes.[19] While Resnick survived this well-funded attack from the business community, the larger effort did succeed in reconstituting the court with the election of conservative justice Deborah Cook in 2000 and the election of former prosecutor Maureen O'Connor in 2002.

A *Metro News* editorial concluded that the election itself—and the election commission's decision to allow the attack ads aimed at Resnick—demonstrated what the Citizens for a Strong Ohio was suggesting in its critique of Resnick: that justice was indeed for sale in Ohio.[20] The paper reported that the $13 million spent in 2002 by independent groups opposed to funding education, groups that refused to disclose their finances as required by law, exceeded spending in all other U.S. state court races across the country combined, concluding that "secretive spending on television ads that destroy basic notions of judicial fairness and impartiality promises a further erosion of public confidence" in the law, the courts, and the school system.[21]

As the director of the Ohio Coalition for Equity and Adequacy of School Funding argued in two separate press releases, the 2002 election also "precluded enforcement" of the *DeRolph* decision and continued a legacy of state-level neglect of education in Ohio. "In truth, the educational neglect the State unconstitutionally imposes on its children will forever impoverish Ohio."[22] For our purposes, this is yet more evidence of state-level neglect of educational funding, and, more important, as the Ohio Supreme Court has now ruled on four separate occasions, it is an extralegal form of elite-led violence to the public sphere that disproportionately disadvantages inner-city and rural school districts in the state. Further, the *DeRolph* case demonstrates that this particular approach to governance no longer resonates (if it ever did, given longstanding local support for school levies and the resounding reelection of Justice Resnick) with local communities frustrated with skyrocketing property taxes and a deteriorating public school infrastructure, a combination most lethal for schools, like UHS, located in inner-city neighborhoods.

Today, state leaders are still and again targeting educational funding. An October 2003 article in the *Lake Erie Ledger,* quotes the finance chair of the Central City Public Schools (CCPS) Board of Education as saying, "the 2003 state legislature had taken whacks at our finances." According to that report, the Ohio General Assembly chose to reduce the aid rates for schools from 2.8 percent to 2.2 percent per year for fiscal years 2004–7 (a $964,000 reduction for Central City schools). Legislators further chose to "eliminate a provision that helped districts such as Central City, which is experiencing declining enrollment" (another $257,820 loss). And other state decisions amounted to an additional reduction of $859,000 (for the next biennium). The finance chair concluded, "We need a reality check. There's a major erosion on the revenue side coming from Columbus."

> [A *Metro News*] analysis of state data and records shows that while lawmakers have campaigned for better schools, they have siphoned hundreds of millions of dollars from the classroom for other purposes. As a result, property owners are under constant pressure to approve higher taxes—and the gap separating tax-rich school districts from middle-income and poorer districts is growing.[23]

From the mid-1980s the push for education reform at the state level has focused not on failed state leadership but on avoiding taxes[24] and punishing schools as alternatives to increasing funding. First, schools that perform poorly on proficiency tests must divert already scarce resources into developing a plan for the state and continuously providing data for auditors to demonstrate plans to improve that focus on accountability to avoid punishment rather than on teaching and learning. At the same time, schools are punished by state programs (vouchers and charter schools in particular) that redirect public funds from public schools and toward private schools.[25]

> Republicans, who now control state government, have stated publicly that it is their plan to continue shifting the school funding burden to local property taxes, which vary widely from one district to another. In fact, the per-pupil revenue gap between the richest and poorest districts grew by 40% between 1984 and 1994. Instead of $10,930, the gap now stands at $15,252 when adjusted for inflation.[26]

But it gets even more troubling. It is not simply that state leaders fear taxes and refuse to fund education. They are also using education as a magnet to attract state lottery and urban renewal funds they can use for other purposes. I will examine these in reverse chronological order, because the decision to redirect lottery funds from education falls under state leadership and the decisions to redirect urban renewal funds were made by national, state, and local leaders (and are analyzed in the section that follows lottery funds for this reason).

Lottery Funds Fail to Find Education

A *Metro News* investigation found that "lawmakers, with the approval of governors, have used millions of dollars over the years intended to educate Ohio children to win friends and reward supporters." The paper provides a detailed account of how public and private state leaders amplified citizen fears of taxes to mute citizen fears about deteriorating public education. These efforts mobilized reluctant support among conservative voters for legislation establishing a state lottery into a free pass to divert funds from education altogether. The paper concluded that the funding patterns that resulted, not surprisingly, favored the wealthy. "Wealthy districts have received state dollars for buildings that are already built with local money, while districts with fewer resources did without."[27]

A study of states using lottery funds for education, cited in the *Metro News,* found that Ohio's diversion of educational funds made Ohio and Indiana the only two states where educational support showed significant declines after the lotteries were established, making each state "an example of what is wrong in education funding." According to the reporter,

> Lottery profits grew rapidly between 1986 and 1990, but records show the state legislature repeatedly under-budgeted lottery profits by $100 million annually, according to state records. When the school year ended, there was a big fanfare announcing an unbudgeted windfall, or what lawmakers called "excess lottery profits."[28]

The excess profits were used for school textbooks, building repair, or debt payments. While this process did not always distribute the excess funds according to educational need alone, beginning in 1991 the state legislature began a process whereby 97 percent of lottery profits were now targeted for basic classroom needs, meaning budget predictions that would create an artificial windfall were no longer possible. Instead, the lottery funds were now being used to free up funds previously committed to education for other uses.

After voting in 1990 to use $63 million in "excess profits" from the lottery for classroom aid (freeing up an equivalent amount from the education budget), state senator Roy Ray made the connections between educational funding, the antitax tradition of many state leaders, and fearmongering when he noted, "At the time, it was a good vote. We had a pretty serious financial problem. The governor cut spending, and then we scrounged around to find additional revenues. The (other) option would have been to raise taxes." But this was not how the lottery was sold. "State Rep. Ron Motti, D-Parma, father of the lottery, told people that if they approved state-run gambling, they would never have to vote on a school levy again. . . . Instead, the number of levies increased, as did the number of districts seeking state-backed loans to continue operating." Local school leaders are left to manage the consequences of these state decisions not to address deteriorating public education. "The public really has been misled," said superintendent Tucker Self in the same *Metro News* report. "What they [state officials] fail to say is that normal money that came in prior to the lottery has been taken away."

As Central City population declined steadily from its peak in 1960, mirroring deindustrialization capital flight, state-level leadership and investment strategies encouraged these challenges to be addressed along the race and class lines characteristic of white flight to Central City suburbs. In 1960 Central City was 81 percent white and 17 percent black; in 2000 it was 67 percent white, 30 percent black, and engaged in a losing struggle with prospering new suburban fortress communities for state educational support chronicled in the *DeRolph* controversy. State-level leaders were reluctant to invest in education and regularly prevented educational spending through electoral campaigns that frightened voters with promises that business would leave the state if taxes were raised to pay for basic quality-of-life services, including education. The empirical reality of businesses stampeding out of a state that refused to invest in education for three decades did not dampen right-utopian willingness to frighten citizens with antitax rhetoric in opposition to public education. In this context, how have local leaders responded?

III. *Local Educational Leadership and UHS*

As we saw in the previous section, the state lottery was justified by claiming it would make future school levies unnecessary, but levies have increased since the lottery was created and the funds have become routinely diverted out of education by state leaders. This shifts the burden of educational funding to the local communities, a shift that has revealed support for education in those communities who can afford it and has created growing disparities between the richest and poorest Ohio districts, challenged in *DeRolph* and found to be unconstitutional by the Ohio Supreme Court. But ten years later, after consistent efforts by state leaders to demonize the court's decision altered the court's composition, the court backed off before any changes were made to educational funding mechanisms in the state. The state story is clear: hostility to funding for education expressed as a part of a more generalized and utopian antitax sentiment that dominates the conservative leadership of the state. At the local level, and here we are focusing on the CCPS in particular, support for education as expressed in the passage of school levies has been more impressive.

According to the CCPS, the county board of elections, and a comprehensive study of Central City school funding completed in 1949, "the voters in Central City have consistently approved tax levies for funds to operate schools," and while bond issues for capital and plant improvement have been more difficult to predict, a $5.9 million bond passed with 72 percent of the vote in 1944 (Scholar 1949). While results are certainly mixed, local willingness to support education exceeds support at the state level.

The Construction of a School without a Neighborhood

On January 9, 2002, President George W. Bush came to Hamilton, Ohio, to sign his education bill, the No Child Left Behind Act, which the *Metro News* called the "most far reaching federal education bill in 40 years." The president, pictured along side Senator Ted Kennedy (D-MA) and Representative John Boehner (R-Hamilton), promised $26.5 billion for states to teach and test children. Ohio expected its share to be $170 million that year, increasing the federal share of the state's education budget from 6 to 8 percent.

A spokesperson for the Ohio Department of Education focused on the fact that the legislation increased required testing that will need approval from the state legislature. The Central City Education Association expressed concern about the idea of still more, and more pedagogically central, competitive testing. President Bush emphasized that the bill was designed to give parents options, but when he included charter schools among those options, the paper reported "only polite applause," because there is a growing sense in Ohio that the "parental choice" provided by charter schools is not evenly distributed.[29] As will be discussed later, it is better understood as a form of patronage for affluent parents that simultaneously punishes those power-poor parents with children in the state's poorest performing schools.

As the president was signing his education bill, 125 parents and teachers "with panic in their voices" gathered at UHS. According to the *Metro News,* the message for the district leaders was that "residents fear closing" their neighborhood schools, as an extension of feelings associated with the long unpopular city busing-for-integration plan and an articulation of a positive vision of community captured in the often repeated image of their kids being able to walk to and from school. The district proposed (for the second time in the decade) eliminating UHS and selling the building to the university because "it has the fewest students living nearby." But when parents were given the options of selling the building, leaving it as is, or converting it into a magnet school, only the option of selling the building "had little support."[30] In fact, the most common preference expressed was for a lot more time and information to allow for a thoughtful decision.[31]

While a desire to bolster state and district agency credibility drove the meeting agendas with a levy looming on the horizon, resident discussions at each meeting focused on support for their own neighborhood buildings, with a healthy dose of cynicism about the real political utility of these community meetings, according to the *Metro News.*[32]

> The planners have a job to overcome the reflex skepticism among ordinary residents when officials swear that their opinions really count. As one participant observed to general agreement at the one table Thursday, "they already know what they want." The inference was understood: school officials are just putting us through the motions here.[33]

But these controversies central to the credibility concerns, according to editorials in the *Metro News,* were neither on the meeting agendas nor part of the public education campaign that led the city and district to schedule these public meetings. By Valentine's Day the resident meetings were concluded. Residents learned that the message from the meetings, according to an assistant superintendent, was "clear as mud," meaning that the only policy decision to come from these was to spend another twenty thousand dollars to hire a consultant to conduct a phone survey.[34] The survey data provided to us by CCPS indicated that from the 989 questionnaires collected from eight community meetings "the biggest concern was funding" and "most did not support selling Urban High."[35] It was also clear from the voluminous individual and group comments reported that numerous residents were angry about these "community dialogues." One resident's comment from a group session focused, like many others, on the lack of information and time needed to provide meaningful input. In response to the question "As we move forward, what ideas/concerns would you like to share?" this resident replied,

> We decided this process was ridiculous—you gave us very little information. Our answers would not be informed enough to make this truly important decision. Give us more visuals, answer more questions, think on a more holistic level. We want to know how neighborhoods will be affected. We also want to know how the school designs will be developed. We are an urban center, not suburbia. Urban communities are very different from suburban communities—that must be considered. History is important to us. New buildings are sterile and lack character.[36]

But UHS survived this process and was neither sold to the university nor torn down (this time). Being a school without a neighborhood, however, at a time when the CCPS were moving to take advantage of state and federal funds to "fully embrace neighborhood schooling" not only put UHS on the defensive, but it also provided the financial and discursive context for school officials' announcement that they will eliminate a controversial effort to integrate city schools through forced busing, an effort that started in the 1970s with the closing of "eight inner city schools serving mostly African-American families." According to a prominent religious leader in town, this plan may also "bring some turmoil because some people don't want their children to go to their neighborhood school. But that's where we have to bring all our schools up to par, so people will want to send their children to these schools."[37]

University Encroachment and Urban Renewal

As it turns out, the perception of no neighborhood is likely a combination of two related factors. First, it is even more of a downtown school today, as the residential character of its surrounding land has been transformed by public and private leaders seeking to revitalize downtown through expansion. The university, partnering with developers and the city, state, and federal governments, annexed enormous residential sections to the south as part of federally funded urban renewal efforts (replacing 234 mostly single-family homes with a large athletic field). This expansion of the downtown core also included the publicly funded construction of the (nearly unused) Waterfront highway, a new museum (always empty and a recent recipient of community development funds to stave off bankruptcy—over objections from community leaders), and the expansion of a hospital (all consuming either a part of or entire residential neighborhoods that previously supported UHS).[38]

Second, dismissing UHS as a school without a neighborhood serves as a focal point for citywide displeasure with forced busing, the darkening of Central City neighborhoods and schools, and the severe economic decline that has plagued the area since so many large manufacturing firms closed shop and took their jobs with them. These two factors make it difficult to imagine an old, new, or renovated UHS satisfying the public school system or city council, as they join forces to build school buildings as dual-use neighborhood-friendly "community learning centers" and a basis for revitalizing Central City communities.[39]

As early as 1967, immediately after the university purchased Marshall Elementary School from the city, parents were articulating their fears that UHS would be closed as university expansion replaced its residential neighborhoods with athletic fields and parking garages.[40] A report written by a prominent local judge provided the following resident survey data (which can be read as sort of retrospective push polling data, since the questions tell us as much about the political struggle as the responses):[41]

Survey Question:

> As university development absorbs Urban High School, a comprehensive high school should be built in the central part of the city to replace it. 55% agreed with this statement. 15% disagreed. And 29% were undecided.

Survey Question:
The population of each school should reflect as wide as possible a range of socio-economic, cultural, and racial diversity, so all children have experience with others of different backgrounds as they are growing up. 43% agreed with this statement. 40% disagreed. And 17% were undecided.

Survey Question:
School attendance should be determined solely by neighborhood boundaries. 70% agreed with this statement. 18% disagreed. And 12% were undecided.

It was only with federally funded urban renewal funds in the 1960s that the city found it within itself to utilize its local college "to finesse the issue of blight" and acquired a downtown neighborhood housing 234 families, clearing the land for athletic fields. When President Kennedy's Higher Education Facilities Act made construction funds available (the state revised its constitution to allow the issuance of bonds for campus construction), a series of grants brought in more federal (and some state) dollars to build over a dozen new buildings for the university campus (Booster 1996, 166–78). The most glamorous of these buildings was a performance hall that attracted financial support from First Steel Production and was named after a former president of that company.

The expansion of the university was thrust upon a reluctant city by the availability of federal grants through the 1960s and 1970s, but this luxury turned to a necessity in the 1980s as downtown business anchors closed. By the early 1990s most of the downtown area was boarded up, awaiting the aggressive redevelopment strategies of Central City's longest-serving mayor. These strategies would again cast the university, and the public schools in general, in the role of magnets assisting the city in attracting private investment as well as state and federal grant funds.

A second scholar researching the city, in a detailed empirical analysis of the racially disparate impact of two large urban renewal efforts in Central City, concluded that two central claims made by city leaders to justify these urban renewal efforts were "not supported by the data." Leaders claimed that "there would be no difference" between black and white relocatees with similar socioeconomic characteristics in terms of where they will relocate to and, more specifically, in terms of "their pattern of movement into future urban renewal or rehabilitation areas." Newspaper stories at that time make it clear that the thousands of families and hundreds of (mostly black-owned) businesses that were forcibly relocated did not support renewal of their neighborhood, because it meant either displacing them for private developers or replacing their community with a six-lane highway.[42]

Contrary to the promises of city leaders 52 percent of white residents relocated into neighborhoods that were less than 5 percent black, while 45 percent of black residents relocated into neighborhoods that were 40–90 percent black (and another 42 percent of blacks relocated into neighborhoods that were 5–40 percent black). Only 7 percent of white residents relocated into neighborhoods with more than 40 percent blacks, and only 9 percent of black residents relocated into neighborhoods with less than 5 percent blacks (Scholar 2 1966, 72). These proportions remained when this scholar controlled for income, occupation, home ownership, and age.

> When a relocatee was white but had a lower status occupation, a lower income, was a tenant, received less for his home or was older than Negroes, the tendency was still to move to Area IV [less than 0.5% black] on the periphery of the city. (Scholar 2 1966, 90)

In the early 1960s, the first large renewal effort was a one-hundred-acre renewal project just southeast of the central business district that replaced "obsolete factories, scrap yards, and overcrowded substandard multi-family dwellings" with "an attractive industrial and commercial park with an adjoining new moderately low and medium income residential development," according to local planners.[43] In a second phase of this urban renewal effort the city moved 234 families, clearing twenty-seven acres for university athletic fields. At community meetings in 1957 the university president reassured concerned residents that any expansion was "years in the future."[44] The 1959 revisions to the Federal Housing Act of 1954, however, provided two federal dollars for every one local matching dollar for urban renewal linked to higher education. The city was able to use monies spent in the previous five years for campus construction (and already planned expenditures for street repairs and utility upgrades) as its $1 million match and the $2 million of federal funds to purchase the land and relocate 234 families who sent their children to UHS while it was the premier school in the city.[45]

While these two initial urban renewal efforts clearly exacerbated racial segregation in the city, placing a larger burden on black families and their communities for the costs of renewing city neighborhoods left to decay as a result of irresponsible public and private leadership in the white community, subsequent renewal efforts in the same decade then forced more black (38.8 percent) than white (9.8 percent) residents to relocate a second time (Scholar 2 1966, 93). From 1960 to 1969, these two additional renewal efforts impacted the UHS district directly and when combined with other renewal efforts completed in rapid succession the planned dismantling of neighborhoods that once constituted a mixed-class and mixed-race school district and the construction of UHS as a school without a neighborhood.[46]

Waterfront Park was the last major federally funded renewal project in this period,[47] with core work completed by 1970. This was a four-hundred-acre section just south of the central business district that had long been home to one of the city's leading manufacturing facilities, but as one city planner commented, "no one was willing to put up cash for much needed capital improvements—streets, sidewalks, street lighting, parks" dating back as far as 1910.[48] As a consequence, this section of the city suffered from double the population density of the rest of the city, double the rate of substandard housing (41 percent), a 30 percent higher unemployment rate, the worst city services, lower incomes (22 percent earning less than three thousand dollars a year compared to 13 percent citywide), and a concentration of the city's least educated residents (25 percent with less than an eighth grade education). "Skyrocketing costs and segregation blocked all avenues of escape for most of the people." By 1966, the schools in this area were highly segregated, "matching the segregated neighborhoods in which they are located."[49]

This project relocated over eight thousand individuals from "a recognized trouble spot of the city" with a population in 1960 already 60 percent less than in 1950, and "indications [were] that the 'blight' [was] spreading southward."[50] But even these frightening statistics were not enough to get one of the nation's largest renewal efforts going, however. The $42 million project was saved when the large manufacturing firm that would benefit most from the renewal contributed $3.5 million toward the city's local matching funds. "[O]nly two years after the city was faced with threat of economic disaster . . . [when] its largest employer with its national headquarters and plant surrounded by 403 acres of blight, seems set to pull out of Central City and move elsewhere," that same employer created a "unique partnership" with the city.[51] What was initially advertised as a project that would renew the area with twenty-one hundred family homes, however, ended up financing several thousand apartment units (further subsidized with low-interest federal loans), another large parking garage ($6.4 million), another highway project ($4.2 million) to link downtown to northern suburbs, as well as routine street and utility repairs ($1.5 million).[52]

Not surprisingly, as the city moved to renew this area in a way that would force these already disadvantaged, poorer, mostly black workers out of the neighborhood, a 1970 report found that citizens generally lacked adequate information about urban renewal and that participation from the families to be moved was minimal. This report found that citizen opposition to relocation and to the proposed highway was high, because it would "insulate and isolate the white segments" of the city and "destroy . . . [a] concentration of black-owned businesses." The report notes that residents strongly supported renewal that would build detached housing rather than track housing or apartments, because they "fear[ed] the image of what they've seen in other cities."[53] These fears fell on deaf ears.

> Residents have become wary, indeed frightened of a city-wide decision-making process which hangs like the sword of Damocles over the heads of residents. Citizens are afraid to make repair investments. Businesses cannot plan. . . . The planning and decision-making are not done with the idea of maintaining community, cohesion and common bonds.[54]

Despite the articulated fears of Central City residents, the renewal projects displaced enormous numbers of poor minority residents, creating even greater concentrations of disadvantage in the neighborhoods on the other side of what would later become the Waterfront Highway, westside neighborhoods now outside of, and cut off from, the Central City business district. And the renewal built mostly low-income housing in the form of high-rise apartment buildings and townhouse track developments that now constitute the most unappealing blocks of housing stock in the city, far from UHS, but with subsequent school boundary adjustments these became UHS neighborhoods-at-a-distance. These federal renewal dollars also made possible the acquisition of eleven acres of land long sought by one of the city's major manufacturing firms (as we write, no longer providing any jobs in the city) that surrounded its fifty buildings, all of which would be granted the exception sought by other property owners—allowing it to be renovated rather than renewed. Promised rehabilitation of existing detached housing stock adjacent to the renewal areas—powerful rhetoric about ensuring that relocated residents would live in the quality neighborhoods of Waterfront Park—was implemented only through clearly ineffective efforts at more punitive code enforcement in these areas, efforts that, to be effective, would simply off-load the cost of achieving the promise embedded in the powerful rhetoric from the city or state to the already poor homeowners in that neighborhood.[55]

A 1975 Planning Department memo concluded that 3,197 families had been relocated in all the renewal efforts, at a cost exceeding $180 million. While the earlier areas annexed for athletic fields by the university were neighborhoods directly adjacent to UHS, the choices made regarding the Waterfront Park area also impacted UHS. Before renewal, this area was covered by South High School, which was closed in the 1970s over strong neighborhood opposition. Each of these renewal efforts forced black residents to concentrate in this area and the neighborhoods just to the west. As a result, the city's premier (and largely white) high school in the 1950s (Lincoln-West High) was 96 percent black in 1994, catalyzing the flight of white residents north into what would soon become the Rhodes High School Cluster, when two new school buildings were built in the early 1960s. Without South High School and with the darkening of Lincoln-West High, school boundary adjustments became the tool for responding to the fears of powerful white residents by insulating their children from poor, black students. Lincoln-West's enrollment area shrank, giving way to Rhodes High on its northern, whiter boundary. And UHS's boundary moved west to include the northern section of the Waterfront Park Urban Renewal Area.

In the ten years from 1983 to 1993, one of Central City's newest suburban communities experienced a 41 percent increase in student enrollment. One explanation for this rapid growth while Peak County student enrollment as a whole was declining was offered by the dean of the Central City University College of Education. "If [public] schools continue to be charged with the responsibility for curing all social ills, more parents will be choosing to pull their children out."[56]

Modifying the Integration Plan

In 1963 it was clear that three of the then nine high schools were located in entirely white neighborhoods. An article in the *Metro News* at that time noted that the city had one all-black school and twenty-five all-white school buildings.[57] Further, the only high school building located in a largely black neighborhood was closed (along with the elementary and middle schools in its cluster) by the city because it was old (though the data shows these were not the oldest buildings). These school closings "caused property values to drop," according to one black city council member in 1999 discussing the proposed removal of the Waterfront highway, which had replaced "culturally-mixed, working class neighborhoods" in areas immediately adjacent to both the area previously served by South High School and the area still served by UHS today.[58]

In the early 1960s, on behalf of several black parents, the local chapter of the National Association for the Advancement of Colored People (NAACP) sued CCPS for discrimination as a result of segregated and inferior schools. A federal judge ruled that school segregation was a result of residential housing patterns, not school district policy. CCPS responded to the articulated fears of these black parents with a voluntary busing plan designed to preempt court-ordered busing and to ensure that nearly all the students to be bused would be black. The Central City Plan closed eight schools in the 1970s, which meant that nearly all of the three thousand students to be bused would be the black students from these neighborhoods whose schools had been closed over the strenuous protest of residents. A federal judge ruled the plan to be unconstitutional, but the reopening of one school that satisfied this judge did not alter the deeply racially biased approach to school construction, busing, and education central to the plan.[59]

In 1993, when the city modified its controversial voluntary school busing plan to reduce the number of minority students bused to Jane Addams High (all white in 1963) from the west side (the neighborhoods where most black urban renewal residents relocated to), a school board document, *Modified Central City Plan* pointed out that crosstown busing "grew out of the need to close school buildings in the mid-1970s" and was now being modified in response to calls from parents to reduce busing, "especially from West Central City to Jane Addams." A second justification for this modification of school boundaries was that Federal Magnet School Grant funds would not have been available to the city if the city's implementation of magnet schools would have had a segregationist impact. Given that the city's "open enrollment" policy, which denies requests from black parents to move their children into schools that are already majority nonwhite, would have meant that the magnet program at UHS (and two other majority nonwhite buildings) would have become inaccessible to black students, the new school boundaries could be justified as an effort to increase parental choice, and particularly for black parents.[60]

By the time the CCPS superintendent resigned in 1997, a superintendent who was a compromise replacement for the previous superintendent, in charge for only the five "strife filled years" that centered on efforts to modify the integration plan, it had become clear that the "biggest problem at present is the obvious divisiveness of the current board over race" manifest in white opposition to an Afrocentric school as segregationist and in black opposition to hiring practices that were forcing qualified black candidates to accept positions in other districts.[61]

Federal, state, and city battles provide a macrocontext in which public and private choices consistently treated public education as a secondary concern, behind the concerns of developers and industrialists as the region struggled to carve out its initial identity and behind the menu of concerns articulated by the conservative antitax leaders who have inherited their leadership mantle today. The data show that, while the situation is more complex at the local level, support for education remains reluctant and state and local leadership tends to combine forces to target public schools for punishment, as seen in the voucher and charter schools reforms discussed next.[62]

IV. The Charter School Debate: Redirecting Citizen Fears

Conflicts among school leaders are rarely highlighted in the news in the ways youth conflicts are routinely represented—as dramatic and frightening threats to community and family.[63] But when elite consensus is incomplete, as on the charter school issue, and the normal coalitions are disrupted because people are being divided in new and challenging ways, we are provided a rare, indeed exceptional, opportunity to examine conflicts among leaders over education. In general, we are encouraged to focus our fears and anxieties on "their kids," on amplified images of rising school violence, and on the "excessive permissiveness" of a criminal justice system with more inmates per capita than any civilization in the history of time. Even within the charter school debate elite-amplified fears of permissiveness and unruly youth are represented as central explanations for our failing educational system (rather than consistent underfunding), justifying an elite-led combination of democratic rhetoric about parental choice and a plutocratic reality of privatizing public education that is punishing our public schools.

In 1999 the *City Post* ran a series on education that documented both the political forces driving this assault on public education and the manipulation of parental fears at the heart of the movement. Under the banner of increasing parental choice, which President Bush emphasized to only polite applause four years later, the move toward charter schools ignored the history of failed leadership manifest in antitax fearmongering to redirect the fears of parents sending their children to these crippled schools from anger at state legislators and governors toward underpaid and overworked public school teachers.

> Ohio, already No.1 in the '90s for putting public dollars into private schools and last in the nation for placing children in safe and sanitary buildings, is on course to earn a new distinction in the next decade. The state is ready to rival Arizona, California, Florida, and Michigan for funneling state and local tax dollars to a new class of schools—charter schools—that are public in some ways public and private in others. Two years ago, Ohio did not have a charter school law on the books. But state lawmakers, former Governor George Voinovich and current Governor Bob Taft have made up for lost time—paving the way for 48 charter schools to open statewide in just the past 15 months.[64]

The rhetoric of charter supporters, reflecting the president's rhetoric, continually emphasized increasing parental choice. According to the *City Post,* private leaders—such as one leader who runs a for-profit EMO, controlling eleven of the state's forty-eight charter schools in 1999 and receiving $16 million in state funds to do so—"say a market driven by parents will decide the fate of charter schools." The governor, referring to the voucher program that evolved into the charter school initiative, noted an intent to "offer Cleveland school district parents—and particularly low-income families—new opportunities to choose a public or non-public school for their child."[65] A state senator asserted that charter schools allow "the community to make significant contributions to the process."[66]

But practice has not matched the rhetoric, unless "community contributions" were to be measured by the need to support even more local school levies as public funds flowed into charter schools with test scores far worse than the public schools. While polling data showed that the public, unlike state leadership, strongly supported public education, another antitax attack on public education was about to begin. The first step was to change the law, redirecting public support for education into support for parental choice that turned out to be support for EMOs. "They opted to bully charter laws onto the books. They granted the state unchallengeable authority to create charter schools in existing public school districts. And they denied local communities any say in the matter, not even allowing public hearings."[67]

Members of the Ohio Board of Education complained that the law gave them nearly no power to reject proposed charter schools, just as the law failed to adequately fund oversight efforts, leaving parents without information, due process at the front end, or redress once privatization was complete.[68] The more business-friendly Ohio Department of Education was chosen to review applications, and state board authority was restricted to only reviewing the degree to which applications met the formal Department of Education standards established in the law. Neither the Ohio Board of Education nor the Department of Education was authorized to follow up to ensure that charter schools, once approved and operating, actually met these standards.[69] Local school boards, and the parents they represent, were conspicuous by their absence from this process. But it was local building or health inspectors, arriving at state-approved new charter school buildings, who were the first to notice no textbooks, no toilets, no fire alarms, and other failures to live up to the standards established in the law. While these conflicts may support dramatic headlines about elite-led extralegal violence harming our children, some might forgive these as learning curve problems if the new charter schools have been living up to their promises about educational achievement. They have not.

Academic Achievement? EMOs promised parents that when they chose charter schools they would be escaping failing inner-city schools and choosing a superior educational experience for their children. "First year test scores indicate that students in charter schools are doing dramatically worse than public school children." One percent of charter school sixth graders passed all five parts of the test, compared to 33 percent in the public school system.[70] While this elite-led violence to public schools, justified by amplifying the fears of inner-city parents about declining school performance, might have supported headlines about failed leadership, perhaps charter schools require more time to demonstrate their success because they are adopting innovative curriculums missing in our public schools, as they promised when they advertised their commitment to parental choice and the innovative nature of a free market released from burdensome government interference (such as regulations requiring fire alarms, textbooks, and safe buildings). But these promises too have proven to be wholly without substance.

Educational Innovation? Advocates argued that "charter schools can make it really easy to innovate in the classroom," according to one state representative. However, a refusal to share curricular information with public officials makes this difficult to fully evaluate, though what we do know is not encouraging.

> Many charter school operators rely on nationally developed, alternative education programs that many public schools would experiment with if money was available. . . . [And] the large EMOs often bring the same cookie-cutter approach to their schools that charter school supporters have argued are problems with the public schools. . . . David Brennan, who denounced the cookie-cutter approach used by public school "educrats" as chairman of Gov. George Voinovich's school choice commission in the early '90s, has opened two types of cookie-cutter schools. His Hope Academies and Life Skills schools rely on the Josten computer-based education program, which is used throughout the nation.[71]

While one might expect that this bait-and-switch approach to education reform would be identified as an elite-led effort to do further violence to public schools (and to political discourse), taking advantage of the fears of inner-city parents whose schools were already in extreme decay as a consequence of earlier decisions made by these same state leaders and now are being punished for the challenges they face, the rush to fund charter schools has not abated. It is possible, despite the lowest test scores in the state and the clearly right-utopian rhetoric about innovation in a free market without government restrictions, that the democratic rhetoric about parental choice is best understood as the politically expedient mechanism for what is a fiscal imperative: perhaps charter schools are simply a more cost-effective allocation of public funds. But they are not.

Cost-Effective? "Profits are being reaped, but there is no evidence that charter schools are reducing education costs or saving Ohio taxpayers money—despite lower pay for teachers and exemptions from 191 state mandates that hike the cost of education in public schools." In 1999 Ohio redirected more than $52 million from public schools to charter schools. The mandates that charter schools are exempt from include record keeping, notification of parents when students are absent, per-pupil ratios for librarians, programs for gifted students, transportation, the 11.5 percent state cap on increases in funding for new students enrolled in public schools (charter schools are guaranteed 100 percent funding for each student enrolled), curricular requirements, and licensed teachers (whose salary at one charter school averaged nineteen thousand dollars a year with two years of teaching experience).[72]

Increasing Parental Choice? EMOs decide where to locate a school and who to enroll. Parents cannot get information from the EMO "other than sales pitches" or from the Department of Education "struggling to monitor and understand the rapid expansion" of largely unregulated and unsupervised schools. The local school board or teachers association, where parents might otherwise go for information, are not the decision makers driving this reform. "After release of first-year charter school proficiency test scores, which were abysmal, state lawmakers and Governor Bob Taft waited less than 10 days to slip a line into the state budget exempting the [charter] schools from issuing performance report cards to parents and the public for two years." It seems clear that state leaders have confused responding to the business community with increasing parental choice. One public leader, responding to criticism about implementation, argued that the state is "trying to go as fast as possible and not be inhibitors for choice for parents and their children," despite the fact that the haste serves the EMOs and trumps the informational, educational, and safety concerns of parents.[73]

Parental Fears? The *City Post* tells the stories of several parents "desperate to flee the public school," who were "afraid for their children's safety" in the inner-city public schools. These are real fears. But the charter school rhetoric that directs these fears toward individual failing public school buildings remains unmatched by safer charter school buildings. One charter school "has been a regular stop for Columbus police," despite the fact that the law allows charter schools to cherry-pick the best and the brightest students. The *City Post* suggests that it might be the nature of charter schools—their rhetorical commitment to innovation is manifest only in their approach to discipline—that accounts for this failure, noting that the many and varied violent incidents at this particular school "might stem from the fact that [the principal] routinely throws students out of the school without calling parents," an option not readily available to noncharter public schools.[74]

Extralegal Violence? Not only have charter schools failed to improve test scores, save taxpayers money, and introduce innovation to school curriculum or choice for parents, but this enormous charter school failure was initially created by public and private leaders in a most heavy-handed manner. Ohio state law prohibits bills that cover more than one subject, but when voucher reform efforts that evolved into charter school reforms could not secure enough votes, then governor Voinovich (in an action later ruled to violate the state constitution by the Ohio Supreme Court) included the enabling statute in his 1995 budget proposal. This created an opening for the key advocates to massively expand a program they could not get even a legislature hostile to public education to endorse on its merits, by circumventing established procedures—structurally reducing parental choice with legislation that takes control away from local school boards. First, state senator Watts proposed legislation to raise academic standards in the public schools. Then,

> Voinovich, Watts and other Republicans met privately to make dramatic changes to the bill, including new, costly mandates for public schools and dramatic expansion of charter schools to all major cities. Charter school sponsors could go directly to the state board of education. . . . Ohio suddenly became one of the easiest states in which private groups can open charter schools, but because the provision was sandwiched in a massive overhaul of public school academic standards, there was no separate vote on charters.[75]

Here we have state law that cannot survive the light of democratic public scrutiny but includes provisions to protect charter school providers against legal liability if charter schools are sued by parents.[76] Now that the legislation has been passed and schools are being approved at a rapid pace, the importance of parental choice has waned further, even in the rhetoric of supporters. "Gone is the talk of communities controlling a local school building," according to the *City Post* series. "More and more, charter schools are a privatization of public schools although supporters are reluctant to acknowledge this idea."[77]

And this privatization is one driving force behind the choices current state leaders are making about public education. During the Voinovich administration public funding for private schools grew faster than funding for public schools, as the voucher program worked as a public subsidy to existing parochial schools (educating fewer students than they did just prior to the voucher program, while receiving $3.3 million in new state funds through the program in 1999),[78] "merely slowing an exodus from Cleveland's Catholic schools to the city's public schools . . . [making Ohio] No.1 in the nation in providing aid to children in private schools." Voinovich acknowledged as much in letters to bishops and speeches before the Catholic conference.[79]

David Brennan is a powerful local businessman who, like Voinovich, is also a Catholic, and he has, according to the *City Post,* profited from charter schools, contributing nearly $1 million to many of the powerful Republican lawmakers who made charter schools a profitable reality in the state: Governor Voinovich, Attorney General Betty Montgomery, Secretary of State Kenneth Blackwell, Ohio Supreme Court justice Deborah Cook, and more than one state legislator. The intersection of Brennan's religious and commercial interests, his political influence, and these educational reforms is apparent in this statement published in the *Cleveland Diocese's Catholic Universe Bulletin:*

> While Brennan admits the voucher system would be an enormous boost for the Catholic schools . . . he says, "The death knell of this idea would be if it is identified as a Catholic movement. The public distrusts all of this because of the religious involvement, but that is the very thing we have to restore to education."[80]

"Documents obtained by the [*City Post*] show that state officials often delivered new laws and policies that aided Brennan in the building of his chain of schools. Some of those officials bent rules—or rewrote the rules—to his benefit. In at least one case, their actions violated the Ohio Constitution."[81] These documents show that Brennan negotiated with the governor, to whose campaign he had just contributed eighty-nine thousand dollars, to serve as the chair of a state commission to create a voucher program for Ohio, a precursor to the charter school initiative in the state. A democratic state senator noted that the governor "turned this issue over to Brennan at the beginning and it set the tone for years." The influence included allowing Brennan an exception to convert an existing school he was already running, exemption of his schools from "remedial steps demanded by the Department of education" if his students performed poorly on state-mandated proficiency tests, permission to accept schoolchildren from across school boundaries, and praise from now U.S. Senator Voinovich on the Senate floor, despite a state study showing Brennan's schools had less parental involvement and worse performance than public schools in all areas.[82]

It was not just Brennan driving this process. Another powerful organization in the state, the Ohio Roundtable, was also pushing hard against a teachers' union they continuously portrayed as favoring sex education and gay lifestyles over prayer in schools and school choice.[83] The Ohio Roundtable president, David Zanotti, with five thousand dollars from Brennan, led the successful 1992 state referendum establishing term limits for legislators, forcing one-third of the state house to retire. Zanotti is also the driving force behind a political action committee that has directed significant sums to conservative leaders, including the chief justice of the Ohio Supreme Court—who dissented from the *DeRolph* decision in 1997.[84]

Today, Ohio spends more per student than any other state on private, religious, and charter schools. In the current two-year budget cycle, the state will invest $420 million in private schools, while in the 1990s the state dropped from twenty-fourth to thirty-second in the nation in per student investment in public education. According to William Phillis, director of the coalition of public school districts still suing the state over funding issues, "there just seems to be a philosophical position that Ohio is really more interested in alternatives to public education rather than in fixing public education."[85]

One question lurking beneath much of the fearmongering about public education in Ohio is the degree to which public schools really are failing. Since manufacturing left, Ohio leaders have focused on providing more accountability but less money for public schools; instead of maintaining safe school buildings or increasing per student investment in our children's education, they have consistently chosen to divert public funds raised for public schools to private and religious schools. One of the most common justifications for this two-pronged approach at the state level has been that public schools are failing. But a 1989 national study commissioned by President Bush found that the quality of public school education—despite consistently stingy budgets—was neither failing nor in decline. The most frequently cited evidence of decline is the decline in SAT scores, but this study demonstrated that the minor decline in scores is a result of more students taking the exam (that is, of more students taking education seriously enough to want to go to college). When controlling for this and other factors, the study found that "the public education system in the United States was one of the best in the world." At the same time, a Rand Corporation study came to the same conclusion, arguing that public and private leaders "have misused test score data in the debate to give education a bad rap."[86]

But despite educational failure in charter schools, the Ohio charter school experience continues to be attractive to business-minded legislatures across the nation.[87] And in a context where state investment in education is only forthcoming when it is paid for with federal dollars and coincides with the interests of industrialists and developers (and when it does not, even a state supreme court order is insufficient to pry loose funds), it should come as no surprise that the debate about the value of education is so impoverished that the Ohio Board of Education recently included strong support for the inclusion of "intelligent design" in the state's science curriculum, criticized by the *Metro News* as another effort to encourage educational mediocrity.[88] While the state has had a track record of disdain for public education since the war, there have been many local areas, including the Central City area, where dwindling state funds and rising unfunded state (and federal) mandates have been met with frustration, distrust of government leaders, and a remarkable willingness to regularly increase local taxes to pay for public education.

The politics behind charter schools, *DeRolph,* redirected lottery funds, and urban renewal show three things. First, the few times leaders did support educational funding was when local leaders used educational needs to secure federal funds for urban renewal efforts, reinforcing existing racial and class inequalities at the expense of UHS, or lottery funds to divert state money from education. Second, the willingness to oppose educational funding by linking these efforts to job-undermining tax increases had no relationship to the implicit message of any antitax campaign: fiscal responsibility. The antitax leadership themselves demonstrated no record of fiscal responsibility, failed to address evidence that $1.00 invested in education produces $1.87 in tax revenue without raising taxes, and ignored the fact that despite their antitax rhetoric their administrations continued to spend growing amounts of tax dollars on policing, prison construction, and enormous tax subsidies for businesses with no loyalty to the state (not on human services, as they claimed during election years), passing on these costs to local communities in the form of multimillion-dollar unfunded educational mandates. In fact, as we have seen here in the charter school reforms and will develop in our conclusion, where one might expect fiscal responsibility we often find elite-led, extralegal violence toward public education and toward a more democratic public sphere more generally. Third, a willingness to invest millions of dollars in fearmongering campaigns to unseat judges seeking to compel the adequate educational funding required by state law by those private leaders who benefit most from millions of taxpayer dollars each year in profits redirected from impoverished public schools to charter schools with test scores many times lower than their public school counterparts (or to financially struggling private religious schools) reveals not a lack of funds for education but a disdain for public education at the state level. It is in this context that we now turn to the place of UHS in Central City politics.[89]

Chapter 5

The Place of Urban High School in Central City Political Culture

President Bush says that our kids must be taught to read. He says if his aides never learned to read, they'd never be able to tell him what's in the newspapers every day.

—Jay Leno

You see somebody younger than you, don't be afraid of him. That don't cost you a dime; might cost you some heart.

—Chuck D, response to what we can do to help our local schools

In an article noting that Ohio has lost House seats after every census since 1960 and projections have the state losing two more seats in 2010, Director of the Ray C. Bliss Institute of Applied Politics, Dr. John Green, concluded, "That's not in the least bit surprising. . . . Ohio has been unwilling to make the kind of investment in education and public infrastructure other states have made."

—*Lake Erie Ledger*, 2004

It is clear that while some see UHS as the city's flagship school, others, including most of the city's current public and private leaders, see it as a frightening school without a neighborhood, a building coveted by a rapidly expanding university neighbor, and a dumping ground for the school system's behavior problems. Part of the explanation for this gap can be explained by the transition over the last one hundred years of the UHS residential neighborhood into a much less residential, largely university-occupied track of land that is no longer just next to downtown but part of it. While this chapter details local trends that mitigate somewhat against statewide forces hostile to educational funding, the previous history makes it clear that even leaders hostile to education line up behind school funding in the form of federal dollars for the renewal of "blighted" mixed-race, working-class, inner-city neighborhoods as university recreational facilities. In our final chapter we argue that this prevailing perverse perspective on public education represents a particular approach to limited government, and in this chapter we argue that it has constructed UHS as expendable if not outright dangerous and the fears of UHS parents as unreasonable, punishing them for the challenges they face as a result of a history of malign neglect at the hands of state (and to a lesser extent city) leaders.

The debates over educational funding, charter schools, and school construction detailed in chapter 4 illustrate the conflicts central to understanding both the rhetoric and the reality of UHS as a school without a neighborhood. At the same time, many other familiar conflicts consumed the time of the superintendent: overseeing the forcible transfers of principals, managing new state rules prohibiting students from changing schools for athletic reasons, negotiating the creation of dual-use schools as community centers,[1] administering "new high-stakes" proficiency tests as required by state and now federal law (without the commensurate funding to pay for these mandates), finding a new football coach for UHS, and firing nearly two hundred teachers.[2]

But now it is time to focus directly on the competing stories about conflict and conflict management within UHS itself to illustrate how these larger political struggles are both reflected in and challenged by discursive struggles within this one educational environment. Many have argued that our recent fascination with all that is punitive is rewriting our present as a "culture of control," displacing our democratic imaginations (Hanson 1985) with a culture of fear (Glassner 1999) that governs through crime control (Simon 1997) and transforming education—the foundation of strong democracies—into enforcement (Saltman and Gabbard 2003; Giroux 2003b) or, as Foucault noted, another site for "the integration of law into the state's order" (1988, 162). In schools, we have already seen that the rhetoric and reality of "zero tolerance" provides one important analytical lens for understanding today's emerging visions of social control (Ferguson 2000; Cohen 1985).

> Seen as a technology for exercising power, however, it is more apparent who the real winners and losers in zero tolerance are. At the heart of zero tolerance in schools is a fundamental reconfiguration of the expectations placed on power and its subjects. Zero tolerance creates two important forms of burden shifting. First, shifting the risks of adolescent life from the class as a whole, on to those marked as crim-

> inally oriented. This makes zero tolerance a kind of right held by conforming students against non-conforming ones. Second, shifting the responsibility for maintaining good order in schools from teachers and administrators to recalcitrant students whose disruptive behavior is redefined by zero tolerance from a failure of administration to a trigger for power. (Simon 2006, chap. 7, 34)

Ferguson's (2000) work makes it clear that the process of being "marked as criminal," which begins by separating white schoolboys from black troublemakers, is itself marked by anything but due process and may even be designed to be criminogenic (Reiman 1995). It is certainly at least a form of institutionalized and official scapegoating—arguably elite-led, extralegal, and violent—designed to sanctify the communities and property of a growing conservative right electoral coalition. As our reading of Glassner (1999) suggests, this has the political utility of redirecting public anger and frustration (and dissipating public energies) from failed leadership to the dysfunctional lifestyle "choices" of our already most victimized citizens. But as Simon (2006) adds, this is not a benign move; this is also a trigger for the power to patronize some and justify the more extreme punishment of others. It constructs a coalition of the passive, encouraging the articulation of an electoral demand for more aggressive and less accountable forms of state agency in our schools, prisons, and shopping malls. Before returning to these larger political questions about power, patronage, and punishment in our final chapter, we must first examine the micromanifestations of these in our second case study: UHS.

Conflicts Colonizing UHS

UHS is a comprehensive high school with grades 9–12. It is the oldest and most centrally located school in the entire CCPS system. The students rally around school colors of red, white, and blue and their proud mascot, the owl. The average class size today is 26 students; enrollments have been falling from a high of nearly 1,200 in 1994 to just over 800 a decade later, while the number of students transferring in each year through open enrollment has remained fairly constant.

First in response to Governor Voinovich's educational accountability initiatives and more recently to No Child Left Behind requirements,[3] UHS (like all schools in the state) is now evaluated with an annual report card that records student proficiency test performance (proficiency tests are in the process of being replaced by achievement tests). The most recent available report card (2002–3) places the CCPS district as a whole and UHS in particular in "academic emergency."[4] Of the twenty-two state indicators, K–12 district students only met five; UHS students met only two of five indicators used to evaluate high school performance (reading and writing). UHS students failed to meet proficiency standards (to earn at least a score of 60 percent) in citizenship, math, or science. Probing further behind the 2000–2001 data, we find that in the ninth grade proficiency test (taken for the third time by students then in the tenth grade) white students at UHS did meet proficiency standards in all but the math category and UHS black students only met standards in writing. When we look at separate scores for the twelfth grade proficiency test the results for UHS students get worse. At that level, the only standard met by any group of UHS students is the writing standard, met only by UHS black students. In fact, the scores in all other categories are far below the state-set proficiency standard of 60 percent.

According to the *2002 Building Report Card* for UHS, the average teacher salary in the building was higher than the state average. The *2003 School Report Card* shows that the amount of money spent per student at UHS was above the district average and considerably higher than the state average of $7,505. The school had fifty-five white teachers, twelve black teachers, and one Hispanic teacher.[5]

While the twelfth grade scores are perhaps the best tool for evaluating the quality of the education students receive at UHS, after 2001 the school report cards no longer list the twelfth grade test scores, only the ninth grade scores. In the ninth grade results we see that in the 2002–3 report UHS students still only met two of five state standards, reflecting improvement over reports issued from 1994 to 2000 (where UHS students failed in all categories every year except 1995, when they met one of the five) but no improvement over the previous year's report card.

Two Perspectives on Difference

As noted previously, one of the reasons UHS has come to be seen as a problem school without a neighborhood is that the racially disparate impact of urban renewal and university encroachment undermined large parts of its residential neighborhood, and leaving it standing as the only school in an expanding downtown core has contributed to its being seen as an inner-city, black, and therefore frightening school by city and suburban residents. In this sense, the fact that so many students come from all over town through open enrollment was offered by many as evidence that UHS is a problem school without a neighborhood. That so many students come from elsewhere was suggested as one cause of low school spirit and low parental involvement. "If you grow up in an area, it's like 'this is my neighborhood.' The kids grow up together," according to the PTA president at UHS; they "go to school together and grow close. Urban's not like that."[6]

At the same time, however, there are those who use these same statistics to defend the school as one that attracts students as a result of its unique academic and vocational training programs. "The fact that about four hundred of the school's eleven hundred students come from other areas—attracted to programs only offered there—cuts both ways. Some say it creates a special atmosphere, others say it only creates a colder atmosphere." As a new school building was built and UHS stood at yet another crossroads, this 1973 statement by the school board president at the time highlighted the prominent role this school played as a magnet for diverse and talented students in Central City history; "I just hope this new UHS can produce the type of leaders in the community that the old has. It will be well worth it," the president added.[7] UHS graduates echoed these sentiments during the demolition portion preceding new construction. "I felt proud to graduate from such a modern building as UHS as in those days after the addition," said one graduate of the class of 1925. "I'm really sorry to see the old school go."[8]

Despite well-funded renewal plans undermining its neighborhood support, a strong alumni network and a lingering (if weakened, shrinking, and relocated) residential base continued to defend the school against city and district efforts to sell the building, insisting that its diversity (and its tradition of success on the basketball court) was one of its strengths. Three hundred residents met and angrily opposed the proposed sale in the early 1990s. According to the *Metro News*, "many were concerned that a sale would pull yet another bulwark from the inner city, and that the programs now restricted to this magnet school—such as ROTC—would be lost. . . . Some in the audience feared the decision already has been made."[9] The superintendent responded to the gathered parents by saying that he agreed that selling the school was no panacea but, with the *DeRolph* case in the courts and future funding uncertain, UHS needed funding immediately. The school without a neighborhood lacked the luxury of long-term planning in the best interests of the students, in large part, he concluded with reference to state leadership, because "this is out of our control."[10]

Extralegal efforts by the governor to advance vouchers and charter schools and by state legislators to ignore repeated court orders to create a fair school funding formula, in the mind of this school superintendent, had taken control of education away from local communities. These efforts, combined with leadership choices regarding urban renewal, university expansion, taxes, and business subsidies, also institutionalized the scapegoating of power-poor parents, already disadvantaged students, inner-city teachers, and their unions. These efforts reflect a decision to choose one of these two perspectives on difference, combining to construct the most diverse schools—and their communities—as frightening and omnipresent threats to a particular order—order, not law and order, since the leadership was already demonstrating contempt for the law when constitutions or court orders obstructed an active state agency mobilized on behalf of their electoral coalition. For UHS this meant that their school was sitting in the crosshairs, the trigger for a power to punish that increasingly governs through patronizing some to support the increasingly severe punishing of others.

The new curriculum set up with the new building in the mid-1970s (and still in place today) reflected both the working-class traditions of Central City and the desire to provide for a better life for our children through an academically rigorous education. In this way, the curriculum blends the different elements seeking to define UHS by focusing on six different career clusters: business; communication; engineering, science, and math; medicine; performing arts; and social sciences. A former factory worker might look at this curriculum and wonder why we ought to invest in performing arts or social sciences, just as educational scholars would wonder if this curriculum might not be skewed a bit too much toward the vocational end. An assistant superintendent commented that UHS "will have a totally career-oriented"[11] curriculum that will include other educational initiatives that were fashionable in the mid-1970s, such as team teaching, classrooms with movable partitions, and large-group teaching rooms.[12] But the vocational aspects of this new curriculum—often noted in interviews as an opportunity many students miss at the school—have yet to translate into improved job opportunities upon graduation for the majority of UHS students, and the academic aspects have not translated into even moderately acceptable test scores. Neither aspect has been successful enough to overcome the dominant sense at UHS that the conflicts bringing it down are a plague upon the school coming from the outside world.

The new school building enrolled 1,125 students "from most areas of the city, making it sort of a magnet school for both vocational and academic programs."[13] But as the school began implementing this new curriculum in a new building, the changes in the city and its neighborhood—reflecting leadership decisions taken at the national, state, and local levels—began to manifest themselves in the ways that news stories covered the school. UHS's diversity was becoming a threat. In 1980 the school got a new track and soccer field, and the school was no longer seen as the training ground for Central City's future elite and began to be seen as a two-dimensional school. Being a school without a neighborhood, a new situation without a history, came to mean being a school with a strong basketball program and frighteningly unpredictable and out-of-control teenagers.[14] The school's neighborhoods had largely disappeared not because citizens voted with their feet but because national, state, and local leaders tore them down. New programs (in UHS and including charters, vouchers, and No Child Left Behind) were producing mixed results, and outsiders began referring to UHS as a school without a neighborhood to conjure up frightening images of a blackening inner-city location demanding more punishment than pedagogy. This final section will try to unpack the meaning of this school-without-a-neighborhood question for conflict and conflict management at UHS.

Conflict Management within a School without a Neighborhood

The last section of this chapter will focus on the final pieces of data compiled about conflict and conflict management in punishing schools. Here we focus on an inner-city school, UHS, shifting from newspapers, consultant and government reports, and conversations with city planners to in-depth interviews with the key players within UHS, who know best what kinds of conflicts and conflict management strategies are constitutive of the culture at their particular school building.[15]

UHS is nearly 70 percent black today. There are no athletic fields surrounding the single, impressively large, and forbidding building that sits right up on the edge of Euclid Avenue, a narrow, heavily trafficked, two-way city road with single lanes in both directions, where UHS parents still sit in their cars on both sides of the road waiting to pick up or drop off their children, creating both a frustrating and an unsafe situation twice daily. No one, including passing police officers, seems to care that "No Parking" signs clearly prohibit this small-town behavior, perhaps because Central City as a whole still clings to a small-town past where routine insider violations of the written law such as these were commonplace enough to be seen as simply redefining law and community. But a school building nearly without windows, with large parking lots to the south, east, and west marking its shrinking boundaries with the university, and with its only green space (about the size of a suburban lawn) to the north, where more incoming students are dropped off, does not fit with this friendly small-town self-image.[16] Not surprisingly, then, one of the most commonly referenced aspects of conflict at UHS focused on its being a school without a neighborhood. As one teacher put it, using language I heard so often that it seemed like the party line in the building, "there is no neighborhood around here, so everybody is from somewhere else here. So we don't have like a neighborhood type thing. So, this guy's coming from King [High School] and this guy's coming from Lincoln-West, and he's come from South, and his cousin hates that guy at South and now he's here, and it's just, it's like a soap opera."[17]

In the course of our interviews several persons strongly urged us to be sure to speak with Officer Smith, because the students respect him and he contributes positively to managing conflict at UHS. We were able to observe the officer on several occasions successfully intervening with black male students to prevent the escalation of a conflict, and it was clear that his reputation was earned and that the power of positive black male role models is not exaggerated in the halls of UHS. This officer also focused directly on the neighborhood question,[18] but perhaps because he was a city police officer he was able to provide a more citywide and less building-parochial perspective. In our field notes from this interview we wrote: "this officer should be training other officers about conflict management, because he gets it in a profound and communicable way." Here was his response to the question, What is the most common type of conflict at UHS?

> *Here it's mostly territorial. You have a lot of Northside—Westside, that type of thing that goes on here. Other than that there's really not too much conflict. You have your regular girls that get into it for cosmetic reasons, stuff like that. Mostly it's street life that brings all the conflict in. Basically it's the side of town you live on. You have a certain group of people stays on Northside and just because they on the Northside they don't like the West-*

> *siders. It's our local [pause] your little street gangs. They try to pertain to, so this is certain things they try to claim. Most of what spills over is you can't walk over to the Westside if you a Northsider. And it's more just like gang stuff. [Question: Real gang stuff?] Wanna-be gang stuff. Just something that they cling onto. Some people have music; they have where they live at. It will play out at school, because we are one of the central locations, so we get 'um from, we're not just a Westside school, we get 'um from all over. [Question: Other than geography do they differ in any other way?] No, same clothes, same music. It's just what they claim. Those are the two main, known groups that you have, that when they get to fighting, basically something happens in the neighborhood that's what they are fighting about.*[19]

Officer Smith highlights two important aspects of the neighborhood dimension to conflict at UHS. First, the definitions of neighborhoods, even among the students, are just "things they try to claim . . . Just something that they cling onto. Some people have music; they have where they live" to construct a sense of identity and community for themselves as young people. Second, the link between neighborhood and conflict that is so salient in the dominant media discourse about UHS is also about the connection between different experiences with "street life" and education (later interviews will also include family life, both references to the different challenges that define growing up in the different communities within one city). The sound bite condensed version of this relationship is mediated through an information system that prefers official and dramatized ways of framing inner-city identity to normalize political support in places like Suburbia for the criminalization of these challenges as frighteningly dysfunctional lifestyle choices constructed to sanctify a sense of identity and community for their kids that is, in part, premised on a vision of state agency limited to the punishment of black inner-city bodies at a distance.

While reading street life and family life into the constant references to neighborhood whenever conflict is discussed at UHS might suggest to some that this turns a difficult challenge into an irresolvable indictment of our way of life,[20] one parent who shared the same frustrations provided a short illustration of how seeing UHS conflicts in context might also provide a valuable resource for more effective and sober problem solving. This parent was still actively involved with the PTA, and we interviewed her while she was doing volunteer duty monitoring the school parking lot, which invited discussion about students (and teachers) who arrive late so often that it becomes a serious problem.

> *Why is the student late every day? And they'll threaten them. You have to get up in the morning, get that bus, get here on time. There may be a problem. I worked at [a local elementary school] and there was a kid that was late every day. They kept just giving him detentions. I took it upon myself to ask the student, Why? He said his mom works, single mother, he has four brothers and sisters, it's his job to get up in the morning to see that those kids get off to school and so he comes in late. When he gets home, mom's gone to work, he had to see to them. So I talked to the school, I said, "Can we work something out? Can we move his study hall to the morning, allowing him to 8:30 to get to school? And see that he gets some help from an agency, mom gets some help with the little ones?" Problem solved. His grades went back up. All I'm saying is that sometimes we need to say, "Hey look here, there's a problem here, why is this happening over and over?" And that's all it took. And I was just a parent concerned. 'Cause he was a good kid. Problem solved. Just little things like that. Now there are kids that carry a chip on their shoulder, I admit that. But then those kids don't need to be here. They need to go back to their neighborhood school.*[21]

Zero tolerance, as the numerous stories about children being suspended for trivial offenses following Columbine demonstrated, undermines problem-solving efforts like these. In fact, as Barber (2003) argues in a different context, it undermines the possibility of negotiation, compromise, or cooperation. Instead of problem solving and conflict management, where all adults demonstrate leadership in practice and adult educators teach in the way they manage their schools and mentor their students, a zero tolerance culture promotes leaders who choose discipline instead of democracy, enforcement in place of education, and compounding rather than resolving the conflicts that we face as a nation and that disproportionately victimize our already most disadvantaged communities.

It is also apparent here, and throughout her interview, that, contrary to the dominant media discourse, this parent (whose children had recently graduated from UHS) considered attending UHS to be a privilege for those students who chose to attend from across town, a privilege that, in her view, the school needed to be more willing to rescind. This parent did not articulate a preference for a lifestyle without education; she defended working hard and valuing education more vigorously than the choices we examined from state leaders in the previous chapter. But her willingness to punish those who do not work hard, here and more broadly, is conflated into a support for punitive state agency and stripped from its context, where she was equally insistent on utilizing flexible problem solving, creating the conditions for more effective parental agency, and holding insensitive school bureaucrats accountable for their conduct.

While it is clear that the most punitive Americans are not those who live or work closest to crime and violence (Lyons and Scheingold 2000), the more ambivalent attitudes, sober perspectives, and balanced approaches of those who live in our most dangerous neighborhoods (and the particular menu of fears that animate them) are routinely parsed in this way to mute the ambivalence and to amplify those frustrations that reinforce punitive state agency. As Bowers, Vandiver, and Dugan (1994, 79) put it in their study of public opinion around capital punishment, "the 'prevailing wisdom' of 'strong,' 'deep-seated,' public support for the death penalty is mistaken and the polls are misinterpreted" by an information system that presumes public opinion will punish any candidate who fails to articulate strong support for punitive approaches like capital punishment, creating a self-fulfilling zero tolerance culture without empirical referent.

Similarly, Tyler and Boeckmann (1997, 255–57) found that "support for the three strikes initiative, as well as overall punitiveness, is linked to judgments about moral cohesion," because in a world "without moral values or social ties to use as a basis for changing lawbreakers . . . there seem to be few alternatives to simply incarcerating criminals for the rest of their lives," suggesting two important caveats to our parents' expression of a desire to educate through punitive enforcement: the context of statements like this provides the keys to understanding their meaning, and, in the case of three strikes and with this parent, our currently dominant zero tolerance culture excludes those aspects of that context that articulate ambivalence about punishment, criticism of punishing schools, and a vision of limited government where state agency is limited to enabling the political action of informed citizens embedded in resilient communities.

This parent is black and active, American and punitive. But excessively punitive approaches to crime control in America are often packaged as a democratic response to the fears of our poorest and our minority communities on the basis of a generally presumed consensus across racial lines about the commonsense value of punishment. But a closer examination of polling data reveals that "[t]he tendency of nonwhites toward punitiveness results from a greater fear of criminal victimization while whites tend toward punitive attitudes as a result of political conservatism. . . . Simply put, whites tend to be punitive because of racial prejudice while blacks tend to be punitive because of fear of crime" (Cohn, Barkman, and Halteman 1991, 288–89). Those who live closest to crime have less expressive and more instrumental approaches to punishment. They are more ambivalent about excessively punitive approaches (Miller 2001), and to the degree that their attitudes about punishment are expressive, they express as much fear of unaccountable state agency as they express fear of crime or unruly teenagers (Lyons and Scheingold 2000). But their punitive attitudes, and the more expressive ones of white Americans, are packaged in official frames for crime that focus on fears that there is a declining "respect for authority" to displace fears articulated by nonofficial sources that focus on extreme economic inequality or threats to civil liberties (Beckett 1997, 75).

As one of us has written elsewhere (Lyons 2000, 234), this "official preference for framing crime as an issue of collective permissiveness and individual failure, succeeds in mobilizing fear because, according to Beckett, it resonates with two central values in American political culture: individual responsibility and family." Framing crime as a lack of respect for authority encourages the linking of crime and poverty as lifestyle choices threatening traditional family values.

> [T]hese findings suggest that the conservative focus on street crime and the heightened fear that discussions of violent crime seem to engender . . . may also help account for growing popular punitiveness. *Under these conditions,* it is quite possible that fear of violent crime—like American individualism and concern about social and familial breakdown—enhances the acceptability of the conservative discourse on crime. (Beckett 1997, 81–82; emphasis added)

The fears of parents like this are as real as the victimizations that disproportionately burden their communities, but only the subset of their fears that reinforces zero tolerance and state agency fits with our current conditions and comes to be articulated as a part of UHS's approach to conflict management. Her fears of unresponsive state agents or enormously unfair burdens placed on children from economically marginalized families were repeated by others at UHS, though these fears were conspicuous by their absence in the previous chapter analyzing the response of state leaders to school conflicts in Ohio. Whether or not it is a privilege to attend UHS, her analysis focused on a more complex picture of a school that experiences conflicts seeping in from the outside, a school without the kind of resilient neighborhood structures that might prevent that seepage without additional and heavily punitive forms of state intervention. One illustrative teacher comment identified the most common kind of conflict as "he-said, she-said," where "a lot of that comes from outside the school."

> *As a matter of fact I would say the majority of it [is] things that are happening in their neighborhoods and then it spills over into the schools. . . . It's usually about their reputations, to be real honest with you, it's usually defaming, especially the girls, and saying they are sleeping around, or that they are cheating on so-and-so's boyfriend, or did you know that girl B called girl A's boyfriend and is trying to take him away from girl A. Those kind of things, relationship type things. Basically boyfriend-girlfriend. It ends up in mediation, as the year progresses some of those will be self-referred but right now [our interviews were done at the start of the school year] it will come into the building and there will be a lot of, obviously, animosity, between the girls, and then they'll side up, my girls against your girls or my boys against your boys. And it usually leads to an exchange of words and then the words will sometimes come to blows. We try to nip it in the bud while it's still in the words stage. But usually there'll be an altercation in the classroom or in the hall, between the girls, yelling at each other, usually using profanity, a lot of street talk, and then one of the unit principals or a teacher will refer it to us. It's mostly girls, but it usually involves a guy.*[22]

This teacher refers to mediation as a school effort to interrupt a pattern of escalation from neighborhood to bus to hallway to classroom and identifies relationship issues as a central driving force behind the conflicts at UHS. As Nader (1993) argues in her analysis of mediation, however, the reduction of complex conflicts to communication problems does enormous violence to the conflict management process in general, undermining respect for (especially in a school context) our understanding of due process of law. At the same time, it disproportionately harms the weaker party in any dispute, because transforming larger neighborhood conflicts into communication issues makes the invisibility of existing power imbalances a precondition for successful conflict management. Mediation, in this context, means something different than it does in Suburbia, suggesting more like what Katznelson (1976) referred to as "managing the consequences of our inability to solve urban problems" than the kind of conflict management designed to diffuse the knowledge and skills necessary to live in safe communities and attend safe schools. At the same time, several interviewees shared the view explained in detail by the following teacher, if in a somewhat nonlinear fashion, that even the neutral-sounding "relationship issues" refers us back again to the thicker understanding of neighborhood we have been developing and to school policies that may exacerbate conflict. This teacher was responding to a follow-up question about the number of students observed sleeping during a study hall.[23]

> *I bet if you asked the sleepers what their grades were I bet they all say ninth or tenth, but if you ask them their age the kid may be a seventeen-year-old freshman. He's just going down the toilet until he decides to wake up. Then also in this building, and not to criticize anybody here, but electives are tough to come by. You've got like three electives and if you can't fit them into your schedule you gotta have a study hall, there's nowhere to put ya. And they don't have early releases, like they used to. If you have study hall eighth period, there's no reason for you to be here, it's zero credits, have your mom say "yeah you can get out of school" and off you go.*
>
> *But around here everybody never leaves, they mill around, they go to the U, they wait until the end of the school day. It's like here at this building, when they tell you to leave ya stay and when they tell you to stay here you take off out the back door. And that's only that 10 percent that ruin it for everybody. . . . Some kids, it's like "where do you live?" but for a lot of them it's "where do you stay?" So I guess home life rolls into school here. My parents are still married. I poll my kids every year, "whose got their original biological parents?" And I don't even get a hand anymore, so I have no idea what that must be like. I got kids in foster care and CSB [Child Services Bureau], one girl it's like her fourteenth home this year and she's a junior. Stuff like that.*
>
> *The cops hear a lot too. There's a lot of law and neighborhood issues, they'll ask the cops. A couple of the cops get along real good with the kids. They see them working and see them doing stuff and say, "What if so-and-so hits that dude, what happens to me?" and they go, "How old are you?" "I'm eighteen." "You go to the big jail." [Question: What strategies does the school use?] There's a peer mediation group, you go to your counselor and you go try to hash it out, you know trying to just say "calm down, let's chill out." Me and the other teacher will do schedule changes. A lot of other people do that. The standard taking time-outs and things like that. Then there's*

all the negative, like the suspensions. Parent calls seem to work great, if you can find some parents. So many times you dial the phone and the recording is "we're disconnected."[24]

Here we see school study hall, early release, and electives policies linked to the perverse phenomenon that those students they want to keep in school flee to their neighborhoods (at least some are known to do so to care for family members) and those students the school would like to stay out linger in ways that allow neighborhood conflicts to trump educational concerns in the battle over defining the character of UHS. The school is aggressively attempting to preempt some of this by investing in a Freshman Academy to reduce the number of eighteen-year-old freshmen roaming the building. This team-taught, intensive focus on working closely with freshman to ensure they are ready for high school academic achievement is in its second year. Those students who do not pass are required to pass the classes, at their own expense, during summer or night school before they can graduate. They are not allowed to linger in the freshman classroom a second year, and the hope is that this will, over time, reduce their influence on the hard-working students and reconstitute a culture of excellence at UHS. While the Freshman Academy demonstrates innovation and promise, this interview also identified more challenging aspects of the link between neighborhood and school conflicts at UHS: broken families, law and neighborhood issues, and parents without working phones. Another teacher, providing a detailed description of one conflict she observed, elaborated on these connections. She explained that they were "lucky" that, with students from at least twenty different countries, conflicts are rarely interracial and then turned her attention to describing a conflict from two days earlier.

It was a black female, three black males, and it started just as an exchange of words. And that's really another one [common kind of conflict], it's not really a "he-said, she-said" but they will tease each other and it escalates and then one of them loses their temper. And that is exactly what happened. It went so far as the girl took off her boots, she was wearing boots that day, she took off her boots and she had on a shirt and tie, she undid her tie and was taking off her tie. We got her in the hall, talked with her first, and then one by one I brought out the boys, but the sad thing was that in talking to one of the gentleman, he did not understand. I was trying to get them to the point, the girl was apologizing, that's what it was, which, I knew the girl very well because I had her last year as a student and this year as a student, and she's very hyper, she flies off the handle very quickly, so it was not a surprise to me that she was involved in this, but I was surprised at two of the gentlemen involved.

But she, on her own, apologized to them, even though from my perspective they called her a black ass, a big fat black ass, she called them a nigger, and obviously it went from there, but she apologized to them even though it started with them, she was trying to get the teacher's attention and one of the boys started teasing her about the fact that she was calling for the teacher's attention and that was how the whole thing started. But the thing that surprised me was that when she apologized to the boys, I myself thought that the apology did not need to come from her, it needed to come from them because they called her a fat ass first, but the boy said, "you don't need to apologize to me" and the point he was trying to make was that there are always arguments, and you don't need to apologize for an argument because that is a way of life. And I found that very sad. I talked more with him, and the more I talked with him the more I realized that this was an ingrained belief system that he has.

And as we continued the discussion, he and I, I remember saying something to him about, these are seniors, when you're married and have a family of your own you mean to tell me that it's okay that your child lives in a household where everyone always argues with each other, and he just looked at me again like "that is the way that it is." I could see that no matter what I said, that that is a firmly held belief and that he wasn't disrespecting me, he was just saying that this is the way it is lady and that I was being naive if I thought it was going to be any different, and that therefore the girl owed him no apology and he really owed her no apology, because that is just the way it is. That's life.[25]

Within a School without a Neighborhood: Violence as a Way of Life

This illustrative conflict extends the meaning of our neighborhood theme to include an implicit conclusion—for students, teachers, and administrators—that in poorer and blacker neighborhoods, for reasons that are generally left unexamined by the interviewees, the students grow up with "violence as a way of life . . . handling conflict with conflict."[26] For this teacher, the consequence of the concentrated disadvantages victimizing her students' neighborhoods and families was a poor and deteriorating school environment. Her analysis of the school environment involved examining the intersection between family, community, and education central to the culture of conflict at UHS.

> *I think the environment in our building is something that we need to tackle, and we just really haven't done a very good job of working with the environment. As that boy expressed, many of our students are used to handling conflict with conflict. They are very overt. They're very aggressive. It seems to be part of their culture. Obviously they want to save face. There is a lot of street talk that goes on in the building and quite frankly when they use the street talk I have a hard time understanding what they are saying, but you can tell by the body language and the tone. [Question: Environment?] I mean the affective domain, the respect, and I think a lot of times it has to start with the respect that teachers give students. I don't think that we listen well enough. And then, we have a hard time with the fine line between enabling our students and giving credence to the lives that they live and where they are coming from.*
>
> *On the one hand you don't want to disrespect their homes, or disrespect the inner city, or stereotype what life is like in the inner city and family life is like in particular, because there are a lot of fine kids who come here from a lot of fine families, but on the other hand, there are a lot of kids that come here, and as this student said, their way of life is a way of life of violence. I remember one girl. As a matter of fact she was a white girl, she came to school one day very nervous and upset, her bedroom happened to be in the front of her house and there happened to be a drive-by, and so she was going to have to change her bedroom. It just wasn't a safe place for her to sleep anymore. She was upset enough that she was sharing with the kids, and I gave them a forum to talk about it, and in that particular class the majority of the kids had either experienced personally within their own family the death of someone or on their street the death of someone by violence. We've had many kids this week and last week attend funerals for peers, not in our building, peers of theirs who have been shot.*[27]

Here one of the most impressive and sensitive teachers in the school begins with her summary of a student saying, "you don't need to apologize for an argument because that is a way of life," and concludes that this is a tragic expression of resignation to a violent way of life, to "their way of life," which is "a way of life of violence" seen by the teachers as an "ingrained belief system" immune to the efforts of educators to instruct students to the contrary. But is conflict not a normal part of life? Would it not be the abnormal family or community that did not experience arguments on a fairly regular basis and in fact depend on the conflict management skills developed in response to these routine conflicts to prepare future leaders? Rather than follow Vygotsky (1978) and meet this student within his zone of proximal development, this teacher frames conflict at UHS in a way that reflects the colonization of education by enforcement. Rather than pedagogical insights about how students learn, her operative analytical frame reflects prevailing political insights from leaders who have determined that we ought to fear conflict and aspire to the no-conflict, nonchangist view of the world animating *Pleasantville* and supporting the currently dominant national electoral coalition we will discuss in some detail in our final chapter.

At this point, suffice it to say that it is at least arguable that conflict is normal (Cohen 1995; Mayer 2000), meaning that educators who have not been transformed into enforcers ought to consider emphasizing the important democratic uses of conflict and disorder (Lyons 1999; Sennett 1970; Schattschneider 1975), particularly with regard to skill development to support leadership in a democratic culture. The conditions teachers work within in punishing schools contribute to teaching practices more about enforcement than education, and even within that narrowed vision of schools the practices are more about enforcing their own authority than enforcing the rule of law (which, even when done poorly or in place of education, would at least have the benefit of enhancing respect for the rule of law),[28] as this same teacher continues, highlighting both the atrophy of and the enforcement-centered redefinition of mentoring as a critical aspect of effective teaching and learning.

> *So, on the one hand I don't want to disrespect family life in the inner city, but on the other hand we need to be realistic about what some of the kids come to school with in experience. So you're almost fighting a culture. But that's the environment. This needs to be a safe place, but it needs to be a place where you're respected, and we need to believe seriously, we've got teachers here who will use profanity, who will lose their temper with the kid, now how can you do that on the one hand and then talk about conflict resolution on the other, you know, if we're not the models for it?*[29]

This criticism of teachers who use profanity—premised on the taken-for-granted and inaccurate assumption that schools are unsafe and the suggestion that this undermines developing a less conflict-driven school culture—came up in more than one interview. This, and the enormous frustration with which teachers explain the difficulties they face daily in their efforts (and their perception that other teachers do not always contribute to these efforts) to enforce dress code prohibitions on wearing hats, for instance, always struck a discordant note with us, seeming to represent a strenuous effort to draw a line in the sand over one of the more trivial conflicts teachers have with students. Perhaps this makes sense in a context where the conflicts seem omnipresent and the resources available paltry.

But as the teacher's description makes clear, the claim that adult profanity or wearing hats undermines conflict management is also given meaning as a rhetorical construction of what is "realistic" in this particular context and what, by extension, is irrational or chaotic or disruptive. And one way to read what is created as realistic here is that teachers and administrators are enlisted to "fight a culture" in their enforcement of a particular school environment. They are fighting a way of life where arguments are normal and, at least in the official mind, associated with a predilection for violence. They are fighting for safe schools by enforcing no hats and reducing the expectation that teachers will mentor their students to an admonition against profanity. Students who emerge from this violent culture with leadership skills, however, are excluded from one of the primary positive tools the school uses, even if in a limited way, to diffuse conflict management skills.

> *I just really believe that we are going to train fifteen kids out of nine hundred [to be peer mediators], all of our kids need to be trained in conflict resolution, you know, that should be an established class, like maybe a nine-week mini-course or done in homeroom, but somewhere our kids need to be given that information. . . . I am trying to think who our new mediators are . . . [interrupted by a student] . . . If you ask me who the leaders are, among the students, I'm gonna tell you it's black females, but is that because [pause] that's the largest population? [Question: Do you choose these students to be mediators?] We try to choose kids [pause] we try not to choose those kids. Some of them obviously are, but we try not to choose those kids because they've got lots of avenues, and they usually have the skills that they need anyhow. So we try to choose other students.*[30]
>
> *The biggest obstacle is the culture that they come from. If the culture tells them, then we have to convince them that this way does work. . . . We do what's called progress report pick up, and we had our first one and I had 25 parents and I have 125 students. That was a very good year for me. As a*

building we had a little over 200, and that was a very good turnout for us, for 900 students. Last year I had maybe 12 parents and that was very good. A lot of the teachers will see nobody or 2 parents. So we can't even get our parents to come when it directly involves their child. However, I would like to do an evening program of CR [conflict resolution], because it is not just the students who need it. Obviously the parents need it also. . . . [F]or some of our kids violence is just a way of life. I think that is the one thing that people just do not understand. You'd be amazed. And I guess as an English teacher I am privy to more of their personal lives than other teachers, through the writing and discussion of literature, so I think I get to know the kids on a more personal level, and as long as I have been doing this I never cease to be amazed, what some of these kids live with and live through.[31]

A Clash of School and Neighborhood Cultures, State Agency, and Citizen Empowerment

It was not only teachers and parents who agreed that the clash of school and neighborhood cultures could be seen as driving conflict at UHS. One unit principal explained to us that, while the volume of neighborhood conflicts spilling into hallways and classrooms declines as the school year progresses and everyone gets used to each other, he does deal with two to three such conflicts a day at the beginning of the school year and "maybe one a week" after that. We asked him whether, when he expels a student, he has any control over the new student that UHS will get to replace the expelled student.

No. If we get rid of one, we're gonna get one. And your earlier question was, you wanted to know if it's effective, sometimes, but I would say that daily when I go to my mailbox and get the flick sheets [for skipping school] and the referral sheets, which is the discipline referral that was made to me, I would say by this time of year I see the same thirty or forty kids, maybe same thirty, for sure the same twenty. I'll see them from almost the beginning of school to the end of school. They'll get in-school suspension for three days, for two days, I'll give them Thursday night detention, out-of-school suspension. Is it effective, for that core, the certain core in school? No, because they don't care. They don't care about the consequence, they don't care about their own education, they don't care about disrupting the school or classrooms.

Many times the parents, they try to support us, they either get real angry with us, they think we're trying to get their student, we're out to get 'um, we don't like 'um, or I'd say most of the time they're causing the same prob-

lems at home and in the neighborhood and they're desperate, they're just beat down. They'll tell me they have the same trouble at home. So, I think it, our discipline works for probably quite a few of the kids, but a certain core it doesn't work.

If I was the superintendent, I would . . . close one high school, disperse the kids, use that as an alternative program, a regular eight period a day high school, and where you take the twenty kids I have trouble with on a daily basis, maybe ten of those twenty, because many of them they're not violent, they just do dumb things, they do immature things, but they do 'um repeatedly. I'd say take that core group that prevents learning in our classrooms, when they get to some point they're removed, they're sent to this alternative school for maybe, however long it's determined by the alternative school it's gonna take them to change the behavior, get them turned around, get them on task, and send them back to us. But we need an alternative school that, instead of suspending them out, for so many days, they go to the alternative school. And then they can earn their way back out of that school. They don't go for three days, ten days, thirty days, they're permanent. They have to earn their way out. They have to get the grades, they have to change their behavior, and then send them back to their home school. I think we need that badly.[32]

This principal connects neighborhood and school conflicts through his observation that the kids "don't care" and that often the parents of these kids are dealing with "the same problems at home and in the neighborhood," but he adds yet another dimension to the story about conflict at UHS. These parents might be a problem for him at times, but not because they don't care or are permissive or unwilling to work hard. Instead, they are "desperate and beaten down" by the intersection of neighborhood, school, and work conflicts that is their everyday experience, an intersection examined in the next chapter as another manifestation of what Wacquant (2002) calls the emerging hyperghetto. This unit principal similarly explains the desperation and beaten-down feelings of these parents as more about the power-poor status of their neighborhood than about their individual laziness or choice of dysfunctional lifestyle.

They [students] always say the teacher's lying, I didn't do it, call the rest of the class in, I'll get witnesses. Many times they deny it, and that's why I like the teacher to be the first one to call home, because I have to make the call that I just suspended your student for five days for calling the teacher names,

> *and the teacher has never made the call and they ask me questions I can't answer, because I wasn't in there. Then it goes to an appeal and takes a lot of time. We have to get statements and narratives and go down and present our position and the students present theirs. Very common, takes a lot of time. Depending on the school, we had a lot of appeals at Kennedy, more so than we do here, and I think it was because Kennedy had a neighborhood, more of families intact, and the parents were more empowered and they knew they could do that, which is fine if they have a legitimate complaint, but a lot of them they just do it just to mess with us, make us be inconvenienced and jump through hoops.*[33]

The Easy Fit of Violent Approaches to Conflict in Our Neighborhoods, Schools, and Beyond

The bringing together of diverse neighborhoods in the city's most centrally located high school creates conflicts outside of school as well. One parent with two children at UHS explained that, while her son has had no problems, her daughter has been caught up in a yearlong conflict with another student that has played out on the city bus they take to and from school each day—and in UHS hallways.

> *I don't know why they don't like each other, but her and these other girls, they don't like each other and the things she's experienced are, you know, they may walk opposite ways in the hallway and bump into her and maybe she'll go into the locker and it will look like it's an accident when it's on purpose or they unfortunately ride the same bus to school and they have had arguments on the bus. A lot of it is if an adult doesn't see it she doesn't have any proof that it happened. They don't live in the same neighborhood, but the bus that they catch comes all the way up from Sandusky Hill and so they end up on the same bus going to school and coming home.*[34]

This conflict resulted in a bloody brawl outside of the bus that the mom described as a "knock down drag out." Her daughter needed four stitches on her forehead. Both girls were suspended. The mother we spoke with wondered why, since the school knew these two were in conflict, they kept them in the same classes and why it was only when she appealed her daughter's suspension that she learned that "the counselor already knew their history" and "her unit principal got statements from people that saw the fight . . . all the other girl's friends." Her son was there but was not asked for a statement. This parent was perhaps one of the most calm and reasonable persons we spoke with, frequently pointing out that she understood school officials had a tough job but also emphasizing that her experiences with conflict management at UHS were disappointing. She was still confused about how the school authorities could threaten that her daughter might lose the privilege of riding regular city (not school) buses to and from school. When asked what tools the school used to manage conflict and how effective they seemed to be, she articulated a frustration commonly heard from all interviewees:

> *It seems like a lot of it is through either in-school or out-of-school suspension, depending on what you do. But I don't think they really go to the heart of the matter of trying to stop it from happening again, it's just that you'll be suspended for these amount of days and you go back to your same class, you know, same problem. If you are out for five days you have five days to make up your work after you get back. I know they expel people, but besides threatening a teacher I don't know what would get you expelled.*
>
> *[Question: How effective?] I wouldn't say it is too effective, because this has been a year and a half that she has been having the same problem with the same one girl. I think if something were done about it, she wouldn't still be picking on her. . . . Part of it is the kids, because they won't tell on each other. That's what they look at it as, tattling. Until the point of somebody getting hurt it doesn't seem like they are willing to say anything. Then when they get hurt it's like "well they did all this other stuff" and then all the stuff comes out. And then a lot of it is, I think, the teachers don't see a lot of what the students do.*[35]

Another parent described their big, but "very gentle," freshman son as similarly somewhere between distracted and tormented by the ongoing nature of minor conflicts that always contain an implicit threat of escalation. This student was one who chose to attend UHS because his father graduated from UHS (and played on the basketball team) and he also wanted to play for a basketball program with a state reputation for excellence.

> *He's always wanted to go to UHS. We took him from private school to UHS, the contrast was just like, "oh my god." He's overwhelmed here. But he loves it. He's bringing his grades up. Everything is playing basketball. We're proud of him. He says there's a fight every day. And I just think that's terrible to know every day that there's a fight. That's like living here thinking*

"we're gonna get bombed every day" and I think that's a terrible environment to have to go to school in. And usually it was girls, last year. This year I think it's both boys and girls. . . . You hate to take him away from something he loves. A friend of ours told us he could make phone calls and we could send him to [a Catholic school very close to UHS] free of charge. He didn't want to go. So what can you say?[36]

Students also made the connections being developed here between neighborhood power and school conflict. One black male student commented that when conflicts are "student-student, whatever their problems outside of school, things like that, when they see each other in school they have problems with it. Most likely start off with an argument or become physical fights. Hallways, classrooms, anywhere where, bathrooms, wherever they see each other at."[37] Another black female student made the connections more explicit in response to a question about where the conflicts she was describing take place.

Well, the classrooms I've been in, it hasn't been so many, it may have been one or two, but you see it most in the cafeteria at breakfast, at lunch, or just walking in the hallway before class, you don't really see it taking place in the classroom. Actually it could be anybody. It depends on what the situation is and who's involved. Like harassment, I see a lot of that. Like, I think it's more of a jealousy thing, and then you have people who see you doing better, sometimes they wish that they could do that but instead they try to bring you down. I see that a lot. Then you just see people who doesn't like you because of who you are and what you do. Stuff like that.

[Question: What do they do to try to bring you down?] Talk about you. Like I have a friend, she's a cheerleader too, and she's not having the best life right now, but she's going through things that people talk about it and they don't, they don't look, they don't know what she's going through, so she does walk around the school looking sad and stuff, but they'll talk about her, call her names and stuff like that, and I don't think that's right. And then it's like, the person that's doing this, I think it's a bit of jealousy. That's just what I think; I could be wrong. Teachers know, because the person that's doing this to my friend, she got caught. She does it in front of like the whole school, like at pep assemblies and stuff like that. She tried to embarrass my friend, but she got caught, so they know what's going on. I think before that happened, she just let our coach know what was going on. My coach, I don't know what was said, but I think she tried to handle it too. They just look out

> *for it, try not to let it happen. They keep them as far away from each other as they can. They just try to make sure they are not placed together.*[38]

Student-to-student conflicts, from the perspective of students, are also manifestations of neighborhood conflicts, conflicts driven by living in a consumer-driven and radically unequal political economy that strike this student as hurtful and just not right. Another student, who also commented that "teachers most of the time are right," widens the lens again from individual students to their families and communities. Her comments can be read at least two ways. First, she is clearly reflecting prevailing cultural prejudices about single-parent families and racial subcultures. Yet, it is also possible that her halting prose is expressing a critique of these prevailing articulations—that is, that she is confused by the inadequacy of categories that require her to make what seems to her to be a nonsensical assertion, that one of society's most important institutions, the family, is responsible for the conflict she experiences.

> *Now, the students' problems can be sometimes dangerous. Some sort can take more personal than other students, like it depends how people are raising their kids, some kids are from female led, kids take care of their family, love their family, you know, and some kids are who are like mommies daughters and daddy daughters, you know, who are, they get everything they want, and they have the last word and they'll say their word, how they say it's like that. That can be a problem, that can be really big problem.*
>
> *'Cause some kids they like fighting, for example, there is a big family, like most of the kids are fighting for their words, they're like, they want to say something, or they don't want to do something, or just they're fighting, you know, for their words, and some kids, like, for example, one or two kids in the family they have whatever they want. Most of the time. And when they get to school and they meet each other, they're fighting for their words and they want, and they know that they'll get, you know, they used to get stuff from their parents and they let do stuff, but now that be really big conflict. Two different types of kids getting together in one school. That's a problem. And you can't do anything about that.*
>
> *You know, if, for example, if I see that someone is like that, you know, who they want to have everything, they wanna be right, I just go on. I don't want to argue with anybody. I used to argue, before, but now that, not worth it, just not worth it, really waste of time, because if you fight and you argue*

> *with kids then you go on and on with fighting and arguing and just you lost time in your school, for your homework, for everything, you know. Personally, I don't have time now for myself. My mom can't walk, she doesn't have a job. I have two sisters who go to this school too. So, pretty much everything is on me. My dad he works overtime; I never see him. He comes home at 3:00 at night and I'm at that time in bed, then he goes to work at 3:00 during the day and I go home at 3:30. So, I never see him. Maybe Sundays. Because he might get day off. So, it's not worth it for me to come here, argue with teachers, argue with students, listen to their stories, and you know, I don't care what others say. Really. They can talk as much as they can talk. It just, as long as they don't hurt me physically. I really don't care how much they can say or how strong words can be. Now I really don't care about that. I used to care. I get into a fight, back in my country. But not here. And the conflicts with students, most of those are like, their fault, you know. They get themselves into that, and then they bring somebody else, you know "he told me, she told me, they told me." No. It's not right. Your fault. You got yourself into that; get yourself out of that. Nobody will.*[39]

This student is clearly articulating a discourse about how to be an immigrant that is reminiscent of nineteenth-century Irish or Italian immigration stories or even model-minority Chinese immigrant stories today. The parents, and subsequently the home lifestyle, center on sacrificing their present (their lives, their time with their kids) so that the next generation can get ahead. That sacrificial attitude comes out in their child, here, as "I have responsibilities and don't have time for petty childhood arguments, for the conflicts you bring on yourself, because I am dealing with bigger, real conflicts." It makes us wonder if the legacy of slavery, understood to mean the concrete persistence of race-based discrimination to prevent self-advancement—in forms from Jim Crow laws to ghettoes to hyperghettoes—has not transformed black families and communities such that some (or even many) parents had parents who themselves grew up without hope or dignity.

Is this the nihilism that Cornell West (1993) talks about and Tupac Shakur angrily raps about?[40] And does this transform the adult form of this hopelessness, which can be seen as a form of loving their kids similar to the immigrant father in this student's story? Perhaps the adult form of that hopelessness is to say, "Well, if nothing works then at least we can enjoy the experience of family now, the dinners, the decent clothes, the respect in the community," such that rather than sacrifice the present, the present becomes all that can realistically be hoped for?

And when this presentist attitude—fully supported by the power of a consumer culture and representing a competing construction of what is (and who are) realistic or irrational—is manifest in their children (in UHS hallways) it might sound like, "We will not back down from the smallest slight today; we demand respect even if we are kids and you are the teacher, because even the most minute amounts of respect we might be able to squeeze out of your stubbornly self-righteous approach to conflict will likely leave us with a respect deficit at the end of the day, the week, the month, and the school year." Certainly something like this presentist attitude is manifest in the comments of this black female student about a conflict with her best friend that resulted in their no longer speaking to each other. Her comments begin in response to the question, What is the most common type of conflict at UHS?

> *Too much "he-say, she-say," and that's where a lot of conflict come from. They go by what other people say, rumors. That's the main problem. Some students feel like if they go to peer mediation they are, like, punks. . . . Basically they won't come to peer mediation and if the problem continues it gets worse, just maybe it might lead to fighting. . . . [Students] complain that there's a lot of drama, that's basically what they say about our school. Basically everything in the hallway, screaming, yelling, passing notes, whatever, however it can get around. I have got caught up, in two conflicts, but they were resolved. My mom called into the school. Because I am a good student. She talked to the principal and it resolved like that, nothing ever happened, we didn't go to peer mediation. But we did talk with the principal and the officer. Well, it was between me and my best friend; she used to be my best friend. We was just having like problems, and something had happened over the weekend between me and my cousin. And my cousin is her good friend, so she came back and she was like telling everybody what happened and I asked her could she not tell people what happened because it was a family affair and it didn't have nothing to do with nobody at school. So, basically she just got rowdy with me and stuff, so we just [pause]. That type of person, she don't want to go to peer mediation, 'cause she tough. Yeah. Like tough like, people think, they label her as, "oh, she a fighter" and stuff like that. And so, she want to keep her rep. So, she don't want to go to peer mediation, so they be like "yeah she scared." I think about it. That's my best friend. We been best friends since elementary. But for something like that, simple for us to fall out over it, it was stupid, so I don't talk to her, she don't talk to me.*[41]

In this response, the student explains that not only is there no tradition of respect for authority (an observation commonly made by interviewees), but there is also no tradition of the kind of independent thought needed to combat rumor mongering. This student describes a process of deterioration in a relationship that was important to her as if there was no recourse. As if the distracting and exhausting melodrama she sees as characteristic of UHS hallways was not frightening enough, she is also aware that the behaviors she observes reflect a profoundly passive approach to education and citizenship, which turns responsible students into "punks" without agency. The school itself becomes a stage for a spectacle where students are only able to construct themselves as learners or decision makers in ways consistent with a passive, consumerist framing of democratic public schools. As graduation approaches, according to this student, the calculus begins to change for most students.

> *It's basically like, I don't know, your peers around you, if you want to satisfy them, then, that's how you do. But if you looking to satisfy yourself, then do your way instead of they way, you be straight. Instead of worrying about what somebody think about you. When you a senior you think about that stuff, because you got a lot to lose if you get suspended, you got a lot to lose, when you a senior. If you think about it, if you fight or something, you automatically lose out. Seniors, we need like, our credits that you have to learn up, we have to class participation, those count. If you don't be in school, you missin' out. Probably you won't graduate or you'll have to take another course over summertime.*[42]

But by senior year a lot of water has passed under the bridge, and efforts to remake the environment as less frightening and unruly are likely to meet overwhelming resistance in a school where only most of the seniors get it. One highly publicized incident at UHS helps cement this evolving view of the school for outsiders. Police reported that in the late 1980s a fifteen-year-old male student punched and kicked a female police officer, causing injuries that required twenty stitches, while his seventeen-year-old sister held the officer's arms. This incident catalyzed demands for returning to corporal punishment (still allowed by state law but prohibited by district policy), building an alternative school for unruly teenagers, and spending $153,000 on metal detectors for schools. The students were expelled for eighty days, and county prosecutor Maureen O'Connor (now in the Ohio Supreme Court majority opposed to enforcing *DeRolph*) demanded that both be tried as adults. This would mean the possibility of a sentence of twenty-five years rather than a maximum of three and a half years if the boy were tried as a juvenile.[43] Eventually the teens were tried as teens, but the state-level political career of Justice Maureen O'Connor was launched to have a larger negative impact on UHS.

This moved the struggle to the state level but left a residue at UHS, an image of the school as more frightening than other schools in the city. And this public image also impacts how insiders frame the routine conflicts common to UHS. In fact, the perspective of the school as overwhelmingly disorderly—and the connection between that view, the neighborhood question, and respect for authority—emerged in many interviews, including the following one with a black female student, who was responding to the question, What are the most common types of conflicts at UHS?

> *A lot of arguments and fighting. Definitely a lot of fighting. They are very violent. A lot of people fight over boys and just stupid stuff. It's very violent and they have to call the police all the time. . . . I'd say there's a fight like every week. Literally. . . . I'm trying to remember the last fight I seen. I didn't get to see it really, but everybody ran into the cafeteria and there's these two boys fightin' over a girl, and this boy hit 'um in the face, but before he could hit him the teachers grabbed him. He was acting real wild, and he knocked over a couple tables, because they wouldn't let him go. He was mad, cursing and all that. And they just took him away, and his parents had to come get him. They separated them, so one on one floor and the other on the other. They got suspended.*
>
> *They get rid of you, but it doesn't last, because I got in an altercation with, the girl I got in the altercation with, it happened last year and they only suspended her for like one school year. They told me that she wasn't supposed to come back at all, period. And now she's back. And she's trying to start trouble, already. It was only her first day back and she's already in the cafeteria talking about "she beat me up." No she didn't, but, talking a lot of mess, trying to start already.*[44]

Like the unit principal, teachers, and parents quoted previously, students are frustrated with the fact that discipline problems never go away. And for some of the students this failure has become a defining characteristic of UHS classrooms, student-teacher relations, and the possibility of getting a good education.

Personally I think this school is backward. Instead of getting rid of the troublemakers they bring the troublemakers in. And when people aren't trying to cause trouble, they [word unclear] get in a lot more trouble than the kids that are causing trouble. I really don't like this school that much, but I'm gonna graduate and try not to let people intimidate me and make me not be focused.

Kids tend to disrupt the class a lot, instead of paying attention to the teacher they disrespect the teacher a lot. Sometimes people will call the teacher or the subs a lot of names and stuff. Subs just sit there, they don't say anything to them. They just look at them. Write a detention. And they don't even let the kid's detention go through, they just write to scare you, but nobody in this school is scared of detention or a write-up. So, you can basically do, I think, the students run this school, rather than the teachers. I don't know. I think that's a fact, not an opinion. I think the students run the school. [Question: Are the teachers afraid of the students?] Uh-huh [yes]. [Question: Are students afraid of other students?] Some of them. But you can mess with, a person that seems like they're scared of you, nine times out of ten they're just being humble. They're gonna end up wildin' out on you, gonna get mad at you. They're gonna go crazy too, so, I don't know if the students are really scared of each other, but I know the teachers act like they're scared of the students. Cause if they weren't there'd be more control in the school.[45]

Where we might expect there to be fear (students afraid of teachers) as part of the motivation for academic success, students experience little. Where we hope to find relationships built on respect or friendship—and preparing students to be productive members of their communities—we find fear of our children squeezing these things out of the UHS experience for many—and, if this student's assessment is accurate, many more than official school statistics indicate.

I think about 75–80 percent of the students here at UHS cause trouble. A lot of them cause trouble. Most of them cause [student-teacher] trouble. Every day. Every day you, like, I'll sit, I'm an office helper fifth period, and I'll sit in the office and all you hear is teachers yelling at the students, "shut up, be quiet, sit down." Then you hear the students yelling back, "you don't tell me what to F-in' do, you not my mama." They don't, students don't care. Every day you'll hear a teacher yelling at somebody, written somebody up or havin' to call the police to escort somebody like, students they like to walk in the class that they not supposed to be in, they'll sit there and when teacher tells them leave they'll just sit there until the teacher calls the police. [Question: Why don't they care?] Because they have no home training.

Sometimes, like my Dad told me, like some kids they're from, they're not, they don't have parents like I have parents. Like my parents are married, you know I live in a good home. And not everybody has it like that. So, they don't have any home training. Some are from foster homes. So, they don't know how to act. They're just bad. They're trying to get attention. They don't know how to get it. So they act up in school, they need help. Some students I really don't think can be helped unless they want to be helped and a lot of students don't want to be helped. They just want to do what they want to do. There's a lot of kids here do drugs. I've heard them talk about it. A lot of kids here sell drugs. I don't think there's anything teachers could do. Like there's a lot of programs that the kids go to, but it takes two. You can't just be the teachers. The students have to want to do it too. If you don't have two, then you can't do anything about it.

[Question: Does UHS have lockdowns?] No. Last year, they were talking about getting metal detectors and having dogs come in and sniff the lockers and stuff like that. They never did anything about it. They say, they talk a lot a stuff, but they don't do anything. They talk the talk; they don't walk the walk. [Question: Have you ever seen dogs here?] No. I remember a lot of people say "'m gonna have to get this stuff out my locker. The dogs about to come up here." We was waiting all day and the dogs did not come. And I know that students ain't dumb enough to leave their stuff in the lockers after school, so they didn't bring the dogs after school. They didn't bring the dogs up here. They don't have any metal detectors. I know a lot of kids probably got knives in their pockets. They don't care about us. We're just, we're just another student, they don't care. They just try to pass us. Some kids already ain't supposed to be in the grades they're in. They just get passed on.[46]

Not surprisingly, these experiences contribute to the larger perceptions of UHS already discussed, as a frightening school without a neighborhood. What this student adds to our understanding is that, while this might be true, it is also the case that she experiences the CCPS system as without viable alternatives, despite the fact that she is clearly a student from a family that has lived long and prospered in Central City.

Like some people say it's [UHS] a school known for fighting. . . . 'Cause Lincoln, if you go to Lincoln, that's a school known for having fun. But Urban I heard that it was a school that you go to for getting your education. But I learned something when I started going here. So a lot of people say it's a school for fighting and having fun, that's it. Well, I can't really say having fun, because we don't have fun here. 'Cause there's so many fights we can't have any pep assemblies. And when we do have pep assemblies, they're boring.

[Question: Why not change schools?] Well, my dad wanted to send me to another school, my mom wanted to send me to another school, but there ain't no point because every school . . . is the same. I heard Lincoln was worse, my sisters went to Lincoln. I don't know. I might as well stay here. Gonna be the same everywhere you go. [Question: Rhodes?] I got a lot of enemies at Rhodes. But I don't think anything would happen, because I don't think they really tolerate anything there, because it's a performing arts school. I think that's a good school. You never really hear anything about Rhodes. I don't think we really even consider it Central City Public Schools. Some try to say it's a private school, but it's not. The reason people consider it a private school is because, you have to have very good grades to get [pause] you have to get accepted into that school. Here at Urban they'll just take you, they don't care who you are. But at Rhodes you have to have good grades or you have to have some sort of talent. My Dad went here to Urban. My mother and all her sisters and brothers went to Lincoln. My uncle was a football player here, he played with [the current] principal.[47]

When Adults Retreat into Bureaucratic Enforcement of Their Own Authority

In this context, UHS parents advise their children to tell the counselor or teachers when there is a conflict brewing. But one parent identified the impersonal, bureaucratic nature of teachers and administrators as the main part of the problem.

At UHS? Mainly are the teacher conflicts. Disrespect, being belittled, not being paid attention to. A lot of students complain about that. Very rude and I have also experienced a teacher being rude with me. Going up there to check on my son one day, and the teacher waived me off and was very rude. I talked to the assistant principal and the principal and got a big runaround pertaining to my son, over three hundred dollars of equipment that I purchased and it came up missing, and just back and forth. My son was put on suspension, in-school suspension, because I came up there and voiced my opinion about it. I have had security called on me because I tried to talk to the teacher. They know me up there. So, we've had a lot of problems. I used to direct the traffic coming out of the parking lot after school, helping them

> *do that, and I didn't like dealing with them. . . . I think with most of the teenagers over there they just mostly deal with it themselves. They may not say anything to their parents, because they fear their parents may come up there and embarrass them, or the parent and teacher might get into an argument and make it worse on them. I think most of them probably take the detention and just blow it off and vent their frustration elsewhere. . . . You know what there is the racial difference, the academic difference, if you have a good student there that they know that's really good academic-wise, they will probably be more willing to help that student. To me it seem like the opposite. You don't ignore the kid that's doing the A-B work, but you kinda like look after that kid that's C-D and really trying. To me it seems like they just pushed those aside and concentrate on those that's actually doing good and really don't need the help.*
>
> *[Question: What advice do you give your children?] Guys, be quiet. You don't talk back to me, you know I have always teach you to respect your adults and your peers and just sometimes the least said the better the thing off. They hated that advice, because to them it made them feel like they were punkin' out or something like that. It's like, well, no, sometimes you might be right, but you're dealing with a teacher, you're the little boy and they are the big giant and nine times out of ten you're fighting a losing battle. . . . The adults there need to learn how to deal with the conflict. If they give the kids the opportunity, the kids will probably show them how to better deal with their issues.*[48]

This sentiment was echoed by another parent, focusing on yet another aspect of the relationship between neighborhood and school conflicts in schools where nearly all teachers and administrators are white and upper middle class and nearly all students are black and often lower middle class or poor—even in implementing one of the school's most progressive, innovative, and costly new programs, Freshman Academy. This parent was so soft-spoken it was sometimes hard to hear every word, and she was always careful to recognize that she only has a partial picture of what is going on, but her observations strike deep into the heart of UHS's conflict management culture.

> *The teachers don't seem to care about only certain students. And, like last year, when he [her son] was in the ninth grade, they were supposed to have a program [Freshman Academy], and they were supposed to follow up with you if your kid has problems or fallen behind, and we never once got a phone call. And then when I made a phone call, they acted like "well, he's failing*

and you should know that" and I thought it was terrible. And one teacher said, "the other teacher said the same thing." And I thought he couldn't call me back? I left a message for him to call but I had to get the message from her, and I thought that was tacky. And the same teacher, she had a student teacher, and my son was having trouble with English and they were saying if she had the extra time she would give help. But she wouldn't. I don't know why she kept saying she was, but she never did. So, I was sort of disappointed in that.[49]

While teacher communication with parents was lacking, even in the school's new program designed to emphasize teacher-parent collaboration, this was only one aspect of a complex conflict management situation from her perspective.

There seems to be a lot of bullies there. A lot of just bad kids that just pick on, this one kid everybody knows, picks with everybody, and they don't seem to address that bad kid. When we had a problem, our son is big but he's an only child and he's soft, okay, and so when my husband went up there and talked to the counselors, well they didn't tell the students, but they moved the other student to another class, which they resolved the matter, but it's like they know that they have problem students, but they don't really deal with them and they're always, like, beatin' up other people and they get their ten days and they're back! Sometimes I think, well maybe there should be a policy of three or four fights they should be out. That's just how I feel.

Unless you as a parent go up there and say something to them I don't think they intervene. I don't think they do. Now we go up, my husband more so, goes up there and talk to them when my son tells us there's a problem, you know, and it's usually where he's at the end of his rope, and he can't deal with it no more, like I'm gonna hit somebody if they keep pickin' with me. And you figure somebody'd have to see the same kid doing stuff day after day, but it don't seem like nothing is done until the kid does something. I don't know if you can, well you should be able to, if he's verbally abusing people and things like that.

My cousin, her stepson, he's a ninth grader and this eighteen-year-old boy just beat him up and he's only in the tenth grade, the eighteen-year-old, and I'm thinking should he really be at that school if he's eighteen in the tenth grade, because, and he is beating up a smaller ninth grader? I thought his mother should have pressed assault charges. They gave him ten days and he's back and he's still same kid, pickin' with everybody again, you know so, and it seems like the kids, my little cousin too, because it's like you big and

> *you picked on this little boy, you know, even the kids know he's a bad seed and he's still there and he's still pickin' with people, talking, I don't know, if they don't consider talking, I think it's harassment.*[50]

Seeing the complexity of the conflicts, knowing the parents of the troublemaking kids, and being consistent with the public opinion research referred to earlier in this chapter, this parent tries to be innovative in response to thinking about possible solutions in a more complex way that is sensitive to the real struggles of actual parents like herself. Her punitiveness is moderated by her proximity to the conflicts and her efforts to balance her fear of unaccountable power, both in the form of unruly kids and in the form of teachers as enforcers.

> *I think they need to, it just seems like the ones who cause trouble, make them cut grass or something. Put them in time-out and study hall, it don't seem to phase them. That's what I think. But maybe making them work, maybe even making them mop the floors in front of other kids, something, because to me, this is not getting to them, that you're in trouble. And I'm not someone, the kid's parents, who are not troublemakers but they're lazy and they're at their wit's ends too, but I think maybe they should make them work or something, because sitting in study hall all day, they just sleep or whatever, it doesn't phase them. So, I think they need to change how they discipline, I mean punish them or whatever. I think most of the parents have tried, I know two situations where they have one model student and the other one, you know they are raised in the same house, one kid is no problem, straight A's, the other one is totally opposite. You know they take stuff away from him, they you know, they try. I don't understand it either. Maybe it's psychological. I don't know. "This one is so good, I'm just gonna be rotten." That's sometime what you think. A lot of them really try, like if you don't do this this week you can't go bowling, if you're in a bowling league or, it don't seem to phase them. I don't know.*[51]

Teacher accountability and parental responsibility are as important to this parent as is addressing the ways that CCPS policy constructs UHS as the problem school it never was, making it into a school without a neighborhood and then into a dumping ground for the problems other neighborhoods would rather pass on than manage themselves. And it is in discussing this aspect of the situation that the parent's most passionately articulated fears are expressed.

> *Where kids get kicked out of every other school in Central City they end up here. I don't think it's deserved, because I think there is a core of very smart kids, very good kids, that you know, he's plays basketball, track and stuff, that you'd be around and you think that this kid is really nice and they're very talented and they could go far, you know but, as long as you got these other ones agitatin' them, where they can't grow, I think, during the day, when you're agitated it's hard to learn. I think they need to find a way to eliminate, I don't know. They try to spread them around, but I don't know. This year a lot of kids have come from [an area parochial school], from Lincoln, so they got a lot of good kids in too, but you get those few bad apples that disrupt it for everybody, it's like I don't know if they can't because of their rights discipline these kids or say "look this is your next step," I don't know, I never talked to them about it.*
>
> *The first day I took him to school in ninth grade, you know his first year of high school and I drop him off over here, and all these kids are in the parking lot smoking, and I'm like, I was traumatized. One of my friends is a teacher there and said "with your old self you probably thought they were smoking cigarettes!" [laughter] I was like, "well yeah," so I mean, yeah, and the things he tells me that happen, you know, they're eatin' lunch or playing basketball, usually he's playing basketball, and you know people want to do stuff to you but when you do it back they want to retaliate or they always say "we'll go get our gang," you know, so I said just tell them you'll get your gang. So, yeah, I think you be afraid a lot. When you get up there and everyone has brothers and got cousins, and they got a gang and you're the only one, your intimidated. . . . One time, and he said the kid hit him and he just hauled off and hit him back, and it was right in front of a teacher and they didn't say anything because evidently this kid, they just felt like he deserved it, you know, I guess it's a problem I guess. . . . The kid tried to, two of them attacked him from behind, and so he picked up the one and threw him down and the other one, when he saw him do that to him, he ran off, but the teacher didn't really say anything to him. And I think that is how some of the teachers feel, like, they're really not going to do anything to him, you got him, they let it go and they never bothered him again. I don't like violence, but I understand sometime you gotta protect yourself.*[52]

Our examination of SHS in chapters 2 and 3 demonstrates one aspect of punishing schools, where the conflicts central to that school culture are generated largely from within the school building and indirectly reflect the mass-mediated impact of consumer culture in ways that divert student energies from larger economic inequalities and focus them intensely on consumerist reproductions of prevailing gender, sexual orientation, and (indirectly) racial prejudices. At SHS the students and teachers experience their palace of a school as a prison, in large part because it is run like a prison. In the two chapters on UHS we see another aspect of punishing schools, where the conflicts central to this school culture are repeatedly identified as coming directly from outside the school building, encouraging the unmediated and disruptive colonization of education by enforcement reflecting a consumer culture managing the consequences of our unwillingness to address inner-city problems.

Another aspect of punishing schools is manifest in the virtual relationship between SHS parents and UHS parents as citizens, a relationship highly mediated by the mass media, federal and state leaders, and the race- and class-coded fears these leaders have determined we ought to focus on today. SHS parents' construction of their identity depended to a large part on their relocation away from the inner city, punishing UHS with white and capital flight. Their suburban identities, reflecting what Mike Davis (1998) calls an ecology of fear, also punish UHS in a second way. As we have argued, the construction of identity and citizen agency in SHS also depends on the absence of the racial and lower-class Other from the inner city, an absence that, when translated into policy positions through the mediation of a powerful electoral coalition we examine in our final chapter, supports the further punishing of inner-city schools in many of the ways we identify in chapters 4 and 5: the diversion of funding from schools to prisons and corporate welfare to support job creation (even as jobs are not being created), infrastructure investments, and fortress communities outside the city.

These two chapters on UHS, taken together, try to make some sense out of the data presented about the relationship between neighborhood and conflict at UHS. The relationship is clearly central to media portrayals and political decisions. It is also a central aspect of perceptions that students, parents, and teachers shared about the most common conflicts at UHS. Key players at UHS describe a complex picture of conflicts that seep in from their neighborhoods, connecting school conflict management with different experiences of family and community life in Central City and both to the disempowering impacts of the punitive framing of these experiences as dysfunctional lifestyle choices by federal, state, and local leaders. School funding conflicts (and the perverse policies that resulted here) sent a message to UHS parents that they must do more with less and that government support will increasingly come in the form of a variety of punishments that increase the burdens on their already failing schools. School funding conflicts (and the perverse policies that result) also send a message to already overworked teachers, continuously more burdened with additional bureaucratic mandates that have less to do with education and more to do with enforcement and social control.

Leadership choices on funding, taxation, and what we ought to get from our schools (vocational training, jobs, community learning centers) provide the meaning-giving background consensus to explain salient UHS concerns about school conflict that comes from the outside, colonizing their educational efforts, suffocating these with unfunded mandates that they cannot fund themselves as a suburban school might (however unhappily) have the capacity to do and that together punish their children for living in—and attending schools within—neighborhoods of concentrated disadvantage (Sampson and Bartusch 1998). Finally, one cultural consequence of this situation is reflected in students without fear of losing their teachers' respect or support, and teachers afraid of developing the close personal connections with their students that make education work suggests that to some degree the irresponsible adult leadership at the state level has left the kids in charge of inner-city schools, creating what Michael Dyson (2001) calls a juvenocracy that punishes both parents and their kids in ways that we argue constitute both SHS and UHS as punishing schools.

Chapter 6

Zero Tolerance Culture
Fear as Punishment, Patronage, and Pedagogy

The state may hold a monopoly on imprisonment, but the carceral form, recast as a kind of prophylactic exile, has become an influential model for governing in other settings. It may take the form of expulsion or suspension from school, dismissal from work, or denial of insurance coverage. In the last decade a thriving market in private juvenile prisons for recalcitrant teenagers has popped up, some in the United States, some over-seas. These institutions market not to juvenile justice agencies but directly to parents looking to address behavior defiance in the wake of a nasty divorce or other trauma to the juvenile. *Prison has become a technology of parenting.*

—Simon 2006; emphasis added[1]

I. Introduction

The homogeneity of Suburbia has a history. The differences we found there were less physically visible and more emotionally stark than initially expected. There were nearly no black bodies, and even the poorest students were from solidly middle-class families. But difference still cast a long shadow over Suburbia in three ways. First, even without black bodies to target, the fear of association with blackness remained present in the stories we heard from Suburban students, teachers, parents, and administrators. In the absence of black bodies, we read these stories as evidence of the presence in Suburbia of mass-mediated images of being black, poor, dangerous, and frighteningly undeserving of anything other than formal punishment through the criminal justice system. Second, in the fear-driven war against this absent yet present form of difference—where locals constructed identity and agency around being white, heterosexual, and consumers—other fears were constructed as worthy of informal punishment in school hallways. These were the fears of any student groups whose sense of identity might challenge white heterosexual normativity or whose sense of agency was not limited to their purchasing power.

Taken together, these two factors contribute to a third way the construction of invisible differences cast a shadow within Suburbia (and extending over a darkening inner city): in a culture that cultivated inattention to power as the privileged form of citizen identity, power relations were less openly contested, and the possibility of subjecting various forms of unaccountable power to critical public scrutiny was structurally and behaviorally constrained by fears of invisible, mass-mediated, market-validated threats to community and property. That is, the mixture of amplified and muted fears in Suburbia appears to undermine the possibility of student identities and citizen agency consistent with developing the republican virtues of moderation and cooperation based upon the experience of living in openly democratic—and therefore inescapably disorderly—communities.[2] Instead, we observed a community built upon an uncritical conformity to a right-utopian vision of democracy, where an amplified fear of democratic disorder supports the patronizing of fortress communities of citizens who self-identify through deference to state agency that punishes those whose fears focus on the disorders of an unregulated market. As such, the punishing schools created in this community, like the market-utopian promises made about charter schools, are less innovative, the communities they reproduce are less resilient, and the forms of citizen identity and agency constitutive of these communities provide a political and cultural foundation for a public opinion made more vulnerable to mass-mediated manipulation by public or private leaders seeking to determine our fears.

Punishing schools target nonconformity and difference as threats, patronizing those who are comfortable with identities that renounce agency and rewarding them by privileging official efforts to reduce their fears. For these citizens, the embrace of freedom as dependence becomes a precondition for them to be recognized as "the community" whose amplified fears the powerful will seek to reduce, patronizing them in ways that disempower—even imprison—them in fortress communities exiled from the disorderly experiences that constitute modern life, spur innovation, and provide opportunities to learn the skills for democratic citizenship. Thus privileged student identities are only linked to their limited agency to the extent that these support the punishment of others at SHS, imprisoning other students for their nonconformist agency (represented as dysfunctional individual lifestyle choices that reflect a lack of self-control). Privileged identities are patronized—exchanging official recognition for their support of punishment within SHS and in the inner cities, where students (and their parents) cycle between the two poles of malign neglect constitutive of their communities: prisons as pockets of fiscal abundance within an otherwise systematically impoverished public sphere.[3]

By focusing on the complex mobilizations of fear in the narratives of both *Pleasantville* and SHS, it becomes clear that even schools built in our most affluent areas become punishing schools when they construct particular notions of individual identity and agency around an empirically unjustified, but politically powerful, image of youth as both dangerous and in danger. Both texts, *Pleasantville* and SHS, are embedded within a context marked by fear, mobilized to gain the consent of the "Whiteys"[4] to punish—formally and informally—other individuals and groups, appearing in color as a visible sign of their lack of self-control, despite the audience's knowledge that the meaning of being in color is more complex. In *Pleasantville* being "colored" means active citizen agency in search of living a rich and full life animated by the American dream as much as it means being a nonconformist and as much as it, eventually, means being labeled a frightening criminal threat to property and community, only redeemable as an identity premised on renouncing agency.

The amplified fears of suburban parents that disempower them and punish others support a zero tolerance culture where a rhetoric of prevention becomes an invitation to perpetual enforcement, where the wide menu of fears about unaccountable power is filtered to exclude concerns about more aggressive and less accountable forms of state or market power. In *Pleasantville* and SHS we see that this fear of youth and difference is mobilized, in part, through a logic of absence, a fear of difference at a distance that amplifies the mass-mediated images of blackness as conflict and conflict as discomfort. And it is clear in both texts that the logic of absence depends on the rhetorical power of a particularly complex construction of nostalgia for the days "when men were men" in the 1950s, a nostalgia that only makes sense for the abstract individual, the "reasonable person" whose identity and agency are made possible by virtue of being a white male and having a wife at home. In this sense, then, the communities redeemed in *Pleasantville* and Suburbia are built upon a nostalgic inattention to power imbalances, a logic of absence that treats difference (female sexual independence or the wrong hairstyle) as a threatening individual lifestyle choice. Difference is the source of conflict, and those who are different are responsible for the discomfort that privileged identities experience when even bodies made invisible challenge their prevailing no-conflict, nonchangist, right-utopian worldviews.

Constructing an image of a past with political utility in the present in these texts encourages an uncritical acceptance of this image as both the way it ought to be and the way it would be were it not for those individuals without self-control, identified by their on-screen, mass-mediated, technicolor bodies. The logic of absence is a replacement of direct experience with familiar images and virtual experience. In *Pleasantville,* when this uncomfortable complexity disrupts David, he turns up the volume to drown out the painful fears and concerns articulated by his struggling mother. When even a culture with black bodies erased through white flight does not actually produce a no-conflict world in Suburbia, adults turn up the volume with (sometimes illegal, often hysterical, and arguably ineffective) lockdowns to drown out student concerns about harassment, or heavy-handed enforcement, or administrators articulating a manifestly inaccurate version of the SHS story right before their eyes (which suggests an implicit fear of speaking freely). And, while the punishing school emerging in Suburbia might imagine itself only indirectly associated with the punishing school in Central City, we argue that they are far more intimately linked.

Schools that create less innovative and more vulnerable citizens—citizens without the democratic citizenship skills that can only be forged by addressing visible conflicts in routine practice—are schools that construct democracy itself as a threat to their communities.[5] As Sennett (1970) and others argue, democratic deliberations and the civic culture on which these depend require citizens who can live comfortably with conflict, who understand that conflict is normal and that leadership is about how we achieve agreements, construct shared values, and create communities in the ways we handle conflict (not in how we make both conflict and the communities we attach to it invisible).[6] This means leaders and citizens must learn these skills in their communities and schools. But punishing schools are afraid of conflict, displacing the promise of practical and intellectual skills developed through rich lived experiences with a fortress mentality driven by amplified fears, and, as such, punishing schools both replace education with enforcement (to contain the conflict contagion in the inner city) and confuse leadership with growing up wealthy. In this way, they encourage a juvenocracy, where adults who should be mentoring are afraid of children, who govern with the sound-bite view of conflict management they are taught so thoroughly by a national leadership unconstrained by proximity to local conflicts.[7] Punishing schools are producing citizens unprepared for the complex challenges we face as a nation and overprepared to support zero tolerance approaches to conflict.

Complementary Forms of Punishing Schools

At SHS conflict centered on two areas: interpersonal conflicts emerging out of romantic relationships and group conflicts based on perceived, if invisible, differences. At UHS interpersonal conflicts were seen as serious, potentially explosive evidence of an inner-city culture where violence was a way of life—incomprehensible to white teachers—undermining the possibility of education, whereas at SHS these conflicts were accepted as a normal part of adolescent life, as conflicts that posed no threat to patronized SHS identities.[8] At UHS group conflicts were constructed by some adults as gang problems and by others as ways for the students to construct their own identities or "ways of being" in contrast to others, arbitrarily made different by urban geography. Most references to conflicts, including interpersonal conflicts, at UHS contained some group element and an associated fear of gang violence, despite the fact that the police officer noted that there was little to no actual threat of gang activity at the school. But this empirical reality did not inhibit the construction of the school as an inner-city pocket of chaotic kids unconstrained by community. In SHS, however, interpersonal conflicts were not associated with gang violence and group conflict. Conflict in the SHS community was framed as a form of individual harassment, ironically normalizing verbal abuse based on class or sexual orientation and in a school culture that did not challenge this abuse, sending the message that the only conflict management skill needed in response to difference made momentarily visible was fearmongering: amplifying homophobic and class-based fears to undercut the fears of those targeted for hateful harassment.

At SHS we heard frequent references to harassment as a consequence of wearing clothing that signifies a family with fewer resources. At UHS the powerful pull of consumer culture was visibly present in the hallways but absent from our interviews for the most part, though one story we heard about a fight in the making included a matter-of-fact description by a teacher of a student taking off her boots and other expensive accessories before fighting, suggesting that the parents of UHS students have less disposable income to replace these badges of consumerist identity than do the parents of SHS students. At SHS overconfident and coddled students struggled over consumer-conformist identities to "be the best that they could be." They struggled to find their individualized invitation to the country club of economic success they feel entitled to join. At UHS, overburdened and variously punished students struggled to get to school at all; that is, they struggled to reduce the negative impact of their neighborhood on their education. This class difference across schools might account for why we found the students at each school appropriating different language from mainstream culture and adopting conflict management strategies surprisingly unsuited for their environment.

SHS students appropriated harassment to insulate their consumerist juvenocracy from difference, analysis, and adult intervention. Students rearticulated this term to reflect larger cultural suspicions about legal efforts to protect women from unwanted contact that democratically targets the narrow and intolerant, nonchangist approach to difference that characterizes their school and community. Instead, this consumerist and juvenocratic articulation of harassment transformed the term into a way to mark other, hardly visible, differences for punishment, making intolerance acceptable and patronizing the "normal" students willing to mobilize this fear in hateful behaviors that suburban administrators frame as just part of being a teenager. UHS students appropriated gang tags and rearticulated these to, similarly, reflect a cultural suspicion of individuals from outside their youth-centered community, even as these tags continued to be used in the larger Central City area to articulate suspicion of their school, their friends, and their bodies as unconstrained by the civilizing influence of a strong neighborhood community.

At SHS the sustained attack on public entitlements advances, without irony or shame, an education that teaches these children that their "terrible sense of [privatized] entitlement" is deserved and forms the basis of an invisible meritocracy within which they will inherit a leadership position. Those at SHS with the economic means to fully participate are disempowered because their participation is reduced to consumption (constructing family values as so self-serving and self-absorbed that they are inconsistent with community). At UHS public impoverishment cannot be supplemented by private resources, leaving those who lack the private resources to replace decreasing public investments with participation as targets for punishment to be seen as uncaring or welfare-dependent parents.

The SHS students are pressured to be deserving, which includes sacrificing their own youth for a perverse juvenocracy and supporting the punishment of those frightening inner-city Americans they have only indirectly met as dangerously undeserving. These students learn that conflict is not normal; it is a consequence of difference. Since the pedagogy of a zero tolerance culture sends the message that diversity causes conflict, conflict management focuses on making differences invisible and citizens insulated from experiencing difference more susceptible to the problematic mobilization of frightening images by the mass media. Unexamined white heterosexual normativity patronizes normalized students to disempower them, denying them direct experience with critical conflicts and, therefore, insulating them from the opportunity to develop the understandings and skills needed to effectively prevent, resolve, or reduce the harms associated with these conflicts. Instead, the weakness of deskilled students is manifest in identities without effective agency, leaving them subject to more aggressive and less accountable forms of power. Even a non-white teacher at SHS experiences his own agency as precariously contingent on the goodwill of the dominant white political culture, disempowered even as his fears are patronized as the black fears that fit with the type of community being constructed in Suburbia.

In both SHS and UHS the adults recognize that it is the kids with leadership skills who are able to handle conflict well, in ways that strengthen the school and prepare the students to be active and productive participants in (sometimes disorderly) democratic politics. But in neither school did we observe a serious effort to identify and transfer these skills through a cultural recognition that conflict is normal, varied, and an opportunity to lead. Instead of embedding skill development into the daily routines of our schoolchildren, we encourage their cynicism and wrath with flavor-of-the-month public relations activities like "Peace Week" or peer mediation programs that few at either school were aware of and that did not seek to engage with the natural leaders in the student population. In this context, to seek adult intervention is to escalate the conflict in two ways: first, our children see that adults favor punishment as the response, and second, since children experience even more directly than adults do that this approach fails to prevent conflict, upping the ante in this way is most likely to just make the situation worse. A process that starts with too little adult educational attention and ends with too much adult enforcement attention at the other end leaves the kids in charge but inattentive to power, a whole series of teaching moments lost by educators, parents, and, most important, legislators failing to lead. In this context, conflict and democracy become spectator sports, dramatic commodities for consumption that teach us to be passive and dependent citizens.

Leaders constructing a zero tolerance culture encourage adults to fear children, citizens to fear informed agency and democratic governance, and middle-class parents to fear power-poor parents in ways that disempower both. In punishing schools, these fears have paralyzed effective mentoring relationships, encouraged reactive and punitive leadership even in our affluent schools, despite opposition (and resistance) from teachers, and supported a juvenocracy in place of community, producing leaders without leadership skills. Those in closest proximity to the conflicts, who research indicates are likely the most ambivalent about strictly punitive approaches to conflict management, are the least empowered to act. Suburban teachers and parents are choking on self-esteem and respect-building programs designed in response to urban school conflicts (Simon 2006) and nationalized by leaders far from both schools who are more interested in building electoral coalitions than in ensuring that we have an education system that will support active democratic forms of citizen agency. Inner-city teachers and parents are starved by programs that work better in affluent suburbs, where affluence can provide private resources to supplement antitax and antiunion attacks on the public sector that blame teachers for their fear of students, parents for being too busy, and both for squandering public investments being diverted into less innovative, more costly, and poorer performing charter schools.

In SHS difference comes to be defined as deviant. Fears of students, of active citizen agency, and of open democratic deliberation displace citizen fears about various forms of unaccountable power—from children without skills, unconstrained by living within resilient democratic communities, to drug dealers; impersonal school bureaucrats; union-protected, deadwood teachers; union-busting charter schools; fashionable professional colonizations of teacher-student mentoring relationships; and aggressively punitive public and private leaders. Fears at SHS about its similarity to Columbine are muted by adults aghast that administrators would even make these similarities known and therefore a topic of discussion, suggestive to students who are already feared because of their potentially disruptive, dangerous power. Fears at UHS included no mention of Columbine, because their school is so dissimilar. But these fears were still amplified and translated into large purchases for metal detectors that were never used during our four months of observation there. SHS experienced three spectacularly expensive lockdowns during our observations; UHS experienced none.

The key conflicts for SHS were internal, and we analyzed these to highlight the ways that even our most affluent suburb schools are becoming more like penal institutions. The students, teachers, and parents at UHS also shared a common discursive construction of the central conflicts and approaches to conflict management constitutive of their school culture, but the consensus at UHS focused on tracing the roots of their inner-city school conflicts to the neighborhoods their students live in. While SHS students and teachers experience their palatial building as a prison, the students, teachers, and parents of UHS experience their school as a target for punishment from state and local leaders for the challenges their students face.

The politics behind such educational issues as charter schools, *DeRolph v. State of Ohio,* redirected lottery funds, electoral fearmongering to reconstitute the state supreme court, near continuous local property tax levies, community-school partnerships, and urban renewal reveal leaders either reluctant or unwilling to invest in the institutions constitutive of a democratic public sphere, preferring instead to mobilize a right-utopian free market discourse (and an electoral constituency whose amplified fears can be rhetorically linked to this) to punish our schools and weaken our ability to produce citizen identities with the practical and intellectual skills necessary to address the challenges we face in democratic ways.

A third aspect of punishing schools is manifest in the power-filled virtual relationship between SHS parents and UHS parents as citizens, a relationship highly mediated by the mass media, public and private leaders, and the race- and class-coded fears these leaders have determined we ought to focus on today. SHS parents' construction of their identity depended in large part on their relocation away from the inner city, punishing UHS with white and capital flight. Their suburban identities, reflecting what Mike Davis (1998) calls an ecology of fear, also punish UHS in a second way. As we have argued, the construction of identity and citizen agency in SHS depends on the absence of the inner-city racial and lower-class Other, an absence that, when translated into policy positions through the mobilization of a powerful electoral coalition, which we examine in this final chapter, supports the further punishing of inner-city schools: the diversion of funding from schools to prisons and corporate welfare as a means to support job creation (even as, in the aggregate, jobs are not being created) and infrastructure investments in suburban fortress communities outside the city.

II. We Fear as Our Rulers Determine

> I don't mean this in a disrespectful way, but Columbine happens in the ghetto everyday. When the shit goes down y'all aint got nothing to say.
>
> —LLCoolJay, "Homicide"

> For nearly three decades, stories of youth violence have claimed front-page news. Early accounts depicted urban youths of color as gangsters and violent predators. . . . Recent stories shifted attention to a string of white student shootings in suburban high schools. . . . Taken together, these stories—about gang warfare, school-yard murders, and bullying—yield images of adolescents as either *uncontrollable* or *unsuccessfully controlled* by school, family, religious, and legal institutions.
>
> —Morrill et al. 2000, 522

Columbine captured our imagination. Eric Harris and Dylan Klebold could have been in class with our own kids, or worse. Columbine catalyzed a national debate about violence in schools, but it was not the first, nor the worst, nor the most characteristic, nor even the most tragic illustration of school violence in America. As the quote by Morrill et al. here indicates and this research project examines, the relationship between conflict and our responses to conflict varies according to the identities of victim and perpetrator that are mobilized in a frightening discourse about crime and punishment that is increasingly colonizing our schools. Our frustratingly ineffective responses to conflict are mediated by amplified fears of stranger predators and muted fears of less dramatic—though often more genuinely threatening—offenders.[9] With a mass media all too willing to simply pass on official frames (Bennett 1996) that excite an empirically inaccurate menu of citizen fears (Beckett 1997), we rush to punish—to frighten other citizens—with astonishingly little regard for what the best available research shows is most likely to prevent or reduce violence (Lyons and Scheingold 2000; Tonry 1995; Tonry and Farrington 1995; Scheingold 1984). Our fears mediate our responses to crime, and as Machiavelli put it, "men love as they themselves determine, but fear as their rulers determine."

In terms of the cases examined here, the fears of some parents are amplified and linked to unrelated fears about social change and economic anxiety and virtual fears of being black, poor, and undeserving. Some citizens are marginalized and punished for it, while others are constructed as "the community" patrons at the foundation of a crime-control state governing through fear. This research project has examined the competing frames, the discursive and material struggles, manifest in our responses to school conflict. Our objective in this last chapter will be to clarify the political utility of amplifying and ignoring, mobilizing and redirecting, citizen fear—fear as a punishment for the marginalized, a form of patronage for middle-class taxpayers, and pedagogy for a zero tolerance political culture.[10] One central aspect of this pedagogy is the cultivation of citizen identities that are inattentive to power and, as such, citizens who are more vulnerable to rulers seeking to determine our fears.

> There is fear. Fear is never an actuality; it is either before or after the active present. When there is fear in the active present, is it fear? It is there and there is no escape from it, no evasion possible. There, at that actual moment, there is total attention at the moment of danger; physical or psychological. When there is complete attention there is no fear. But the actual fact of *inattention breeds fear;* fear arises when there is avoidance of the fact, a flight; then the very escape itself is fear. . . . Fear is one of the greatest problems in life. A mind that is caught in fear lives in confusion, in conflict, and therefore must be violent, distorted, and aggressive. It dare not move away from its own patterns of thinking, and this breeds hypocrisy. (Krishnamurti 1995, 92, 5; emphasis added)

Inattention suggests two important aspects of punishing schools. First, if inattention breeds fears and fears grow through a collective willingness to favor avoiding rather than facing those forces that do threaten serious harm, then what is driving us to be so blithely inattentive? Second, where is our attention being drawn, what fears have our leaders determined we ought to be focusing on, and with what political utility?

As one prominent conservative analyst points out, there are real fears that might account for schools encouraging a more generalized inattention to power in both affluent and power-poor neighborhoods. The proportion of total U.S. income going to the top 1 percent of our population has steadily increased over the past twenty years. In 1981 it was 9.3 percent. In 1997 it had risen to 15.8 percent, bringing it back up to

1929 levels. When we examine family wealth, rather than income, the data are even more telling. The top 1 percent of American families controlled 19.9 percent of total family wealth in 1976, but that has risen steadily since that time to again reach a level not seen since 1929—in 1997 the top 1 percent of American families controlled 40.1 percent of total family wealth. The land of the free and home of the brave now stands, according to World Bank data, as a nation with more extreme economic inequality than that found in any of our closest allies, a gap that has grown through Republican and Democratic presidencies. The changes in income by quintile for the period 1977–94, are shown in table 3 (Phillips 2002, 121–37).

But U.S. income inequality is not only extreme relative to our allies; it is extreme relative to our own history. When compared to the income distribution that prevailed in the four decades following World War II, we get a more accurate sense of what nostalgia for the 1950s ought to really mean. In 1950, when men were men, corporations paid 26.5 percent of total taxes collected and payroll taxes were only 6.9 percent of the total. In 2000, corporations paid 10.2 percent (*before* the Bush administration's enormous tax cuts for the wealthiest individuals and corporations) and payroll taxes made up 31.1 percent of total taxes collected (Phillips 2002, 149). In this context, it is not difficult to imagine a political utility in identities distracting our attention from fears that point to the powerful with fears for our children that target teachers' unions, stranger predators, and political correctness (Glassner 1999).

The mixture of amplified and muted fears bred by a zero tolerance pedagogy reflects a culture where leaders encourage us to cultivate identities inattentive to (the possibility of self-) governance, breeding a paralyzing fear that drives us to demand more aggressive and less accountable forms of state or corporate agency (Lyons 1999; Taylor 1982; Tocqueville 1956).[11] Affluent inattentiveness to bomb making in the basements of the Harris and Klebold homes, or in palacelike schools

TABLE 3. Percentage Change in After-Tax Income, 1977–94

Poorest quintile of Americans	–16%
Lower middle class quintile	–8%
Middle class quintile	–1%
Upper middle class quintile	+4%
Wealthiest 1% of Americans	+72%

Source: Data from the Congressional Budget Office.

experienced as prisonlike warehouses, is driven, at least in part, by amplified fears of lazy, black, and criminal students in inner-city schools and paralyzing fears of economic insecurity should we choose the "mommy track" to spend more time with our children. Power-poor inattentiveness may be similarly driven by the economic imperatives of balancing three jobs without benefits (or, as in our more affluent communities, family- and community-destroying addictions of one sort or another), which makes PTA meetings or parent-teacher conferences a mighty challenge.[12]

This study highlights the continued importance of analyzing moral panics to make explicit the implicit political and cultural utilities driving what may initially appear to be simply democratic responses to citizen outrage about rising crime. Our study also highlights important analytical tensions between national and local leaders. National and state leaders willing and able to powerfully amplify particular fears operate within a context that contains fewer constraints on the strictly symbolic and expressive aspects of moral panic rhetoric, whereas our study again confirms that at the local level punitiveness was moderated to some degree by political interactions that were more direct, more cross-cutting, and less exclusively mediated by a nationalized information system. This translates into the more ambiguous, sometimes contradictory, and analytically revealing policy struggles we observed in local school districts and among parents when compared to the more ideologically rigid approaches articulated at the state and national levels. And our study highlights the impact on our schools of the emergence of a powerful new governing coalition that has displaced the New Deal coalition, directing resources (forms of patronage from jobs to curricular reforms to having your fears legitimized as the conflicts that leaders will invest in resolving) in exchange for continued electoral support (for the more aggressive and less accountable punishment of others).

From a New Deal to Zero Tolerance

The data presented in this book highlight the emergence of a zero tolerance culture animated by a plutocratic vision of limited government that has displaced the New Deal coalition with a right-utopian, antidemocratic, cultural (and sometimes electoral) coalition intent on governing through crime and fear.[13] This zero tolerance coalition seeks to dissipate public energies by focusing citizens on those lesser fears that draw our attentiveness not to power but to blaming the power-poor. A zero tolerance culture cultivates citizen identities as inattentive to failed leadership, amplifying fears that divide and paralyze us, insulating us within a passive and dependent articulation of citizen agency as consuming subjects, and reinforcing state agency and a vision of limited government limited to punishment.

We argue that what began as a Republican strategy to mobilize a punitive, law-and-order, electoral coalition has become institutionalized as a zero tolerance coalition, a political culture as comfortable with Bill Clinton as George Bush. It is built upon an elite-led, extralegal, and often violent intolerance for the disorder inherent in active citizen agency and a democratic public sphere, a political culture that punishes the poor for the challenges they face as energetically as it insulates corporate corruption from critical public scrutiny and justifies less accountable but more aggressive forms of state agency as democratic responses to elite-amplified citizen fears. It is a political culture that enables world-record income gaps between the rich and poor, even as our economic productivity declines more rapidly in response to an overextended military. Right-utopianism makes explicit the aspirations animating this cultural and (inconsistently) electoral coalition. It identifies a zero tolerance vision of the good society to which they would like to lead us.[14] Punishing schools and the larger zero tolerance political culture these schools reflect and reproduce are ultimately premised on an unstable and antidemocratic right-utopian worldview, which means, in part, that, like the Progressive Era or the New Deal era challenges we faced, we will not repair education in America until we repair democracy in America, and that effort requires that we direct our fears and frustrations toward the failed public and private leadership driving the right-utopian mythologies that support our zero tolerance culture.

III. Fear, Pedagogy, and Punishing Schools

Our leaders are punishing our inner-city schools for the challenges they face, as if their decaying buildings, decades of disinvestment, disappearing residential neighborhoods, and status as power-poor communities stand as evidence of parental neglect and uncontrollable youth. We argue that the evidence does not support this claim. Instead, we are persuaded that this approach to conflict management, to teaching and learning in the inner city, reflects a perspective on limited government that Katznelson (1976, 220) calls one that encourages "a politics of dependency," where governance is limited to amplifying largely punitive efforts to "manage the consequences of our inability to solve urban problems," a perspective that Mike Davis (1998) argues is based on an ecology of fear and one that Jonathan Simon (2006) persuasively contends is best understood as an effort to govern through crime control.[15]

Rather than strengthening the families and communities in our most victimized neighborhoods, this combination of more aggressive punishment in communities less able to hold powerful state and corporate agents accountable further fragments and disorganizes urban communities (Santos 1982) and constructs local political networks that are gradually made more responsive to a nationalized and expressive politics of crime and punishment (Lyons and Scheingold 2000) than they are to the parents, teachers, or students attending punishing schools. At the same time, we believe that the data presented here also demonstrate that our leaders, while patronizing suburban parents to the extent that responding to their mass-mediated fears (of difference) reinforces state agency, are also punishing even our more affluent schools by responding to their amplified fears in ways that disempower them as individuals and undermine the social foundations for resilient democratic community life.

Conservative and frightened law-abiding suburban parents are managed as political inputs with campaign rhetoric that amplifies their fears, condensing a wide range of concerns into a fear of crime and channeling broad social and economic anxieties into a fear of the poor, the young, and the disorderly.[16] This fear—and the frightened and dependent middle-class taxpayers mobilized by it—then justifies more prison construction (suburban and rural job creation for these same frightened taxpayers) in place of investment in education, deepening educational inequalities between affluent suburban and inner-city school districts (Schlosser 1998). At the same time, this fear constructs the poor, their communities, their schools, their children, and their parents' fears as dangerous and irrational, appropriately managed as political outputs, a population targeted for extreme, often expressively punitive, criminal justice policy, but also, increasingly, through welfare-to-work social service providers and the public school system itself (Ferguson 2000).[17]

In terms of the cases examined here, the fears of some parents are amplified and the articulated fears of other parents are ignored on two dimensions. First, within the inner-city school those fears that articulate with a punitive educational environment, reinforcing state agency, are constructed as "reasonable and pragmatic," while other fears become problems for the administration and are consistently framed as "beyond our control," and the parents who insist that these fears be heard are constructed as irrational and unstable, as living evidence that "the apple doesn't fall far from the tree."[18] The second dimension is that, while the "irrational" fears of inner-city parents are marginalized and their children punished, suburban parents are constructed as "the community." As the community, currently prevailing approaches to limited government are designed to reduce their fears, as the foundation of a crime-control state governing through fear.

The leadership decisions that have constituted UHS as a problem building were choices that favored responding to the (politically amplified) fears of white suburban parents and muting the fears of black inner-city parents. These decisions by political and economic leaders are communicated to our children in deteriorating classroom experiences, educational funding decisions, extralegal school reform initiatives, and, perhaps most powerfully, popular cultural. Taken together, these political, economic, and cultural messages suggest that punishing schools articulate a zero tolerance pedagogy and support the need for a critical examination of the social foundations beneath punishing schools that highlights the ways that current approaches to school conflict exclude inner-city communities targeted for punishment and include suburban communities in ways that disempower both.

IV. Punishing Schools and Political Patronage

Fear of bullies at Columbine, protected and enabled by a zero tolerance culture, still fall on deaf ears today (Aronson 2000). Fears of official misconduct are muted in police-community partnerships or displaced by fears more consistent with state agency when official violence is transformed into police officers' fear for their safety in the trial exonerating the officers who beat Rodney King. Fears of gang violence and other forms of unaccountable power ravaging our most victimized neighborhoods or fears of impersonal and ineffectual public and private bureaucracies insulated from critical public scrutiny—these are all fears that could challenge efforts to reinforce a vision of state agency that is limited to extremely punitive approaches to conflict in our schools. But these are muted as unreasonable, beyond our control, or the screeds of poor parents that are themselves constructed as part of the problem.

Even in the case of terrorism, a fear-based approach to conflict isolates us from critical resources (the support of our most powerful allies), undermines the rule of law, and thereby increases the long-term costs of public safety. Barber argues that fear itself is the enemy and that a strong democracy "refuses to make room for fear."

> In free societies, Franklin Roosevelt reminded us, "The only thing we have to fear is fear itself." Free women and men engaged in governing themselves are far less vulnerable to fear than are spectators, passively watching their anxious governments try to intimidate others. Preventive war will not in the end prevent terrorism; only preventive democracy can do that. (Barber 2003, 32)

But the current fear-based electoral strategy, while preempting critics with a war on criticism that portrays disagreement as unpatriotic and its own position as realist, is itself profoundly disconnected from empirical reality. As Barber (2003, 35) persuasively demonstrates, in the foreign policy arena, this zero tolerance coalition, in "hubris laced with fear," reveals a deeply ideological, faith-based, utopian approach to conflict that encourages the same nostalgic inattention to power characteristic of punishing schools. Barber, referring to the hawks in the current administration who are driving our invasion of Iraq, argues that they have "become the new idealists—idealists of unilateralism" in an interdependent world.

> In their romantic enthusiasm, they are absolutely certain they can overwhelm interdependence through acts of sovereign self-assertion, override global complexity with nationalist daring, liberate people in bondage by bombing them into submission, democratize women and men who have never known freedom by executing their rulers. [Whereas the doves in the administration] are the new realists. To them interdependence is less an aspiration, the world as they wish it were, than a pressing reality that mandates working with others through the law because this is the only way interdependence can be survived. (43–44)

When polling data before the invasion of Iraq showed that two-thirds of Americans opposed unilateral action, our leaders adopted the same strategy they have long used domestically to make salient our fear of crime and drugs in wars on crime and drugs, begun when public concern and empirical measures of the threat were both very low: they decided to identify our fears, determining for us a menu of fears that will fragment the possibility of effective democratic agency. Polling data show that our leaders did indeed determine our fears, as public concern about crime rose following political initiatives to focus our attention on crime or drugs (Beckett 1997), and two weeks after the invasion of Iraq two-thirds of Americans switched to support unilateral invasion, a number that would be dramatically more if we broke it down to those Americans who exclusively watched Fox News.[19]

Punishing schools thrive in this zero tolerance political culture. When average Americans were concerned about job loss and financial insecurity, President Bush was focusing on fear as patronage, punishment, and pedagogy to make permanent a new tax system that taxes earned income from blue-collar paychecks and does not tax unearned income in the investment portfolios of the wealthiest Americans, punishing those who work with their hands and patronizing the fears of elites "antagonistic to the public sphere" (Scapp 2003, 215). The president is proposing budget increases for drug testing in schools even as drug use continues its decadeslong decline and is shifting drug treatment programs to a core constituency of the zero tolerance coalition: faith-based religious groups who stand to benefit most from this "votes for patronage" arrangement.

> [T]here's a political story that runs through much of what has happened to this country lately, the story of the rise and growing dominance of a radical political movement, right here in the U.S.A. I'm talking, of course, about America's radical right—a movement that now effectively controls the White House, Congress, and much of the judiciary, and a good slice of the media. (Krugman 2003, 3)

We argue here that this is also a cultural coalition seeking to wrest control from teachers (and in more complex ways from parents) over a public education system that has been steadily starved into submission over the past two decades.[20]

Krugman argues that this new regime is frightening because it does not recognize the legitimacy of our political system; rather than improve on what we have accomplished, these leaders have long sought to impoverish in order to dismantle (and privatize) foundational programs average Americans depend on, such as Social Security, unemployment insurance, Medicare, the United States Postal Service and welfare (largely accomplished with Clinton's Welfare to Work program). But impoverishing the public sphere also undermines respect for the rule of law and democratic legitimation (USA Patriot Act, Guantanomo Bay, 2000 presidential election, disinformation campaigns before and after the invasion of Iraq); international institutions *that we built* to project our influence and protect our interests (United Nations, NATO, World Bank, and other international regimes, including the Kyoto Accords, the land mines treaty, and the International Criminal Court); and principles such as the separation of church and state (Krugman 2003, 6–7; Cole and Dempsey 2002; Schlosser 1998). The war on terror hastens and makes more visible this transformation; but analysis reveals it in punishing schools as well.

In the war on terror the context of being under attack dramatically changed the dynamics of domestic politics, the direction of funding priorities, and the priority ranking of competing policy objectives. When our leaders determined that we ought to fear weapons of mass destruction, this justified resource allocations, including our willingness to send our young men and women into harm's way.

> Terrorism can induce a country to scare itself into a kind of paralysis. . . . How he [President Bush] got from the first widely supported goal of suppressing terrorism to the second widely opposed goal of removing Saddam from power is at least in part a story of *fear*—fear instilled by awful terrorist deeds but also *fear marketed and amplified by the administration's response to terror.* On its slippery slope, "rogue states" became fixed targets that could be identified, located, and attacked, but targets that were stripped of their internationally recognized sovereign rights, which otherwise should have protected them from attack . . . . [T]he United States prefers states it can locate and vanquish to the terrorists it cannot even find. . . . *Vulnerability trumps culpability.* Except that states like Iraq and North Korea are intrinsically more suited to deterrence and containment than to preventive war, so when the doctrine of preventive war is applied to them, it rapidly melts down into something that looks very much like a special case of deterrence—in Tod Lindberg's bold phrase, preemption as "the violent reestablishment of the terms of deterrence." (Barber 2003, 26, 106–9; emphasis added)[21]

This leadership choice to amplify one fear—displacing fears of al Qaeda, economic insecurity, environmental degradation, corporate malfeasance, and official misconduct—constructs a limited public sphere around domestic political debates that recognize the fears of selected elite Americans as those that are worthy of the government protections that come with citizenship. At the same time, this is a form of limited government that is silent on the fears of other Americans. As Cole and Dempsey (2002), among others, have argued, this choice has concrete material, political, and discursive costs: weakened individual rights against invasion by public or private leaders (arguably encouraging official extralegal actions like those in Guantanomo Bay, extra-constitutional creation of charter schools, and tort reform or other legislative efforts to insulate private leaders from accountability) and the incremental colonization of impoverished educational bureaucracies by a laissez-faire business model that is hostile to both intellectual inquiry and the kind of democratic citizenship that is the foundation of American prosperity.[22]

Our responses to these amplified and muted fears are constructing some communities as "virtuous citizens" and others as "disruptive subjects," distributing citizenship as a form of political patronage to some in ways that disempower them and denying it to others to justify punishing them (Yngvesson 1993). Understanding the political utility of amplifying and muting particular fears, we believe, illuminates the political-cultural foundation for what has been variously referred to as governing through crime (Simon 1997) our culture of control (Garland 1996, 2001), education as enforcement (Saltman and Gabbard 2003), or a zero tolerance political culture. Following Machiavelli, thinking of fear as a powerful political tool is not entirely new. Hobbes nearly equated sovereignty with both fear and the redistribution of it through state agency. Stuart Hall's critique of policing (Hall et al. 1978) focuses on identifying the political utility of citizen fear by naming police- and politician-initiated, mass-media-amplified moral panics as a mechanism for public and private leaders to manufacture consent for increasingly punitive approaches to crime, social welfare, and governance.[23] While not entirely new, we argue that the more complex analysis of fear presented here contributes to advancing our understanding of punishing schools, citizenship, and identity in a zero tolerance culture.

V. Identity and Agency in Zero Tolerance Culture

Like the New Deal the zero tolerance vision of limited government is built upon the strategic language constitutive of an electoral coalition whose support is secured through political patronage: the provision of resources for votes. Funding for free legal defense clinics, social workers, and teachers—particularly in liberal urban voting districts—is rhetorically reconstituted as permissive and either eliminated or reduced to the point of ineffectiveness, while funding for prisons is constructed as the serious and sober response to the challenge we face from evil individuals to support economic redistribution, funding programs, and booming employment opportunities among conservative rural and suburban voting blocks. Prisons are only the most expensive and perhaps most representative program, but this new exchange relationship includes funding for programs rewriting education as enforcement, welfare-to-work in a context where public leaders reward private leaders for the capital flight responsible for down-waging and massive job loss, and health-care reform that punishes the sick by redirecting funds to health maintenance organizations and insurance companies—a policy that only makes sense in a zero tolerance culture that insulates right-utopian approaches from critical public scrutiny.

These are structural punishments that privatize those aspects of the public sphere that were created to check private ambition with public scrutiny and regulation, patronizing powerful private actors with corporate welfare despite leadership decisions in the private sector undermining secure employment, living wages, and decent benefits. The combination of punishment and patronage constitutive of the zero tolerance coalition is directed at the families who would like to reduce their dependence on big corporations or government and revitalize their own resilient communities dependent on income they earn through their own hard work in order to redistribute the profits generated by their work to the already extremely wealthy plutocrats who derive their support from unearned income. The vision of limited government being constituted here can be read in the steady privatization through starvation, deregulation, punishment, and patronage of already impoverished public schools. This is our read of the political and cultural significance of a charter school movement that is neither innovative nor educationally defensible, rhetoric about unsafe schools that focuses on crime rather than unsafe buildings resulting from decades of disinvestment, and rigidly antitax ideologues who insist—despite the rapid and ongoing flight of capital and jobs on their watch—that shifting funds from education to prisons and corporate welfare is fiscally responsible leadership.

We argue that our traditional understandings of patronage as just about jobs and of fear as just about demonizing target populations are incomplete, because when leaders choose to demonize one (potential) constituency and make their putative lifestyle choices the focus of our fears and legitimate targets for state punishment, these leaders are also choosing to recognize the fears of some as the fears of "the community" that we ought to respond to, prioritize, and invest in reducing. In this way, when our "rulers determine our fears" (as Machiavelli put it), they not only select targets for punishment, but they also prioritize the problems and concerns of particular communities over others, turning fear-reduction efforts into a form of political patronage, as we see in current approaches to educational reform.

Further, we argue that fear can be seen as one critical starting point of this ongoing, contingent, and indeterminate political dynamic, because it is a primary electoral resource used to mobilize support for law-and-order candidates, punitive resource redistributions, and the cultural force we all felt just after 9/11 when criticizing the president, any president, suddenly felt viscerally impossible.[24] Then, as now, there is a zeitgeist that normalizes either social welfare or social control, rehabilitation or retribution, to insulate its prioritization from critique, by constructing it not as a choice but as a given. While there are instructive similarities between New Deal and zero tolerance political and cultural strategies that come to light once we focus on fear as punishment and patronage, there are also important differences that reflect dramatically different relationships to intellectual inquiry, the competing substantive positions constitutive of these very different electoral coalitions, and the consequences for the possibility of identities that can provide the discursive and material foundations for effective forms of democratic citizenship within resilient communities.

Ron Scapp (2003) argues that we currently live in a predatory culture fueled by the financial and social fears driven by a "singular vision" that prosperity is driven by an unfettered free market, which cannot safely allow space for loyal opposition or reasonable dissent. Following Scapp, the amplification and muting of fear is no longer just one tactic, used only when necessary or only by the more extreme elements of any coalition with distance swiftly placed between them and more responsible coalition leadership. Today, fear is the central tactic, defining our punitive political culture as committed exclusively to elite profit and security and "antagonistic to the public sphere." Just as we argued earlier that the new vision of American democracy premised on fear mobilizes some in ways that disempower them to punish others for their disadvantage, Scapp similarly concludes that it is not only the residents of the hyperghetto who suffer in our punitive political culture.[25] The citizenship ideal cast by the limited forms of agency and identities made possible is one where frightened citizens, without the practical and intellectual skills developed in democratic communities, are returned to a state of nature, where their options are structurally constrained to fight or flight, not by natural law but by a punitive political culture.[26]

As one of us found in his study of community policing, the earlier stages of a model police-community partnership were characterized by forms of reciprocity that empowered citizen agents with the capacities necessary to mobilize the informal social controls sought by community policing advocates, but this narrow window of reciprocity was soon closed as the police department came to colonize the partnership and this colonization was marked by the decline of reciprocity and the rise of fear reduction efforts (Lyons 1999, 179). "Policing narrowed to focus on fear of disorder . . . may lead the fearful to voluntarily seek to reduce their freedom through insulation. Instead of learning to cooperate with others, a focus on fear of disorder is likely to encourage more isolation in more fragmented fortress communities." This may encourage citizens to more readily leap to the violent management of conflict (or encourage violent state action in response to frightening conflicts) "long before less tragic responses have been exhausted." When police officers, school superintendents, state legislators, corporate executives of EMOs, teachers' unions, and a parade of "education presidents" all fail to address the conflicts plaguing public education, and fail in ways that weaken the capacities of parents, teachers, and communities to invest in education, our choices *construct* turning to a more aggressive and less accountable state as the most "pragmatic and realistic" approach to managing conflicts over schools in our communities.[27]

In this context, citizen agency is reduced to passive acquiescence to state and corporate power, which can be analyzed as an institutionalization of our vigilante tradition in defense of a plutocratic regime. Even the capacity of communities that might, as in previous times, rise as elite countervailing forces to check the official and corporate corruption that always accompanies plutocratic regimes is undermined by the citizen identities constitutive of zero tolerance political culture. As Barber argues, a punitive political culture that focuses on fear to paralyze active citizenship and democratic identities disproportionately harms the power-poor directly but then also harms the affluent because it also undermines the possibility of cooperation. It "disempowers the powerful by provoking an anxiety that disables capacity. It turns active citizens into fretful spectators. . . . The trouble is, the language of moral absolutism makes negotiated solutions to . . . conflict nearly impossible" (Barber 2003, 26, 59).

Those who despise the public sphere now control its daily operations (Phillips 2002). The zero tolerance vision of limited government is arguably based on an electoral strategy homologous to an institutionalized form of our vigilante tradition, sustained on the basis of political patronage, an exchange model trading on fear. Robert Maxwell Brown (1969, 156) conducted the most exhaustive and respected scholarly study of our vigilante tradition and concluded that, perhaps contrary to some expectations, this tradition is most accurately described as a recurring elite-led, extra-legal, "violent sanctification of the cherished values of property and community." While it is beyond the scope of this book to fully consider the parallels, it is certainly clear—once we understand violence to include punishing schools, an elite-led cultivation of citizen inattentiveness to the harms that most threaten our communities, and approaches to governance that undermine the capacity of our children to become active and informed democratic citizens—that the violent sanctification of patronized communities supportive of a zero tolerance regime has included extralegal actions.

From ignoring international law regarding prisoners of war to undermining international law by failing to support an international criminal court, treaties to ban land mines (used more by the United States than by any other nation) as weapons that continue to actually cause mass destruction, or enforcement of UN resolutions that highlight Israeli violence as vigorously as those that highlight Arab violence, U.S. leadership has increasingly demonstrated a willingness to act outside international law. From dubious presidential pardons, to countless campaign finance law violations, to Enron and WorldCom, to enormous no-bid contracts for corporate allies now under investigation for war-profiteering at the public expense, to state educational reforms passed with extra-constitutional means and new laws to exempt EMOs from burdensome standards (such as sprinkler systems, textbooks, and proficiency tests), to dogs sniffing students, the same leadership has increasingly demonstrated a willingness to act outside our own laws, constructing violence as the only "realistic" approach to conflict.

VI. Competing Approaches to Conflict

Seeing fear as patronage and punishment directs our attention to the relationship between rhetoric and reality, between governing through crime as a set of institutional practices and the zero tolerance political culture as a discursive articulation of a right-utopian plutocratic regime, and between competing ways to divide the public by choosing which conflict or fear is made most politically salient.

> What happens in politics depends on the way in which people are divided . . . which of the multitude of conflicts [fears] gains the dominant position. . . . Democracy is a competitive political system in which competing leaders [public and private] and organizations define the alternatives of public policy in such a way that the public can participate in the decision making process. . . . *The unforgivable sin in democratic politics is to dissipate the power of the public by putting it to trivial uses.* . . . Above everything, the people are powerless if the political enterprise is not competitive. . . . conflict, competition, leadership, organization are the essence of democratic politics. (Schattschneider 1975, 60, 136–38; emphasis added)

New Deal efforts to amplify or mute fears differ in both degree and kind from zero tolerance efforts. The zero tolerance coalition lacks a substantive interest in empowering the structurally disadvantaged power-poor, preferring instead to assert what must be achieved: a level playing field for a mythical meritocracy that draws significant discursive force from the shared aspiration that meritocracy suggests. Current efforts to redirect resources toward faith-based organizations, charter schools, and the penal-industrial complex (including community policing as currently practiced) can be fairly characterized as illustrations of what Skogan (1988) calls preservationist, rather than insurgent, community organization. They are reducing funds to programs that sought to level the playing field for the least advantaged and directing those funds to patronize already privileged communities. Like the New Deal, this is a mobilization of the federal government's revenue-generating capacity to fund local constituencies who support the coalition. It is unlike the New Deal coalition in that this is a shift of resources from one elite (national) group to its already power-rich local constituencies, a retrenchment of existing power imbalances at a time when economic inequality is growing in America.[28]

Their substantive differences with regard to power reveal competing choices to prioritize and respond to the fears of the already powerful, targeting the already disadvantaged for punishment in the case of zero tolerance and for the New Deal to prioritize the fears of the power-poor, targeting unearned privilege (by birth in legacy affirmative action, for instance) and structural inequalities (race, class, and gender discrimination) for a punishing critique. These substantive differences are compounded by the fact that these two coalitions also differ in the degree to which their fundamental objectives included amplifying and ignoring the fears of competing communities to support more democratizing or more disciplinary mechanisms of social control. As we have consistently argued throughout this text, a punitive political culture impoverishes our public policy debates in a variety of ways, including the well-documented cases analyzed in Glassner's (1999) book and Moore's movie.[29] We argue that the more extreme and enthusiastic applications of this strategy constitute a clear case of a systematic effort to "*dissipate the power of the public by putting it to trivial uses*" and that this is, indeed, "*an unforgivable sin in democratic politics,*" because it not only paralyzes citizen action in the present but also extends this into the future as a disinvestment in the social capital constitutive of resilient communities,[30] that is, in the discursive and material resources, networks, and skills that are required to sustain democratic citizenships.

> Political strategy deals with the exploitation, use, and suppression of conflict. Conflict is so powerful an instrument of politics that all regimes are of necessity concerned with its management, with its use in governing, and with its effectiveness as an instrument of change, growth, unity. The grand strategy of politics deals with public policy concerning conflict [metaconflicts]. This is the ultimate policy. The most powerful instrument for the control of conflict is conflict itself. (Schattschneider 1975, 65)

The political struggles over educational reform and the colonization of this public sphere with an increasingly privatized business approach to conflict management do reflect the fact that our ability to effectively deliberate over particular microconflicts can be constrained or enabled by the context created by leaders focusing our attention on one or another macroconflict. While this insight draws our attention to continuities in the structure of political struggle, any normative evaluation of our current conflict over conflicts must also take into account how the selection of some metaconflicts may mobilize cultural forces that weaken our capacities for the democratic "check of ambition with ambition" by constraining the scope of the public sphere, the timely availability of necessary information, and our collective ability to elect leaders who will campaign to govern democratically, instead of being subjected to leaders who govern to strengthen their electoral campaigns.

> Conflicts open up questions for public intervention. Out of conflict the alternatives for public policy arise. Conflict is the occasion for political organization and leadership. In a free political system it is difficult to avoid public involvement in conflict; the ordinary, regular operations of the government give rise to controversy, and controversy is catching. (Schattschneider 1975, 135)

As we studied the two schools that this analysis is based upon, we were struck by the fact that there was an overriding fear of conflict. That teachers and administrators in particular, but also students and parents to a lesser degree, generally sought to avoid conflict rather than to develop and hone their democratic and leadership skills by learning to more effectively prevent or resolve conflicts. In this sense, it was not specific substantive conflicts that invited democratic deliberation, but fear of conflicts condensed into a fear of crime, youth, and difference. Rather than operate as "occasions for organization and leadership," conflicts became opportunities to ascribe blame to the victims and target punishment for the already disadvantaged. Rather than "controversies being catching" and a system where it is "difficult to avoid public involvement" in conflict management, we found a system where students, teachers, and administrators alike saw conflict itself as deviant rather than normal and, as a consequence, demonstrated little willingness for sustained and meaningful involvement in efforts to prevent or resolve conflict democratically. Since conflict did not disappear, this transformed education into enforcement.[31]

And this transformation was accomplished by displacing one set of fears with another. A *Metro News* editorial highlighted precisely this leadership decision to determine what we ought to fear. First the editor describes how leaders "have made matters worse" for local school districts by compelling local school districts to get voter approval each time the state funding formula reduces their revenues. According to this opinion leader the funding system, a creation of the state legislature, directs citizen frustration at schools instead of the state house, further undermining citizen agency by impoverishing public debate.

> Imagine the governor and lawmakers asked to do something similar with income or sales taxes, frequently returning to voters with their hands out, trying to explain the complicated system that drives their requests. Voters would become frustrated and angry. Public confidence would suffer.[32]

Thus, voters are frustrated and angry with public schools, frightened that investing in education will somehow hasten an already record-setting pace of job losses in the state, with no response to a now decade-old legal obligation to repair an unfair and dysfunctional school funding system. And this provides a political and cultural foundation for a form of collective inattentiveness that supports an electoral coalition dependent on the less informed forms of citizen agency resulting from a leadership determined to undermine citizen confidence in the value of investing in education.

VI. Looking Ahead

So, given our analysis, where do we go from here? As citizens we need to recognize that the challenges we face are complex, demanding that we continuously struggle to become informed and develop the knowledge and skills we all need to better prevent, resolve, or reduce the harms associated with the overlapping and routine conflicts that require our individual and collective attention, deliberation, and action. In recognition of this complexity, and in a spirit of intellectual honesty and democratic community, we will not, because we cannot, provide a detailed blueprint for rescuing our public schools, let alone the great American experiment. But we can and do provide our thoughts on resources and directions.

Kevin Phillips (2002, xiv) argues that the "historic confrontations have come from a broad-based national arousal against an abusive sector or stratum and its corrosive-seeming concentrations of wealth and power." As wealth concentrates, so does the political influence of the wealthy grow larger and more bold, leading Phillips to conclude that the United States today is a plutocracy, where the wealthy control both the private economy and the public political systems. For us, what Phillips sees as a near inevitable cycle of concentration and reform is also a broad agreement among Americans on the fundamental value of a free market and private property but a disagreement on the relationship between the private market and a democratic public sphere. There are two dominant views, one we might call the Mr. Potter approach and the other the George Bailey approach, with reference to Frank Capra's classic film *It's a Wonderful Life.* The first insists that the free market works best with little to no countervailing powers organized as a public sphere. As we see in the film, a Mr. Potter approach to the free market greedily inflates profit taking, increasing income inequality without concern for the atrophy of communities, families, and civic virtues in the way Schumpeter (1943) suggested with his concept of "creative destruction."

The second view insists that we are in this together, empowered by two forms of capital: private property and the social capital that inheres within strong community networks. This second view similarly begins with the creative and destructive powers of a free market to raise standards of living but believes we can collectively regulate those energies in the choices we make as leaders to protect communities, families, and civic virtues like citizenship and the centrality of an informed and active democratic human agency. George Bailey was a capitalist, but his profit making was tempered by his embeddedness within community relational networks. His was not a right-utopian free market but a free market where there remains an enormous demand for public leadership like Teddy Roosevelt, Elizabeth Cady Stanton, Progressive reformers, Woodrow Wilson, or Martin Luther King—leaders willing and able to support rising standards of living without succumbing to the mind-numbing zero tolerance, consumerist culture and its associated right-utopian view of the relationship between markets and government. As Phillips (2002, xiv) states clearly, history shows that in prosperous free market democracies "government power and preferment have been used by the rich, not shunned." George Bailey's view of this relationship is one that sees right-utopians as confusing the rhetorically seductive invisible hand that a thriving democratic public sphere must make visible with the thousands of visible handshakes that actually do constitute the wealth of nations when subjected to critical public scrutiny that constrains natural market instincts to destroy community, family, and citizenship.

Building on Phillips (2002, vii), then, one way to think about remedies is to begin with thinking, to "inform public understanding and reform aspirations with a sweep of data and history." While the war on terror is likely to delay this rethinking and critique of capital by making other fears more salient in the public imagination, we need to regain our willingness and ability to criticize unaccountable power and to oppose the corrosive influence of Mr. Potters. The tools for this struggle include mobilizing the kinds of political, economic, and cultural data presented here to resist the right-utopian, zero tolerance, plutocratic political culture whose leaders benefit by dissipating citizen energies. Resistance begins with an insistence on aspirations that are not repugnant to complex and indeterminate empirical realities, that proceed through an analysis of the data to provide sober critiques that inform public understandings in meaningful ways, so we can reform our aspirations, so we can achieve what right- or left-utopians simply assert, the shared values, the ability to manage conflict and secure voluntary cooperation, and the visionary leadership that emerges from strong democratic practices embedded within free, safe, and resilient communities.

Recognizing our responsibilities as educators (and leaders), we conclude with one thought. Even as we passionately deliberate responses to the challenges we face, it is important that we also remain cognizant of the larger conflict over conflicts. That is, it is critically important that we "become the change" we wish to see in our political culture. We can do this by recognizing that even in the passion of our opponents we must find shared concerns about our children and our communities, which might be expressed in religious or secular terms unfamiliar to us and may make us uncomfortable, in order to secure our children's future and our communities' resiliency. It is true that the political dynamics we analyze here have made us more vulnerable to those more passionate voices on all sides willing to demonize us or others to advance self-righteous positions. But we can do more by moderating the extremists who articulate positions closer to our own than by deploying these same divisive strategies to demonize the extremists more closely allied with those who disagree with us on this or that policy reform.

Just as we teach our children to turn the other cheek because more often than not the misbehavior of a friend can be safely separated from the friend to redeem the relationship and strengthen community,[33] we train conflict managers to help disputants let go of the usual fixation on "bad people" as a dramatic but unproductive explanatory framework for conflicts. We need to reinvigorate our classrooms with cultural and political texts that will enable students to greater media literacy, rhetorical savvy; to value the rigorous intellectual inquiry of a liberal arts tradition that helps us navigate a complex, interdependent world; to understand how democratic governments work (and sometimes don't work), so that we can intelligently learn to separate our condemnation of behaviors from more disintegrative approaches to punishment to ensure that our approaches to conflict reaffirm the achievement of our shared values and strengthen our communities.

We can build schools that teach our children to manage conflicts productively. And we should, because when we fail, punishing schools "teach students that adults or authority figures are needed to resolve conflicts."

> [These schools] cost a great deal in terms of instructional and administrative time, and they work only as long as students are kept under surveillance. While they help adults to become more skillful at controlling students, they do not empower students to learn the procedures, skills, and attitudes required to resolve conflicts constructively—for and by themselves—in their personal lives at home, in school, at work, and in the community. (Johnson and Johnson 1996, 322–33)[34]

This is not a utopian vision. Nor is this a repudiation of punishment as one tool for managing conflict. This is a recognition that we can, and should, teach our children to respect George Bailey capitalists and Mother Teresa religious leaders, just as we teach them to welcome, even insist upon, vigorous public sector regulation to contain the corrosive instincts of Mr. Potter capitalists and their counterparts among religious leaders who choose to be like the revolutionary power Kissinger warned against. This is a reminder that democratic governments only "provide for the general welfare" when they are built on informed, thoughtful, cooperative, prudent, and innovative forms of citizenship—and these depend on investing more in a democratic information system that starts with a vigorous education and resilient civic organizations than in prisons or punishing schools. This is the foundation for our prosperity that Adam Smith celebrated in *Wealth of Nations* and the most prudent approach to protecting the "diverse faculties of men" that James Madison insisted was both the first object of government and the foundation for liberty.

Appendix

TABLE A1. Number of Families below the Poverty Level and Poverty Rate, 1959–2001 (Numbers in thousands)

Year	Number of Poor Families	Poverty Rate for Families	Number of Poor Families with Female (NSP) Householder	Poverty Rate for Families with Female Householder
2001	6,813	9.2	3,470	26.4
2000	6,400	8.7	3,278	25.4
1999	6,676	9.3	3,531	27.8
1998	7,186	10.0	3,831	29.9
1997	7,324	10.3	3,995	31.6
1996	7,708	11.0	4,167	32.6
1995	7,532	10.8	4,057	32.4
1994	8,053	11.6	4,232	34.6
1993	8,393	12.3	4,424	35.6
1991	7,712	11.5	4,161	35.6
1990	7,098	10.7	3,768	33.4
1989	6,784	10.3	3,504	32.2
1988	6,874	10.4	3,642	33.4
1987	7,005	10.7	3,654	34.2
1986	7,023	10.9	3,613	34.6
1985	7,223	11.4	3,474	34.0
1984	7,277	11.6	3,498	34.5
1983	7,647	12.3	3,564	36.0
1982	7,512	12.2	3,434	36.3
1981	6,851	11.2	3,252	34.6
1980	6,217	10.3	2,972	32.7
1979	5,461	9.2	2,645	30.4
1978	5,280	9.1	2,654	31.4
1977	5,311	9.3	2,610	31.7
1976	5,311	9.4	2,543	33.0
1975	5,450	9.7	2,430	32.5
1973	4,828	8.8	2,193	32.2
1972	5,075	9.3	2,158	32.7
1971	5,303	10.0	2,100	33.9
1970	5,260	10.1	1,951	32.5

(continues)

TABLE A1.—*Continued*

Year	Number of Poor Families	Poverty Rate for Families	Number of Poor Families with Female (NSP) Householder	Poverty Rate for Families with Female Householder
1969	5,008	9.7	1,827	32.7
1968	5,047	10.0	1,755	32.3
1967	5,667	11.4	1,774	33.3
1966	5,784	11.8	1,721	33.1
1965	6,721	13.9	1,916	38.4
1964	7,160	15.0	1,822	36.4
1963	7,554	15.9	1,972	40.4
1962	8,077	17.2	2,034	42.9
1961	8,391	18.1	1,954	42.1
1960	8,243	18.1	1,955	42.4
1959	8,320	18.5	1,916	42.6

Source: U.S. Census data.

Some Very Preliminary Thoughts on What We Ought to Fear Most

American deaths from work-related injuries per day	16
American deaths from work-related disease per day	137
Total work-related deaths per day	153
Total American work-related deaths per year	55,845
Additional work-related disabling injuries per year	9,000
Total American work-related deaths and disabling injuries per year	64,845

Source: www.ucop.edu/cprc/occuhealth.pdf

Average number of U.S. homicides per year (1976–2000)	21,358
Percent of homicides not perpetrated by strangers	52%
Percent of homicides where relationship is undetermined	34%
Percent of stranger homicides	14%

Source: www.ojp.usdoj.gov/bjs/homicide/intimates.htm

TABLE A2. Outlays for Major Spending Categories as a Percentage of GDP, 1965–2002

	1965	1975	1985	1995	2002
Discretionary					
Defense	7.4	5.6	6.1	3.7	3.4
International	0.7	0.5	0.4	0.3	0.3
Social Security	2.5	4.1	4.5	4.6	4.4
Medicare	0.0	0.9	1.7	2.4	2.5
Medicaid	0.0	0.4	0.5	1.2	1.4
Means-Tested Entitlements (other than Medicaid)	0.7	1.2	1.0	1.4	1.3

Source: http://waysandmeans.house.gov/media/pdf/greenbook2003/AppendixI.pdf

Gun Homicides, 2000

United States	10,828
Canada	183
Germany	103
United Kingdom	73
Australia	65
Switzerland	36
Sweden	33
Austria	27
Japan	27
New Zealand	3

Source: www.helpnetwork.org/frames/gun_death_by_nation_data.htm

U.S. firearms deaths, 1997	32,436
Suicide	54%
Homicide	40%

Source: www.tf.org/tf/lib&data/firearm4.shtml

The U.S. poverty rate increased from 11.7% in 2001 to 12.1% in 2002 (up 1.7 million to 34.6 million), and 43.6 million Americans were without health insurance in 2002, up 14.6% from 2001. A World Bank study found that citizens living in low-income countries have an average life expectancy of forty-nine years, compared to high-income countries with an average of seventy-seven years. Further, where high-income countries average six infant deaths per one thousand live births, only one in ten children born in low-income countries live to celebrate their first birthday.

Source: www.worldbank.org/poverty/voices/reports/dying/dyifull2.pdf

Notes

Chapter 1

1. As a part of the Institutional Review Board process that gave us permission to interview students, we agreed that the names of the students, teachers, administrators, and parents we interviewed would remain anonymous. In our conversations with administrators we also made it clear that we would do our best to disguise the name of each school as well. In order to fulfill these commitments we have selectively altered aspects of each school and the communities each building is located within to preserve anonymity. This process involved disguising several sources that we cite in the book, such as newspapers, books written about the two towns, and historical documents that would identify the locations of these schools. All of these sources are available and on file with the authors. For these reasons, readers will note that our references to newspaper articles are simply to the (disguised) name of the papers, that some book-length manuscripts and historical documents are cited in footnotes (but not in the list of references) with manifestly fictitious, but consistent, names to allow readers to differentiate when references are from different sources.

2. Interview of Suburbia Teacher (ST) 11.

3. Interview of ST11.

4. Interview of ST11 and Suburbia Administrator (SA) 1.

5. Interview of ST11.

6. The Board of Trustees of Suburbia County Public Schools, in their current Suburbia County School Policies, state that "Administrators are permitted to conduct a random search of any student's locker and its contents at any time," but the policy clearly states that "The Board also authorizes the use of canines . . . in detecting the presence of drugs or devices. . . . This means of detection shall be used *only* to determine the presence of drugs in locker areas and other places on school property . . . and is *not* to be used to search individual students unless a warrant has been obtained prior to the search."

7. Interview of ST11.

8. Our understanding of the political, social, and educational trend toward education as enforcement—and enforcement as education—builds on the work of Simon (1997, 2006), Saltman and Gabbard (2003), Giroux (2003a, 2003b), and Aronowitz and Giroux (2003), among others.

9. Wacquant (2002) similarly argues that our prevailing mechanism for racial subordination, replacing the ghettoes that replaced Jim Crow laws that

replaced slavery, is a hyperghetto, where power-poor residents of abandoned inner-city school districts cycle from underfunded schools to overfunded prisons and back. Giroux (2003a, 2003b), Saltman and Gabbard and their contributors (2003), and Simon (1997) also argue that prevailing approaches to the mobilization of political power are having a similarly demonstrable, negative impact on democratic education, either in the form of "enforcement as education" or "governing through crime." We argue that there are two faces to the concept of punishing schools: we punish our public schools politically, economically, and culturally and at the same time our schools punish our children and impoverish our public spheres, each involving the mobilization of fear as a form of punishment, patronage, and pedagogy, identified in detail through the middle chapters of this book. In this sense, then, while we recognize that our inclusion of surveillance techniques, for instance, suggests important distinctions between punishment and discipline, our approach develops a much broader notion of punishment, one that highlights the conceptual overlap with discipline. This is not, however, to suggest that punishment and discipline are synonymous.

10. Our analysis here builds on the work of Simon (1997, 2006), Giroux (2003a, 2003b), Hall (1981), Glassner (1999), and Scheingold (1984), among others. For discussion of the various approaches to zero tolerance found in criminal justice literatures, see Tonry 1995; Tyler and Boeckmann 1997; Harcourt 1998; Walker 1984; and Beckett and Sasson 2000. Consistent with this more narrow reference, we understand zero tolerance more broadly, as an approach to policing (and to governance in the sense of the Supreme Court construction of police powers) that privileges the maintenance of order over competing social values or approaches to conflict management, favors preservationist over insurgent community activism and citizen identities (see Skogan 1988), and articulates what we argue are emerging mechanisms of social control where, as Foucault (1988, 162) argues, legitimation shifts from politics to law to order and it becomes "impossible to reconcile law and order because when you try to do so it is only in the form of integration of law into the state's order."

11. Our data collection strategy was to triangulate our analysis using three distinct sources of information: public school documents, media accounts, and in-depth interviews. We also had several opportunities to gather data as participant-observers as a secondary consequence of our extended presence in the school buildings while conducting our interviews. We conducted over sixty interviews, evenly divided among students, parents, and teachers or administrators at an urban school and a suburban school. The interviews each centered around five questions (with follow-ups): (1) In your view, what are the most common types of conflicts that students have to deal with here? (2) In your view, in what types of conflicts are students most likely to seek adult intervention? (3) In your view, what are the most common strategies used here to prevent or resolve these conflicts? (4) In your view, how effective are these strategies for preventing or resolving these conflicts? (5) In your view, what are the obstacles to more effectively preventing or resolving these conflicts? Since this study was an effort to examine how two different school cultures address conflict, each student, parent, teacher, and administrator was as qualified as the

next to speak to how participants in this culture understand conflict and conflict management. For this reason, we utilized self-selected samples. We put flyers in teacher mailboxes to identify teachers interested in discussing the topic, utilized teacher and administrator suggestions to identify teachers and students, and combined interviews with parents we met on-site with interviews we arranged by attending school functions to identify parents willing to meet with us at another time.

12. In his chapter "Youth at Risk," Glassner (1999) notes, "Municipalities . . . raise taxes . . . to buy more surveillance cameras and metal detectors, and to station more police officers in schools," despite the fact that "Public schools are safer, studies show, than other locations where kids hang out, such as cars and homes. . . . When teachers *have* been asked about the biggest problems in their schools, they responded with items such as parent apathy, lack of financial support, absenteeism, fighting, and too few textbooks—not rape and robbery" (76). Simon (2006) makes the same argument. On safe schools, see also Schiraldi and Ziedenberg 2002; *National School Safety Center Report* 2001. On linking even safe social space to crime control, see Christie 1994; Schlosser 1998; and Davey 1998 on crime control as industry. On media amplification of fear of crime, see Bennett 1996 and Beckett and Sasson 2000.

13. One of the most obvious recent examples of the advantage for political leaders who attempt to define our fears may be found in the public accusation by Education Secretary Rod Paige of the Bush administration on February 23, 2004, that the National Education Association "was like 'a terrorist organization' because of the way it was resisting many provisions of a school improvement law pushed through Congress by President Bush in 2001" (Pear 2004). The political utility of linking the hotly contested, underfunded No Child Left Behind Act to the Bush administration's war on terror seems apparent, if not particularly effective, on this occasion, as Paige and other officials rushed to explain and apologize for the secretary's remarks.

Chapter 2

1. While such fear-inducing statements about youth and crime are not unusual, the actual "pervasiveness" of youth violence is not a conclusion supported by criminal justice statistics when understood within a broader rhetorical and cultural context. For example, statistics showing some form of violence as the leading cause of teenage deaths, Glassner (1999) notes, despite being reported and repeated "early and often," require "a moment's reflection. Adolescents are unlikely to die of cancer, heart disease, or HIV. Those leading killers of adults generally take years to progress. Fortunately, we live in a period and place, unlike most cultures throughout history, where the vast majority of people survive to adulthood. It is far from surprising that those young people who do lose their lives fall victim to immediate causes, which is to say, accidents, homicide, and suicide" (54).

2. These three quotes, taken together, suggest some of the ways in which fear drives electoral, economic, and educational policies and trends. The *belief* that such pervasiveness exists and, in fact, is increasing fuels white flight to the

suburbs and the subsequent hemorrhage of political and economic support from urban neighborhoods and schools.

3. In his discussion of nostalgia and public policy, Simon (1995) notes that in "willful" nostalgia, "the distortion of the past moves from an unconscious horizon to a self-conscious essence. . . . Willful nostalgia seems to thrive precisely on its improbability, falseness, or artificiality. . . . The ultimate retreat is escaping to a past that has been self-consciously and systematically revised to remove its jagged edges." As we will see later in this chapter, and in chapter 3 as well, the fears of teachers, administrators, and parents at SHS and the policies those fears engender are vehicles for nostalgia, implying "that a virtuous condition of the past has disappeared in the present and needs to be revived," despite that, as Simon states, "from the perspective of rational social policy, nostalgia may always seem like a dysfunctional way of literally backing into the future" (30–32).

4. For example, the Nickelodeon network's line-up of popular TV shows, such as *The Andy Griffith Show, Happy Days, I Love Lucy,* and *Father Knows Best,* as well as a host of other widely consumed, popular-culture texts (e.g., Norman Rockwell's *Saturday Evening Post* prints; Tom Brokaw's best-selling *The Greatest Generation* and the related network-produced news segments; and Peggy Noonan's political campaign speeches and anthologized essays that appear in educational textbooks) rely on a nostalgic present view of the past, where traditional values and the heroism of the individual help to construct fear, identity, and policy.

5. *Suburbia Community Vision,* 2003; *Suburbia Plan,* 2003. Section III relies on data from multiple interviews, city, school, and county documents. These texts are referred to with disguised names. See Notes on Sources.

6. *Suburbia Community Vision,* 2003.

7. *Suburbia High School Partnerships,* 2002.

8. *Suburbia Community Vision,* 2003.

9. Multiple Suburbia Student (SS) and ST interviews.

10. *Suburbia High School Partnerships,* 2002.

11. SHS is owned by the county, but it is operated by the city of Suburbia, thus creating jobs through the initial investment of public funds, through the taxes passed in the levy that built the school, and through individual memberships to the recreational facilities on campus.

12. *Suburbia High School Partnerships,* 2002.

13. Part of the Performing Arts Auditorium was funded by the Feckley Foundation, which donated four hundred thousand dollars for additional seating. The Feckley Foundation was established by a local family who have long resided in Suburbia County. See *Suburbia High School Partnerships,* 2002.

14. *Suburbia High School Partnerships,* 2002.

15. Members of the community may pay a membership fee to use the sports and recreation facilities at SHS. Information provided by Suburbia County Schools communications director.

16. *Suburbia Community Vision,* 2003; *Suburbia High School Partnerships,* 2002.

17. *Suburbia High School Partnerships,* 2002.

18. The consensus that violence is rare at SHS, and so then not "serious," is

especially interesting vis-à-vis the fear of violence that motivates both policy and group dynamics among teachers, administrators, and students (discussed later in this chapter and in more depth in the following chapter). The SHS community appears to agree that violence is not an issue at SHS, while continually making new policy and enforcing—even ramping up—old policy that is predicated on vigilantly eliminating the potential violence that is believed to be ever present. The disconnect here is glaring, and the anxiety expressed by teachers on this issue is marked.

19. Interview of SS6.

20. John Gray, PhD, has authored a series of relationship self-help books titled *Men Are from Mars, Women Are from Venus;* they are immensely popular and have earned millions of dollars around the world. Central to the arguments made and advice given in these volumes are the concepts of essentialized, naturalized, and universal gender traits, as well as heteronormativity.

21. Interview of ST1. We found interesting the use of the word *harassment*—a legal term denoting a particular category of behavior that makes certain language usage, physical proximity, and especially sexual intimidation a crime. Use of the word *harassment* across populations in these interviews suggests a deliberate attempt on the part of the administration and law enforcement to categorize a collection of behaviors among and between students as crimes and so necessarily as having serious consequences.

22. Interview of SS5.

23. Interview of SS5.

24. This student's interview was fascinating. His description of the ways in which the tag "gay" is deployed at SHS certainly confirms notions that to be identified as homosexual in a homophobic, homosocial context can be and often is about far more than sexual orientation or sexual activity—it may not be about homosexuality at all but rather about defining and controlling what it means to be male in both sexual and nonsexual arenas. Also, the contradiction between "being gay," for which those boys deemed straight may shove you around, and "getting a lot of girls," for which the straight boys may also shove you around, is ripe for analysis in terms of latent homosexuality, homophobia, heterosexual inexperience and insecurity, misogyny, and so on. What we found particularly interesting, however, was the way in which consumer culture has apparently trumped homophobia at SHS: the "high maintenance" guy—the one who takes great care with his appearance and thinks about, chooses, buys, and wears the "right" clothes—is the *real* man, the heterosexual man, while presumably the gay man is slovenly and does not care about his physical appearance or what is currently in fashion. This suggests a reading of *Queer Eye for the Straight Guy* as accomplishing the same thing: consumerism trumping homophobia and redefining the straight guy as someone who ought to spend the kind of time and money on fashion that gay men supposedly do.

25. Interview of SS5.

26. Interview of SS4.

27. Interview of SS5.

28. Interview of SS3.

29. Interview of SS10.

30. Interview of ST6.
31. Interview of ST1.
32. Interview of ST7.
33. Interview of SS2.
34. Interview of ST6.
35. Interview of ST4.
36. Interview of ST2.
37. Interview of SS7.
38. Interview of ST1.
39. Interview of ST4.
40. Interview of ST4.
41. The bootstrap narrative also constructs the most likely critique of this black teacher (Uncle Tomism) in terms that again deny the blackness—the difference—of his agency and obscure how structure and behavior remain inseparable; see West (1993).
42. Interview of Suburbia Parent (SP) 2.
43. Interview of SP3.
44. Interview of ST1.
45. Interview of ST1.
46. Interview of ST5.
47. Interview of ST6.
48. Interview of ST4.
49. Interview of SA1. Simon (2006) argues that teachers, who are closer to conflicts in schools, see more need for prevention than administrators do because administrators operate at a greater distance from conflict in the school. Both teachers and administrators experience self-esteem-building and respect-centered approaches to discipline as a bad fit for a student culture with a surplus of self-esteem and no experience with widespread (race- or class-based) disrespect. As Simon argues, this is because these approaches to conflict reflect problems unique to inner-city schools. They don't fit because they are externally imposed and irrelevant.
50. Interview of ST2.
51. Interview of SS8.
52. Interview of ST2.
53. Interview of ST7.
54. See Morrill et al. 2000.
55. Interview of SS4.
56. Interview of SP2.
57. Interview of SS6.
58. Interview of SS10.
59. Interview of SP6.
60. Interview of ST1.
61. Interview of SS5.
62. Interview of ST7.
63. Interview of ST1.
64. Interview of ST5.
65. Interview of ST7.

66. Interview of ST4.
67. See Morrill et al. 2000.
68. Interview of Suburbia Counselor (SC) 1.
69. Interview of SS4.
70. Interview of ST1.
71. Interview of ST5.
72. Interview of SP3.
73. Interview of SC1.
74. Interview of ST7.
75. Interview of SS10.
76. Interview of SS5.
77. Interview of SS6.
78. Interview of SS8.
79. Interview of SS3.
80. Interview of SS3.
81. Interview of SS10.
82. Interview of SP2.
83. Interview of SP4.
84. Interview of SP4.
85. See Beckett 1997.
86. Interview of SP4.
87. Interview of SP4.
88. Interview of ST6.
89. Interview of ST3.
90. Interview of ST6.
91. Interview of ST7.
92. Interview of ST6.
93. Interview of SP4.
94. Interview of ST6.
95. Interview of ST1.
96. Interview of SP2.
97. Interview of SS4.
98. Interview of SS2.
99. Interview of SP2.

Chapter 3

1. See Ferguson 2000 and Blumstein 1993.
2. For discussion on film's relationship to cultural imagination and the material consequences of cultural representations, see, for example, Blumer 1933; Eisenstein 1942; Haskell 1974; Huaco 1965; Jarvie 1970; Metz 1981; Monaco 1976; and Mulvey 1975.
3. See Simon 1997.
4. See, for example, Saltman and Gabbard 2003.
5. See Barak 1994.
6. For discussion of popular culture (textual) analysis as an important component of cultural studies' examinations of power and politics, see, for exam-

ple, Adorno and Horkheimer 1972; Barthes 1972; Hall 1985; Slack and Whitt 1992.

7. The pedagogical power of popular texts, and the importance of recognizing that such texts are neither entirely corrupt nor entirely authentic, is echoed in later discussions of the concepts of "volitional" and "structural," which are also pedagogical and also not mutually exclusive concepts.

8. See Hall 1981. An example is the increasingly common use of rock songs and rock stars to sell consumer goods to baby boomers who remember their idols' now classic music as a part of younger days marked by then radical thinking and acts of resistance. Led Zeppelin's music sells Cadillacs; Bob Seeger's music sells Ford Trucks. In addition, for a discussion of counterculture as not just co-opted and appropriated but as having a "direct confluence of interest" with the "official culture," see Frank and Weiland 1997.

9. Powers (2004) argues that, whereas in Singapore and France people are grappling with rising fundamentalism in their cultures by banning the wearing of Muslim headscarves, in the United States people are talking about Mel Gibson's *The Passion of the Christ.* The implication that the U.S. response, whether official or unofficial and cultural, to rising fundamentalism is not reactionary and remains in the realm of discourse, without material consequences to Muslims and others, is suspect but outside of the scope of this project.

10. We chose *Pleasantville* as an example of a popular film dealing with issues related to our project; we gauge this film to be "popular" due to its mainstream, widely acclaimed studio (New Line Cinemas); its director (Gary Ross); its principal actors (William H. Macy, Joan Allen, Tobey Maguire, and Reese Witherspoon); its positive critical reviews; and the dozens of industry awards for which it was nominated and, in many cases, the numerous awards that it won (see http://www.imdb.com/title/tt0120789/awards). We chose to examine one film in depth rather than provide a more cursory textual analysis of several films or television shows, in order to thoroughly mine the text for its multiple and complex alignments with dominant cultural attitudes regarding youth, fear, and punishment within racial, gender, and class frameworks, as well as to provide with this close reading an illustrative example of the kinds of analytical strategies that might prove fruitful in addressing other cultural texts.

11. For our purposes here, we understand *metanarrative* as referring to any narrative or theory that claims to transcend local, lived experience in order to legitimate the mechanisms of social control. Metanarratives are sometimes called "grand theory" and often enjoy a privileged position in the sciences; postmodern theory argues, however, that all narratives are inherently political. See, for example, Lyotard 1985, 1999.

12. See, for example, Gramsci 1994; Ricoeur 1994.

13. Notably, this doubly Othered population, named here as "drug-addicted homosexuals," is presumed to have an increasingly high rate of HIV infection, and those rates are acceptable. It is only the shocking news that affluent, heterosexual white kids are contracting HIV that constructs a frightening future within the world of *Pleasantville*'s depiction of contemporary American life.

14. David's knowledge of Pleasantville—along with his imagination—is key to the pedagogy of this film. David is an outsider in his 1990s world, which is

rife with conflicts and in which he appears to have little power and few skills for survival, let alone happiness or success. His utopian, antipresent aspirations, however, of living in the no-conflict world of Pleasantville reconstruct his inadequacies as unimportant at worst and an asset at best.

15. The questions of why and how one might be homeless in Pleasantville are not important; David's quick and emphatic insistence that homelessness *does not exist* in Pleasantville reveals that what is important in constructing the identity of Pleasantville, its residents, and their lives is knowing what it is *not:* knowing what cannot and does not happen in Pleasantville is perhaps more crucial to identity than is knowing what can and does happen there. The logic of absence in identity construction, and the material, political consequences of such rhetorical sleights of hand, is mirrored in the narratives of SHS and will be discussed later in this chapter. In Pleasantville we see clearly that the logic of absence is driven, at least in part, by a fear of conflict for those in Pleasantville that appeals to David as a world without conflict.

16. In *Pleasantville,* as well as in the hallways and classrooms of schools, a no-conflict, utopian vision of community is premised on gender subordination and lack of agency.

17. The parallels are made explicit here between *Pleasantville* as a popular, nostalgic TV show that David loves and the popular, nostalgic TV shows that we love: Don Knotts (*The Andy Griffith Show*) plays the TV repairman; once David and Jennifer are transported to Pleasantville, their "TV mother," Betty," has the same name as the eldest daughter on *Father Knows Best,* and their "TV father," George, calls Jennifer "Kitten," the pet name of Jim Anderson for his other daughter on *Father Knows Best.* The audience is thus hailed into a community of insiders who "get" the popular culture references and are savvy enough to "critique" nostalgia while simultaneously indulging in it.

18. Among those books most frequently banned from high school libraries and curriculums during the 1990s, according to the American Libraries Association, are *Brave New World* by Aldous Huxley, *The Catcher in the Rye* by J. D. Salinger, *The Grapes of Wrath* by John Steinbeck, and *The Adventures of Huckleberry Finn* by Mark Twain (http://home.nvg.org/~aga/bulletin43.html).

19. The Garden of Eden analogy is made explicit by Ross later in the film. Margaret—the 1950s girl David likes—asks him, "What's it like out there?" and he replies, "It's louder. And scarier, I guess. And it's more dangerous." Margaret says that it "sounds fantastic." She goes to a tree and picks something from it, comes back, and extends her hand out at arm's length to David—in her hand is a big red apple, the only thing in color in the scene—and says, "Go ahead. Try it." Margaret thus embodies Old Testament temptation in the form of woman and knowledge.

20. See, for example, Freire 1973.

21. For a wide-ranging sample of the decade or more of conflict pedagogy and contact zone scholarship in rhetoric and composition, see, for example, Bizzell 1994; Cain and Graff 1994; Fox 1990; Graff 1992; Jarratt 1991; Lu 1992; Miller 1994; and Pratt 1991.

22. The film addresses gender subjugation in the form of domestic work and

female sexuality but comes to the narrow conclusion that white, middle-class, stay-at-home moms shouldn't have to be home at six o-clock with dinner on the table just because their husbands want them to—obliterating the women of color who did (and still do) much of that domestic work for white, middle-class women in the 1950s and refusing any notion of women working outside the home, of women constructing lives outside of heterosexual domestic partnerships, or of the countless women and girls caught up in the sexual-slave trade, a literal elision of labor and sexual oppression of women.

23. Mirroring Betty's sexual choices (sex with George, who "would never do something like that," or masturbation), Jennifer's choices here are comically presented by Ross as sex with Skip or sex with D. H. Lawrence—mediated by herself, through the act of reading and, thus, also masturbation.

24. See, for example, Rousseau 1987.

25. Margaret is pretty, slim, blond, and a high school cheerleader, which lets the audience know that David has overcome his 1990s high school loser status.

26. Interview of SS11.

27. Interview of SA1.

28. See Simon 1997.

29. Interview of SA2.

30. Making connections between prisons and schools is certainly not new; we wish here only to support the contention that those connections do exist and that they are arguably expanding by citing specific local manifestations of the conflation of those two institutional spaces. For examples of scholars making those connections, see Simon (1997, 2006) and Ferguson (2000).

31. Interview of SP5.

32. Interview of ST2.

33. Interview of ST2.

34. Interview of ST2.

35. Interview of SP5.

36. Interview of SS9.

37. See Foucault 1977.

38. Interview of SP5.

39. Interview of SC1.

40. See, for example, Giroux 2003a.

41. See Glassner 1999, which makes a point throughout that our increasing fear of young people—particularly young black males—is produced in (large) part by the fearmongering by news media; it has real effects on people. Glassner notes a study by Professor Esther Madriz in which women in New York City were interviewed about their fears of crime. Those interviewed "identified the news media as both the source of their fears and the reason they believed those fears were valid." Glassner reports, "Asked in a national poll why they believe the country has a serious crime problem, 76 percent of people cited stories they had seen in the media. Only 22 percent cited personal experience" (xxi).

42. In addition to the logic of absence, there exists a logic of ownership in the fears and identities that motor school policies and zero tolerance culture. As an

extension of consumer capitalism and a focus on individualism, the logic of capitalism—private investment and laws that recognize and protect private property—was crucially important in persuading the wider community of Suburbia to invest both economically and emotionally in the new high school; the logic of ownership is also used deliberately within the adult school community to maintain rigid control over "their" facility, lest a breakdown in vigilance lead to the destruction of their property. This logic, however, is curiously not extended to students in any meaningful way; some teachers talk about students' "investment" in the school, via athletics, arts, and other extracurriculars, but the language of "our" school and "our" hallways appears to be reserved for (or at least embraced by) the adults. Law (both written and unwritten) and the up- and downsides of our cultural understanding and legal protections for both place and space (like hallways) as always-owned property create some of the layers and tensions at SHS among and between teachers, students, administrators, parents, and the community. This "ownership" of space and place is a part of the Suburbia community identity (singular and unified), which is troubled by any deviation—aesthetic, behavioral, racial, economic—and certainly by any sense of contention among property owners. Urban schools, where the very questions of "neighborhood" and "culture" are unstable and contested, are much more likely to both identify and be identified as *harmful* to the extent that students' cultures enter into the school, an important distinction we discuss in the next chapter.

43. Spaciousness itself identifies SHS and its members as not black and not poor. According to one African-American maximum security prisoner, in "the projects in the inner cities . . . the U.S. government is trying through these structures to control us. Because wherever you go, east or west, you see African-Americans and low-income people packed in on top of one another, with no real space. When you walk down the streets of most inner cities, you feel indifference to everything: 'This isn't really part of me. I'm just existing here. This is not something I should care about or protect or build up. This is something I gotta deal with until I get out.' I guess that's the same way we look at prison. There's nothing in this building that we particularly care about or we think is precious or should be taken care of" (quoted in Leder 1993, 32).

44. See Giroux 2003a, 2003b.

45. Suburbia's most recent levy was recently defeated nearly two to one. Sentiment among voters was so strong, according to the *Metro News,* that "there are no immediate plans to put a similar request on the ballot." One teacher from SHS said, "I've been teaching for over fifteen years, most of it in a southern state; there are always periodic budget crises and rumors of layoffs, but I've never known anyone who was actually fired. Welcome to Ohio, where people really do lose their jobs" (ST11).

46. We were given a copy of the 2003–4 disciplinary report for SHS by one of the principals, who hastened to point out that most of the disciplinary action taken against students during the first half of the year was due to the unfinished kitchen and cafeteria facilities in the new school, which caused many students to leave school grounds for lunch, which is against the rules; when they

came back for class—and he pointed out that they came back—they were punished. We found it interesting that the students were publicly punished for actions that this administrator privately condoned.

47. Teachers, parents, and administrators who spoke to this issue in their interviews conceded that education as a value in itself worthy of community investment was not articulated as a secondary goal or value, but the economic development, value-added argument was necessary to get voters to pass the levy—it would not have passed on a "quality education" argument alone.

48. We saw this echoed in Bush's recent State of the Union address, in which he offered "incentives" to schools that will randomly drug test students; they embrace, but are also coerced into, participating in a zero tolerance culture to reinforce that culture and to become punishing schools.

49. ST1.

50. See Foucault 1977; Dewey 1966.

51. SS2.

52. Class discussion at SHS; we took notes when students spoke, but all comments from that discussion are anonymous.

53. Comments made by SA2 in conversation.

54. Class discussion at SHS; we took notes when students spoke, but all comments from that discussion are anonymous.

Chapter 4

1. *Metro News,* 2000. Section I of this chapter draws on several books written about Central City or Urban High School. These texts are referred to with disguised names. See Note on Sources.

2. The phrase *right-utopian* will become more central to our argument in chapter 6, but it is meant to highlight two things. First, it is important to make explicit the aspirations animating any particular electoral coalition, that is, to identify their vision of the good society to which they would like to lead us. Second, while conservatives generally insist on framing political debates as if only the left can fall prey to the policy failures inherent in excessive utopianism, this is not supported by the facts, including as most currently pointed out in Benjamin Barber's (2003) powerful analysis of the war on terror as driven by Hawks with a form of right-idealism that insists, in the face of all facts to the contrary, that we do not live in an interdependent world. Conservative analyst Kevin Phillips (2002, xxi) provides a thought-provoking definition of the term when he contrasts it with liberal "utopias of social justice, brotherhood, and peace," arguing that "the repetitious abuses by conservatism in the United States in turn involve worship of markets (the utopianism of the Right), elevation of self-interest rather than community, and belief in Darwinian precepts such as survival of the fittest. Bill Clinton, like President Grover Cleveland during the Gilded Age, showed how Democratic chief executives can coexist with and largely accept these values during a boom era in which corporate and financial interests predominate." His final comment is also important to our analysis. While the current leadership in the White House and the Ohio State House are Republican, and the right-utopian electoral coalition was initially

driven by Republican Party strategists, leaders in both parties currently encourage and thrive on the zero tolerance culture associated with it. This will be discussed further in our final chapter.

3. One powerful reason to start our examination of UHS with a look backward is to disabuse us of any tendency toward a naive nostalgia about the way it was in the glory days of UHS or Central City or the United States of America. This alum's observations make it absolutely beyond question that anyone concerned about disorder, moral depravity, violence, or resilient communities today cannot find refuge in the claim that these maladies are new or that these have worsened as a result of the expanded franchise, a social welfare safety net, civil rights, or women entering the workforce. The record simply does not support such a claim. For a more complete discussion of this point in another context, see Johnson and Monkkonen 1996.

4. Greenhouse, Yngvesson, and Engel (1994) argue that in areas experiencing these type of rapid economic changes the intense conflicts that result demonstrate that the struggles to define community and law are inescapably interwoven and manifest not only in actions of state legislators but also in local efforts to address or avoid conflict and in cultural conflicts over competing notions of individualism, fairness, democracy, and governance.

5. We see this as a vision of government limited to defense and criminal justice, an approach to conflict management in the international arena that overemphasizes a unilateralist (Barber 2003) and dangerously overextended (Kennedy 1987) deployment of military power and in the domestic arena that similarly relies upon a excessively monological and punitive approach to social control.

6. *Metro News*, 2004, reported in a retrospective piece that when the city health department, reinforced with WPA workers and the newly created City Metropolitan Housing Authority, ordered property owners to clean up their buildings, they ignored the law. In fact, according to this article the owner of the city's "worst" building avoided the law until urban renewal "mercifully" bulldozed it "to rubble in May 1970. . . . Today the former slum site is a sprawling lot across the street from the Peak County Jail. It's surrounded by a ten-foot-high, chain-link fence that's crowned with barbed wire. A huge mound of dirt occupies most of the space. Clearly this is a big improvement over previous conditions." The booster's observations highlight the birth of redlining in Federal Housing Authority policy documents, suggesting a move from slavery, through Jim Crow, to a third form of racial subordination, the ghetto. Later in this chapter and the next one, we will document the further movement from ghettoes to something like what Wacquant (2002) calls hyperghettoes through urban renewal and policy decisions to subsidize private firms while impoverishing the public sphere. For another text advancing the same historical argument, in a different medium, see the 2003 PBS three-part series titled *Race: The Power of Illusion*.

7. As one reporter put it in the business section of *Metro News* (2004), the 2004 layoffs have come at a tough time. "In the last three years [2000–2003], Ohio has lost 160,400 manufacturing jobs, or about 16 percent of the state's manufacturing job base, according the US Bureau of Labor Statistics."

8. *Metro News,* 2004, reported that state lawmakers were again considering tax reform, though this editorial noted that the speaker of the Ohio house had a bad reputation on educational funding promises. The editorial pointed out two important facts that support the argument that the antitax ideology is less about fiscal responsibility or good governance and more about patronage: the speaker planned to continue the political pattern described here, steering discussion behind closed doors despite objections from other legislators, and the Ohio tax code is deeply flawed and getting worse. "It doesn't facilitate innovation. It even penalizes manufacturers. It also places an undue burden on individual taxpayers. In 1980, businesses in Ohio paid 37 percent of all state and local taxes. Consumer paid 63 percent. Today, the gap is wider, 28 percent to 72 percent. The corporate franchise tax accounted for 16 percent of state revenue in the 1970s. The amount has declined to 4.5 percent. Ohio ranks near the bottom of all states in per-capita collection of corporate income taxes."

9. Schattschneider will be examined in some detail in the next chapter, but to provide a context for this reference, here is a longer quote. "What happens in politics depends on the way in which people are divided . . . which of the multitude of conflicts [fears] gains the dominant position" (1975, 60). "Democracy is a competitive political system in which competing leaders [public and private] and organizations define the alternatives of public policy *in such a way* that the public can participate in the decision making process. . . . The unforgivable sin in democratic politics is to dissipate the power of the public by putting it to trivial uses. . . . Above everything, the people are powerless if the political enterprise is not competitive. . . . conflict, competition, leadership, organization are the essence of democratic politics" (136–38).

10. Governor DiSalle was elected in 1959 with 57 percent of the vote, defeating a Republican incumbent who, despite weak support from both Ohio business leaders and his own state party organization, campaigned for a right-to-work amendment that was defeated in the same election (63 percent against), uniting a previously fractured labor movement in the state in opposition to the amendment and the incumbent.

11. While the text analyzes how these decisions were greeted by other elites, a recent public opinion poll in the state found that Ohio residents overwhelmingly support educational funding. The KnowledgeWorks Foundation poll data, released on September 16, 2004, found that 96 percent of Ohioans agree that education is essential for a democratic society and a healthy economy, and nearly 80 percent said the state should spend more on education, "far surpassing other spending areas such as health care for the poor and elderly, jobs and economic development, courts and prisons, and roads and bridges" (KnowledgeWorks Foundation, http://www.kwfdn.org/index.html).

12. See http://www.lbo.state.oh.us/fiscal/budget/testimony/grfex2003_sb261.pdf.

13. *DeRolph v. State of Ohio,* 78 Ohio St. 3d 193 (1997).

14. *DeRolph v. State of Ohio,* 93 Ohio St. 3d (2001).

15. *Metro News,* 1996.

16. *Metro News,* 1996.

17. *Metro News,* 1996.

18. See http://www.lbo.state.oh.us/fiscal/budget/testimony/grfex2003_sb261 .pdf. *Metro News*, 1996, came to similar conclusions, noting that "after adjusting for inflation, state and federal spending on Ohio prisons surged 130 percent, or $452 million, between 1984 ad 1994, making Ohio one of the biggest corrections spenders in the nation. On the other hand, state and federal spending on education increased only 16 percent, or $687 million."

19. *Metro News*, 2000. In fact, the campaign linked the justice to Darth Vader by using the acronym DARTH to mean "Defeat Alice Resnick Tax Hike." Resnick defeated her republican opponent 57 percent to 43 percent, but that opponent was then appointed to the court by Governor Taft in 2003 to replace Justice Cook, who was appointed by President Bush to the federal bench.

20. There is currently a lawsuit pending to try to compel Citizens for a Strong Ohio and a sister organization, Informed Citizens of Ohio (whose trustees include the charter schools entrepreneur David Brennan), to disclose the sources of their over $6 million used to purchase television and radio ads in the 2000 and 2002 elections attacking Justice Resnick. Ohio state law requires that funding sources be disclosed before the elections take place, but the court order in November 2003 demanding disclosure (or face fines of twenty-five thousand dollars per day) was stayed on appeal by the chamber of commerce and remains unsettled at the time of this writing. According to the attorney working on this case, "it is clear to me that there were two issues driving this: Resnick's *DeRolph* decision and her decision to overturn the comprehensive tort reform law" (conversation with the attorney working on the suit).

21. *Metro News*, 2004.

22. Ohio Coalition for Equity and Adequacy of School Funding is the lead group in the state urging the Ohio Supreme Court to retain jurisdiction in *DeRolph*, and these statements came from their press releases dated November 11, 2003, and October 20, 2003 .

23. *Metro News*, 1996.

24. In 1976 House Bill 920 prevented property taxes from rising with inflation (making a mill no longer a mill); legislation in 1984 that reduced business taxes passed in part because it was paired with legislation guaranteeing that lottery profits would go to education; and a 1987 $51 million unfunded mandate from the state required students to pass a proficiency test in order to graduate—in the same year that the state reduced educational spending by $34 million, using lottery dollars to make up a portion of the difference but beginning the process of justifying reductions for education because lottery dollars are designated for that purpose. In 1989 the legislature rejected a recommendation from its own committee to put a 1 percent income tax for schools on the ballot, instead exempting schools from building code violations, passing another unfunded mandate to create the statewide Education Management Information System, and denying school districts the right to borrow emergency funds, meaning that between 1989 and 1995 schools lost $56 million in interest they were forced to pay to commercial banks (*Metro News*, 1996).

25. In a conversation with a colleague in the College of Education he noted that "a lot of the pain is in the development of the plan, being continuously watched and audited, and providing data to show improvement." Schools that

fail to develop a plan and eventually move out of the status created by low performance on standardized proficiency tests will, like the Cleveland Public School System, be taken over by the state or city. Despite a campaign promise to raise per-pupil funding, Governor Voinovich, who inherited a $1.5 billion budget deficit, cut school funds by $88 million in 1992. He then saved the state money at local expense by increasing the "charge off," or local taxpayers' share of guaranteed per-pupil spending. The governor defended this action because it allowed the state the flexibility of directing its resources toward the poorer districts, a not so subtle effort to preempt the ongoing court battle. Following the 1994 Perry County Common Pleas judge ruling that the state's educational funding system was unconstitutional because it was grossly unequal from district to district, a $125 million onetime expenditure for computers passed in 1995, artificially boosting per-pupil expenditures to 1987 levels (*Metro News*, 1996).

26. *Metro News*, 1996. According to the paper, the district with the lowest revenues per student in 1994 was collecting only $2,261 (lower than the lowest in 1984), while the district with the highest revenue was collecting $17,513 (up from the highest in 1984).

27. *Metro News*, 1996.

28. *Metro News*, 1996.

29. A more recent *Metro News* editorial noted that since passing the legislation with great fanfare there has emerged a large gap "between the administration's rhetoric and its purse." Funds actually allocated have amounted to $12.35 billion, far short of the $26.5 billion promised. "When students do not make progress," the editorial continues, identifying the locally costly unfunded mandate aspect of President Bush's educational initiative, "the law gives parents an option to transfer their children to a better school, whether there is room or not. It requires extensive reporting of scores and data from local school buildings to the state level, intensive remedial work for students and the deployment of highly qualified teachers in every classroom by 2005–06. . . . [But] for all the Bush team's rhetoric, it offers miserly support of its touted requirements. More frustrating, the administration's failure shifts the financial burden to state governments, most of whom had trouble enough funding adequately their own requirements, even before enactment of *No Child Left Behind* two years ago. . . . The president proved on Tuesday [in his 2004 State of the Union address] how easy it is to make expansive promises and demands when someone else has to foot the bill and answer for the failure to meet goals" (*Metro News*, 2004).

30. *Metro News*, 2002.

31. *Metro News*, 2002.

32. *Metro News*, 2002.

33. *Metro News*, 2002.

34. *Metro News*, 2002.

35. *Central City Public Schools Community Dialogue*, 2002.

36. *Central City Public Schools Community Dialogue*, 2002.

37. *Metro News*, 2002.

38. One high-ranking official in the city planning department told this researcher that "urban renewal was one big mistake," and a coworker added

that the Waterfront Park and Waterfront Highway renewal efforts simply "moved blacks to Euclid and whites then moved from Euclid north or out of town, and we then had to build Rhodes High School" (conversations with city planners, February 12, 2004).

39. *Metro News,* 2002 and 2003.

40. *Metro News,* 1967.

41. Document in Planning Department files made available to the authors.

42. *Central City Waterfront Highway Report,* document in Planning Department files made available to the authors. The highway was expected to carry one hundred thousand suburban drivers per day, but it in fact carries less than twenty-two thousand—that is, it is such a failure that the current mayor is pushing hard to have it removed and replaced with commercial and residential development, though there is strong opposition among the spattering of area suburban residents who use the highway.

43. A statewide planning newsletter (1973), document in Planning Department files made available to the authors.

44. *Metro News,* 1959.

45. *Metro News,* 1959. A 1961 flyer in the Planning Department files, "Building a Better Central City through Urban Renewal," announced in large font to residents: "Don't Be Alarmed. Don't Believe Rumors: Telephone the Urban Renewal Office" (published by the Urban Renewal Commission of Central City).

46. In 1963 urban renewal demolished "a 45 acre tract of decay" in the northwest corner of the central business district that created a two-thousand-space submerged parking garage with a large hotel at ground level and catalyzed pressure for the Waterfront highway, which would eventually have an exit directly into the parking garage (A statewide planning newsletter, 1973, 4). This project did not have much impact on residential housing, other than being consistent with the trend toward a willingness to invest public funds to support private developers rather than to support public education.

47. The Waterfront Highway was a state project, partly explaining why it ran out of funds after only building 2.5 of the 21 miles planned. It is now a highway few people drive on that cuts Central City's central business district off from neighborhoods to the west. The highway sits on land that once was home to thriving working-class neighborhoods, including several of the city's most successful black-owned businesses. The neighborhoods to the west absorbed a disproportionate number of the black residents who were forced to relocate. "Opposition to the [highway] centers around several things: It would dislocate hundreds of persons to benefit commuters. It would box off certain Neighborhood areas, dividing us. It would destroy our sense of community. . . . The Neighborhood shared no part in the decision-making. . . . Residents see this as a sign of their powerlessness. It would isolate black and white residents of the Neighborhood" (*Neighborhood Commission Newsletter,* document in Planning Department files made available to authors). Despite opposition and a foreseeable disparate racial impact, the highway was built at a cost of $65 million.

48. *Model Neighborhood* (1973).

49. *Model Neighborhood* (1973).

50. *Report to the Central City Planning Commission,* 1961, a document in Planning Department files.

51. *City Housing News,* 1966, a document in Planning Department files.

52. A statewide Construction Industry Newsletter, 1971, a document in Planning Department files.

53. *Central City Model City Program Report,* 1970, 7–10.

54. *Central City Model City Program Report,* 1970, 7–12.

55. Various documents in Planning Department files.

56. *Metro News,* 1993. According to a 2001 Brookings Institute study of census data, Central City ranks among the lowest metropolitan areas in the nation in terms of percentage of their population living in suburban areas and it is among the top cities with the highest city-suburban racial dissimilarity (Frey 2001).

57. *Metro News,* 1963.

58. *Metro News,* 1999.

59. *Metro News,* 2004.

60. In 1996 a group of white parents sued the CCPS to allow them to send their children into adjacent suburban school districts, ultimately reaching a settlement allowing limited transfers. In 2000 CCPS opened its first Afrocentric school. In 2001 the first black superintendent of CCPS redefined the open enrollment policy to allow near complete freedom of choice and successfully secured voter approval for an income tax increase premised on the promise to rebuild neighborhood schools (and eliminate busing). As we write, however, black parents are demonstrating outside CCPS school board meetings in protest of the board's decision not to offer a contract to the black principal recommended by the new superintendent to run the new Afrocentric school.

61. *Lake Erie Ledger,* 2000.

62. For national data on charter schools see "Charter Schools Suffer from Ill-Prepared Teachers, Unequal Funding, Says PACE Study," at http://www.berkeley.edu/news/media/releases/2003/04/08_charter.shtml, and the study to which it refers. The *New York Times* reported on August 17, 2004, that national data from the Department of Education show that charter schools, rather than improving student learning, are dramatically underperforming when compared to the public schools they target, in terms of student test scores.

63. Residents in ward meetings are regularly portrayed as "frustrated" about the decline in their neighborhoods, and even when resident input is gathered before ward meetings indicating that salient concerns are "housing, capital improvements, public safety, and jobs," the interaction between two hundred angry residents, city officials, and the journalists condenses this broad range of concerns into stories about fear of student vandalism and violence (*Metro News,* 1986). Neither the article nor the headline after one meeting, "Ward Residents Blame Students for Problems," showed any sign of resident fears about the public and private mismanagement of area housing stock or employment opportunities that left town when the large corporations abandoned the city. But even if leadership failures are generally reported without drama, when they are emphasized at all, there are enough reports to recon-

struct a picture of leaders whose style reflects as much disdain for the value of education as they do for modeling a cooperative approach to conflict management.

64. *City Post,* 1999.

65. *City Post,* 1999.

66. *City Post,* 1999. Cleveland's voucher program would eventually find its way to the U.S. Supreme Court, where Chief Justice Rehnquist wrote for the majority (5–4) in *Zelman v. Simmons-Harris* that the program did not offend the establishment clause and was "entirely neutral with respect to religion." Neutral or not, our research points to the business community and not parents of school-aged children as the community whose choices are driving this process, while parents are coerced into paying for it through additional school levies.

67. *City Post,* 1999.

68. "Diana Fessler, an elected board member from the Dayton area, has criticized the board for not doing homework or addressing important issues. She also could not get the education department staffers to send her contracts to review and was not given access to the thousands of pages until shortly before the April 13 meeting" (*City Post,* 1999).

69. "The state has allowed charter schools to open without textbooks or indoor toilets. One Cleveland school was closed by fire inspectors a month after opening because it had no sprinklers or fire alarms. The state let the school move to a different building without a working alarm—a problem once again cited by city, not state, officials. In October, staff from the Office of School Options made visits to the 36 schools approved by the state board [eleven elected and eight appointed]. Ten charter schools were not in full compliance with fire inspections, 17 did not have completed occupancy permits, and nine schools were not in full compliance with health and safety inspections" (*City Post,* 1999).

70. *City Post,* 1999.

71. *City Post,* 1999.

72. *City Post,* 1999.

73. *City Post,* 1999.

74. *City Post,* 1999.

75. *City Post,* 1999.

76. *City Post,* 1999.

77. *City Post,* 1999.

78. "If the goal was to allow children to escape the public schools, then the assumption would be that Catholic enrollment should have risen as children fled the public schools. . . . Instead, Catholic school enrollment fell by about 220 children" (*City Post,* 1999).

79. "Voinovich's remarks came at the same time a coalition of more than 500 school districts was in court saying that 1.8 million public-school children were relegated to a system that was unfairly, inadequately, and unconstitutionally funded. Separate studies showed Ohio school facilities to be the worst in the nation, and the state ranked near the bottom for classroom technology. . . . The importance of the Catholic electorate to Voinovich can be found in his

archives, which contain a 1995 national Republican Party study showing that the voting bloc was up for grabs." There is evidence that the Cleveland diocese pressured Voinovich for financial assistance for their atrophying inner-city schools and, in exchange, supported the governor's efforts to reform public education (*City Post,* 1999).

80. *City Post,* 1999.

81. Copies of these documents were provided on the *City Post* Web page for review at the time of this series and are in the possession of the authors.

82. *City Post,* 1999.

83. *City Post,* 1999. Ohio Roundtable is distinct from the Ohio Business Roundtable, which, according to the *City Post,* issued a 1997 report on fixing Ohio schools with "only a cautious endorsement to school choice." The paper located Zanotti's response in the Voinovich archives, where Zanotti said, "The educational system in Ohio is not an enterprise as the (Business Roundtable's) briefing intimates. It is, in fact a well established, state sponsored monopoly. The balance of power in that monopoly is controlled by the education bureaucracy. . . . The fuel for this debate is money and the goal is control. The children come last in this equation. Education is only the bi-product [*sic*] of the struggle" (*City Post,* 1999).

84. *City Post,* 1999.

85. *Metro News,* 2004.

86. *Metro News,* 1996.

87. *Metro News,* 2004.

88. *Metro News,* 2004.

89. As we write, *Metro News* (2004) reports that the CCPS plans to cuts $11 million from its next annual budget, meaning the layoff of fifty to two hundred teachers. These cuts are in part in response to the fact that CCPS will lose $14 million next year to charter schools, that state aid and business taxes are falling, and that enrollment is declining. At the same time, if the data presented so far does not persuade readers to consider the connection between conflict and conflict management in our schools and what is going on at the state and national levels we are highlighting, consider this: on the same day that this article was published, the paper provided an update on the second hollow apology from Secretary of Education Ron Paige, who, "speaking last week to a room of governors concerned about unfunded costs of the 2001 federal No Child Left Behind Act, labeled the National Education Association a 'terrorist organization.'" As the *Metro News* (2004) editorial notes, his second apology "did little to repair the damage," because "in this age of real war and real terror, painting the teachers with the same brush . . . undercuts Paige's ability to lead the movement to end the achievement gap." Calls for his resignation led the White House to say that they have the utmost confidence in his ability to bring to education the same vision President Bush is bringing to the nation. After our next chapter examines the conflicts colonizing UHS, we turn, in our final chapter, to an examination of what this new vision of limited government looks like and what it might mean for education and democracy in America.

Chapter 5

1. While there has been haggling between the mayor, city council, and the school board over community access to school facilities for some time, the mayor surprised the city in 2000 when, in a live forum, he demanded that the schools open their facilities, adding that "if it doesn't happen, it's going to become more and more difficult to get some people—including me—to support a levy. It's not a threat. It's just an absolute promise" (*Metro News,* 2000). Here the state funding formula is used by even local leaders to hold schools hostage. *Metro News* responded with an editorial five days later noting that school buildings are already open to the city recreation department, which logged 9,499 hours of activities in school buildings the year before.

2. Central City has over 120 schools, including 19 high schools. The district's students are nearly half white and half black. More than half participate in the free lunch program. Less than half take the ACT. The average ACT score for the district is two points below the national average of 21. The Central City School District runs a variety of fairly small alternative programs, including a Phoenix School, an intense behavior management program for unruly students; a Saturn School, a highly structured program for students expelled for nonviolent behaviors; an intensive summer remediation program for prefreshman; an overage high school for those who did not finish, are between the ages of eighteen and twenty-one, and are referred by a guidance counselor; a new digital academy; Character Counts; High Schools that Work; ROTC; Ninth Grade Academies; a Renaissance Program; and a college scholarship program called BECOME (Business Education Collaboration on Minorities in Education) because the district students are nearly half black but only 14 percent of teachers are nonwhite (CCPS Web page).

3. *Metro News* (2004) reported that these requirements were being dramatically changed by the U.S. secretary of education for the third time in the past two months due to severe criticism from school districts across the country for unworkable standards that reflect more national political promises than an understanding of educational challenges in particular districts.

4. The state report cards are organized into five categories. A schools that meets twenty-one or twenty-two of the standards is considered "excellent"; a score of seventeen to twenty is "effective"; eleven to sixteen is "continuous improvement"; seven to ten is "academic watch"; and fewer than seven earns an evaluation of "academic emergency."

5. An analysis of the UHS yearbooks available in the city public library revealed that from 1925 to 1975 there was only one black person hired to work as a teacher, administrator, or staff (one black, female secretary was hired in 1970). In 1976 the yearbook listed three black teachers. There were six in 1979, three in 1981, and six again in 1982.

6. *Metro News,* 1994.

7. *Metro News,* 1973.

8. *Metro News,* 1973.

9. *Metro News,* 1994.

10. *Metro News*, 1994.

11. While the Freshman Academy (discussed in more depth later in this chapter) has been innovative and successful, one academic effort in this direction seems to have fizzled. UHS tried to partner with the university's strength in polymer science by enrolling twenty-seven students in a four-year program called Lake Erie Science Project. While the program was trumpeted loudly in 1993, a search of local papers shows no article on it after that year, the UHS Web page does not list the program on a long list of "what makes UHS special," and no one at UHS seemed to know what I was talking about when I asked about the program.

12. *Metro News*, 1975.

13. *Metro News*, 1975.

14. *Metro News*, 1985 and 1995. While this is not part of our analysis of UHS, this transformation from elite training ground to trigger for the power to punish was repeated in Central City with Lincoln-West High, which was the all-white model school in the 1940s and 1950s until urban renewal changed its residential population and forced the building of Rhodes High and the expansion of UHS's district to take some of the poor black student population from now struggling Lincoln-West High.

15. We spent a considerable amount of time talking with students, parents, teachers, and administrators at UHS over a three-month period. We also observed numerous classes, including several in which the student discussions were focused directly on questions about conflict and conflict management at their school. We also reviewed hundreds of pages of school documents on discipline, conflict management, curricular innovations, and other aspects of the school environment. This chapter presents our findings.

16. According to data provided to the authors from CCPS, nearly 50 percent of UHS students are driven in from outside the district, compared to 10 percent at Lincoln-West High, 11 percent at East, 19 percent at Jane Addams, 28 percent at Rhodes, 32 percent at Kennedy, 11 percent at South, and 7 percent at King High. According to various reports in local papers the building was initially praised by residents because of its modern facade, but a local architect explained to me that these assessments likely confuse modern with new, since the building is not modernist and is more "like a tomb. It's all focused internally, without addressing the environment that surrounds it. There is no reciprocal interaction with the neighborhood. It's a warehouse, isolated in its completeness, with no way to get in." To me it looks like an enormous box with only a few slivers for windows, lacking character or warmth, perhaps presciently constructed in 1973 as a place to warehouse unruly students on the prison track in the next millennium.

17. Interview of Urban High Teacher/Administrator (UHT) 5.

18. Note that our interview questions did not solicit, directly or indirectly, information about the neighborhood. We asked five open-ended questions.

19. Interview of UHT6.

20. It is certainly our intention to avoid theory for theory's sake, because, as Wittgenstein argued, perennial questions are more useful for keeping philosophers employed than for focusing our intellectual efforts on living. As he put it,

"the way to solve the problem you see in life is to live in a way that will make what is problematic disappear" (1937, 27). When Gandhi said, "be the change you wish to see in the world," and St. Francis added "preach the gospel at all times, when necessary use words," both agreed on the critical importance of doing the difficult work of developing analytical frames and intellectual tools that construct theoretical insights as useful additional resources for effective political action.

21. Interview of Urban High Parent (UHP) 5.

22. Interview of UHT2.

23. We observed a study hall in the school cafeteria with twenty-eight students, fourteen of them sleeping with arms dangling over their desks.

24. Interview of UHT5.

25. Interview of UHT2.

26. Interview of UHT2.

27. Interview of UHT2.

28. See Black 1971 for evidence in policing of the shift from enforcing the law to enforcing the officer's own authority.

29. Interview of UHT2.

30. In other portions of this interview (UHT2) the teacher referred to not selecting these students three times: she suggested that CCPS guidelines for participation in any extracurricular activities precluded participation; she pointed out that the trainer who initially helped them set up the program strongly encouraged them to include these types of natural leaders; and she noted that the biggest conflict about the peer mediation program itself has been conflicts "with the unit principals because we wanted to try certain kids and they had a rap sheet in the office so the principals did not want us to use them and we wanted to at least give them a try."

31. Interview of UHT2.

32. Interview of UHT9.

33. Interview of UHT9.

34. Interview of UHP1.

35. Interview of UHP1.

36. Interview of UHP3.

37. Interview of UHS4.

38. Interview of UHS1.

39. Interview of UHS6.

40. In his song "Changes," for instance, Tupac Shakur angrily describes the chaos of the world he grew up in, directing his blistering critique at both structural (political, economic, cultural) and behavioral factors. For more analysis of Tupac Shakur, see Dyson 2001.

41. Interview of UHS4.

42. Interview of UHS4.

43. *City Post*, 1988.

44. Interview of UHS5.

45. Interview of UHS5.

46. Interview of UHS5.

47. Interview of UHS5.

48. Interview of UHP2.
49. Interview of UHP3.
50. Interview of UHP3.
51. Interview of UHP3.
52. Interview of UHP3.

Chapter 6

1. Another important factor in the analysis here has to be the impact of a consumer culture on children, parenting, and families. Juliet Schor, in *Born to Buy* (2004), argues that the "commercialization of childhood is being driven by a number of factors, including broad social trends. But underlying them all is a marketing juggernaut characterized by growing reach, effectiveness, and audacity" (20). As Schor demonstrates, this marketing assault on children is already having impacts that can be associated with the prison emerging as a technology of parenting, impacts that include rising levels of depression and anxiety among children who recognize two hundred brand names when they arrive at school with record levels of learning disabilities, "social pathologies promoted by the materialistic and exclusionary messages of ads and marketing" (14), and the invasion of the family by advertisers surreptitiously allying themselves with the children against their parents "in an increasingly close embrace that parents find it difficult to penetrate and is even affecting how kids and parents get along" (17). "We have become a nation that places a lower priority on teaching its children . . . than it does on training them to consume" (13).

2. We argue, following Hanson (1985), Boyte (1992), Barber (1984), and others, that moderation and cooperation are among the virtues central to the forms of citizen agency that make democracy both possible and desirable. These are practical and intellectual skills that citizens *learn* in practice (in schools, in families, in churches, and on playgrounds), which is one of the many reasons why strong democracy depends on individuals with rights, empowered and constrained by their embeddedness within resilient, innovative, and progressive communities (Kymlicka 1989). These *skills* are learned when individuals grow up in communities where conflicts are addressed openly, where differences are resolved through compromises that invest in the social capital constitutive of strong communities (Lyons 1999), and where power is open to critical public scrutiny—that is, conflicts are resolved in ways that recognize that any compromise remains provisional, because political struggle is ongoing, agreements are always contingent on changing factors, and the future meaning of any current compromise can only be indeterminate as a consequence. Thus, later in this chapter we will condense these virtues—skills—necessary for democratic citizen agency into those concrete conflict management skills that are developed in and through our individual and collective efforts to manage the conflicts we all face in our families, communities, churches, and schools. (For a review of psychological research in this area, see Huesmann and Podolski 2003.)

This argument is consistent with research on integrated approaches to conflict management in schools. Mayer and Leone (1999, 33) argue, on the basis of a detailed statistical analysis of the School Crime Supplement to the National Crime Victimization Survey, that the zero tolerance approach to discipline is less effective—to the point of being criminogenic—than an approach that transfers skills and knowledge to students: "Creating an unwelcoming, almost jail-like, heavily scrutinized environment, may foster the violence and disorder school administrators hope to avoid." Thus our focus on the transfer of practical and intellectual skills, which is also supported by Stevahn's (2004, 57) research, where she concludes that "the likelihood of creating a safe, orderly school community where students can excel increases when all students not only learn procedures for constructive conflict management, but also use those procedures to resolve conflicts. This requires knowledge, will, skill, opportunity [to practice], and organizational support." Gerald Graff (1992) argues that in order for intellectual positions to be(come) meaningful to students, their opposites are necessary, and, in fact, the intellectual/professional debates that result in particular curricular choices ought themselves to be a part of the curriculum in order to make the inevitable politics of education transparent and to both "naturalize" conflict for students and teach them productive and democratic ways to address conflict. Graff notes what he perceives as a cultural resistance to intellectual multiplicity in general and to teaching disciplinary conflict specifically as important factors in the degradation of American public education.

3. See Wacquant 2002.

4. Whitey is the name of a *Pleasantville* character discussed in chapter 3.

5. And as schools punish our children, we may be exacerbating social trends toward punishing our schools. As Scheingold (1998) commented on Tyler and Boeckmann's 1997 study of public support for "Three Strikes" legislation, which found that the support was more strongly associated with a general anxiety about social conditions than about crime, the data there show a significant relationship between punitiveness and education (the less educated are more punitive), highlighting a possible "self-perpetuating policy cycle," where we build prisons with money from education, creating a less educated and more punitive public, more willing to support shifting educational funds to prison construction. In our view, this highlights the importance of framing this as a right utopian, zero tolerance *culture* that is associated with a homologous electoral coalition but that as a cultural phenomenon represents a broader and more resilient political force. As a political coalition with such deep and self-perpetuating cultural roots, it is able to rely upon prevailing constructions of common sense to preempt the articulation of alternative positions in much the same way as how the cultural milieu of the 1960s made it more difficult to advance the social Darwinist positions now taken as self-evidently pragmatic and sober or more recently how in the months immediately after the 9/11 attacks there was a palpable cultural force that made it nearly impossible to criticize the president or his attorney general.

6. Harrington 1993; Boyte 1992; Fraser 1992; Kymlicka 1989; Habermas 1989; Hanson 1985; Cohen and Rogers 1986; Abel 1982; Zinn 1968; Pateman 1990; Macpherson 1989; Mill 1975.

7. Michael Eric Dyson argues in *Holler If You Hear Me: In Search of Tupac*

Shakur (2001, 36) that "addiction, along with gang activity, fed the rise of the juvenocracy: the shift in economic and social authority from the older to younger members of the family and neighborhood." When President Bush announced that our considered response to the complex challenge of terrorism was "bring it on" he demonstrated this dramatized, familiarized, simplified image over substance pedagogy that our current information system enables. See Bennett 1996 for a critical analysis of the kind of media literacy skills and knowledge we would include within our understanding of the skills essential for effective citizen agency in a democratic society. Schor (2004) provides evidence of a juvenocracy when she points out that "40 percent of urban tweens [a marketing category targeting children ages six to twelve] worldwide are strongly attached to particular car brands and that 30 percent of their parents ask them for advice on car purchases" (13), thus abdicating parental roles as mentors who might consult *Consumer Reports* for data on fuel efficiency and safety ratings to demonstrate the importance of living a thoughtful life where choices are made after examining evidence rather than relinquished to the controlled messages of advertisers in alliance with their children. Another industry study showed that 67 percent of car purchases are influenced by children (24).

8. For a criminological parallel, see Tonry 1995 on differential sentencing for two forms of the same illegal drug—lenient penalties for the form popular in privatized white suburban areas and much more severe penalties for the form popular in publicized black inner-city areas. Similarly, there is a parallel logic in the gender analysis advanced by the Seneca Falls Declaration that argues that the same moral delinquencies that justify the exclusion and punishment of women (their inner-city kids in this case) are deemed of little account in men (our suburban white kids).

9. Glassner (1999) demonstrates that while our children are one hundred times more likely to be molested by a heterosexual relative than by a homosexual stranger and that women caught in the cycle of domestic abuse are most often victimized by family and friends, our information system (media, entertainment, educational, cultural) reflects a culture of fear we have found in our schools, persuading us to redirect our fears toward (black) stranger predators or other invisible threats from unknown students. The real harms and actual conflicts that threaten to destroy our families and communities are muted by an information system saturated with an empirically inaccurate assessment of the harms we face. Similarly, Glassner describes how workplace conflicts over "downwaging" and capital flight are muted and displaced by fears of coworker violence; how conflicts over investing in dangerous highway systems without a national speed limit (versus public transportation and driving 55 mph) are muted by amplified fears of road rage; and how campus conflicts over hiring more diverse faculty to work in less intolerant intellectual environments are muted by amplified fears of liberal political correctness. (See appendix for data on relative harms.)

10. Blumstein argued in 1993 that we react to criminal behavior differently when it is our kids rather than their kids perpetrating the violence. When it is our kids, we fear for what this bodes for their future, and we see their violence as a manifestation of our unsuccessful efforts in schools, in churches, or at

home to teach our children how to resolve conflicts or to provide them with productive avenues for their considerable youthful energy and imagination. When it is their kids, we are afraid they will hurt our kids, and we tend to see their violence as a manifestation of the uncontrollable nature of these particular kids, constructed to be entirely unlike our children. When school violence was a more exclusively inner-city phenomenon, we settled on framing it as a crime problem that fell well below the crisis radar, rarely finding a place in national debates about educational reform. When the Columbine event exploded these particular myths about the class and racial distribution of school violence, however, we did not shift suburban educational funding into constructing prisons and making the juvenile justice system more punitive. These were our kids after all, and "the criminological representations of young people [that] frame youth individually and collectively as violent and in need of discipline and punishment" (Morrill et al. 2000, 522) no longer made sense as the basis for a pragmatic and sober approach to school violence. This political imperative to protect our own by punishing others constructs the fears of suburban parents as different from inner-city fears and creates wider political opportunities to run election campaigns, rally national sentiment, and reinvent government on the basis of the capacity of our public and private leaders to mobilize and direct, amplify and ignore, citizen fears.

11. Lyons (1999) argues that fear reduction, a major component of community policing programs, supports mechanisms of social control that are more disciplinary than democratizing (see Krugman 2003, 6–7; Cole and Dempsey 2002; Schlosser 1998). Taylor (1982) argues that the existence of the state as one solution to collective action problems has contributed to the atrophy of alternative, less costly, and more cooperative solutions, such as community. Tocqueville (1956) argues that the democratic citizen identities he observed in America were already and would continue to be driven by a passion for equality that supports centralizing political and economic power.

12. As Glassner (1999) argues in *The Culture of Fear,* public and private leaders determine fears that make us inattentive to trends likely to be more harmful to us and our children. For instance, over 64,000 Americans suffer work-related deaths (over 55,000) or debilitating injury (9,000) each year (see www.ucop.edu/cprc/occuhealth.pdf), compared to an average of 21,000 homicides per year during the period 1976–2000, but we have no War on the Unsafe Workplace, or War on Harmful Corporate Leadership, or War on the Automobile (43,220 deaths in 2003, according to the National Highway Safety Administration), or even War on Lethal Violence, as suggested by Zimring and Hawkins (1997).

13. Simon 1997; Schlosser 1998; Phillips 2002; Krugman 2003; Broder 2003; Rauch 2003. While the argument developed here is related to the argument developed by David Garland (2001) in *The Culture of Control,* Garland highlights the neoliberal aspects of right utopianism, and our work emphasizes the neoconservative elements.

14. By identifying it as right-utopian we make explicit the empirically inaccurate claims common to zero tolerance leaders, who generally insist on framing political debates as if only a social welfare perspective or social democratic

politics can be impractical and vulnerable to utopianism. This claim is not supported by the facts.

15. See chapter 4, note 4.

16. Giroux 2003b; Ferguson 2000; Aronson 2000; Bauman 2000; Scheingold 1984; Beckett 1997; Sennett 1970; Melossi 1993.

17. Katznelson (1976) argues that the shift from machine politics to bureaucratic politics made city governments better at service delivery. Governments became better at delivering the resource side of the patronage exchange of jobs (and other forms of public economic support) for votes (and other forms of political support). But as governments became better able to craft policy, to produce the political outputs expected from government institutions, this shift also made them less able to mobilize citizens, to ensure that the political inputs on the other side of the exchange of jobs for votes would be forthcoming. This weakened governments. One way to think about the combinations of amplified and muted fears we analyze here is as efforts to revitalize official capacities to mobilize political support (by amplifying or patronizing the fears of particular communities and muting others) by better managing selected fears—and the associated publics—by mobilizing them as political inputs and other fears by punishing them with zero tolerance policy outputs.

18. See Greenhouse, Yngvesson, and Engel 1994 for a detailed analysis of the ways that our ongoing struggles over law, community, and social change impact identity and agency. They argue that in our efforts to manage conflicts we construct meanings for law and community, common sense, individualism, and what is realistic, including some and excluding others in the process.

19. See www.pipa.org.

20. Krugman's analysis begins, ironically, with Henry Kissinger's 1957 doctoral dissertation, which argued that the reconstructed Europe after Waterloo was a system facing a new kind of threat, a "revolutionary power . . . that does not accept the system's legitimacy." Krugman argues that the currently dominant radical right electoral coalition is another revolutionary power, "whose leaders do not accept the legitimacy of our current political system" (2003, 5–6). His evidence focuses, precisely as we do here, on the ways that this revolutionary power seeks to displace the electoral-patronage exchange relationship that grounded the New Deal coalition with a successor regime that we are calling a zero tolerance political culture. While the New Deal coalition experienced only limited substantive success as a class compromise, as an electoral coalition it remained dominant for thirty years. Krugman's framing of its successor coalition as a revolutionary power provides an analytical basis for seeing both the similarities in terms of electoral strategy and the differences in terms of substantive approaches to governance of these two regimes.

21. Barber (2003, 109) continues, noting that the "Bush administration admitted as much: at the beginning of 2003, an unnamed senior administration official acknowledged that in the new preemptive strategy 'there is also a deterrent element for the bad guys.'"

22. Another way to contrast this business model with the one central to the New Deal would be to say that the zero tolerance coalition is advancing what Kevin Phillips calls an "extreme idolatry of markets" or a "market utopianism"

or a Mr. Potter capitalism, in contrast to the lower profit margins of family- and community-friendly George Bailey capitalism famously brought to life by Frank Capra. A *Metro News* (2004) story reported that the Ohio State Board of Education approved, 13–5, the "critical analysis of evolution" curriculum that the scientific community had argued strenuously for years was simply an inclusion of creationism in the science classroom. In the paper that same day, the sports section reported that the CCPS budget cuts would not include cuts in athletic programs because, as the school superintendent put it, "if you take away those programs, there's no need for students to enroll in your system." Also in the same issue, the paper's editorial page argued that schools were in trouble because the legislature ignored a court order for ten years (extralegal action), phased out a tax on business equipment and reduced funding to school districts where the cost of doing business was too high, prevented property tax revenues from rising with property assessments, lowered state basic aid to all schools, and "tweaked the funding formula . . . to add to the burden of schools." This section included a list of members on the governor's blue ribbon task force to fix education. That list of thirty-three names includes four government tax experts, eight politicians (only three of whom are on education committees), twelve business lobbyists, five upper-level school district managers, and three teachers. Finally, in that same issue it was reported that there are other fears, causing real harm, that are not getting the attention through amplification described here. First, racial disparity in area mortgage lending means that African-American borrowers were more than three times more likely to get a subprime loan rate. Second, 88 percent of those teens, in a study of twelve thousand, who made chastity pledges had premarital sex, the same amount got STDs, and those who made the pledge were less likely to know they had an STD, leading the investigator to conclude that "to 'just say no' without understanding risk or how to protect oneself from risk, turns out to create greater risk" of STD, early marriage, and the same risk of premarital sex.

23. A close examination of community policing in a city the National Institute of Justice called a "model partnership" found that the fears of the more affluent, white property owners were amplified to mobilize them in support of a more aggressive and less accountable professional policing targeted against those communities already most victimized by crime, further concentrating their disadvantages. Some fears were amplified to mobilize particular publics in ways that disempowered them but enhanced state agency and police power to punish other publics, both through more aggressive law enforcement and by using the model partnership to screen out fears of police misconduct, redlining, or long-term disinvestment in resilient communities.

> Getting back to Mayberry captures in a single image the complex and intoxicating allure of community policing; an aspiration of all people to live free from fear and with dignity in safe and prosperous associations with others. The same image also encodes a vision of community based on partnerships that exclude the least advantaged, empower state agents, and are limited to targeting those disorders most feared by more powerful communities and most amendable to intervention by professional law enforcement agencies.

> When more resources from the community were needed by the police department, stories about active communities taking responsibility for crime prevention spurred citizen partners to lobby city council or contribute volunteer labor. When these same partners challenged the police administration's failure to extend beat tenure, stories warning against community micromanagement, citizen mobile watches, and a loss of information control constrained citizens, encouraging passive communities dependent on professional law enforcement agencies.

Prevailing stories about community and policing advanced by advocates were efforts to construct history to support state-centered stories about social control. Prevailing stories about policing drew discursive resources from references to empowering communities with specific capacities, while at the same time they narrowed the possibility that policing in those communities most victimized by crime and disorder would invest in the social capital of residents living there. Stories about community revitalization were central to the political appeal and coherence of prevailing stories about policing reform, but the logic of these stories was left to wither as prevailing stories narrowed their meaning to problem solving and reducing fear, both police-led activities that tapped community partnerships only insofar as they were resources for the police departments, reversing the power flow from empowering communities to empowering the police (Lyons 1999, 166–71).

Thus, when it is argued that middle-class "anxieties about crime . . . identify the culprits, name the problem, and set up the scapegoats" (Garland 2001, 153), further inquiry requires that we examine leadership efforts to determine these anxieties, from policing reform to educational reform. Police efforts to reduce fear cannot be seen as simply a positive, democratizing counter-trend, just as the Safe Schools Act cannot be understood as simply President Clinton's decision to allocate more money for schools. It is also about determining what we ought to fear, what problems we ought to prioritize, and what solutions will be constructed as realistic. As Simon (2005, chap. 7, 24) argues with regards to the Safe Schools Act, the legislation "conditioned this funding on states and local school districts adopting techniques of knowledge and power calculated to focus more governance attention and resources on crime in school and assure a more rapid and more punitive response to it." For related analyses, see Greene and Mastrofski 1988; Skogan 1990, 1995; Skogan and Hartnett 1997; Pearson 1983; Covington and Taylor 1991; Donziger 2002; Furedi 1997.

24. It is not only the president who continues to live on September 12. We were all already living there, even before the terrorist attacks brought home the kind of fear many may have assumed was only constitutive of third-world political economies. The culture of fear highlighted by Glassner (1999) and Michael Moore suggests a fear-driven, punitive, political culture that operates as a set of shared assumptions about the world, a background consensus as a cultural force that shifts the burden to demonstrate reasonableness to anyone unwilling to accept the party line without deliberation. This is, of course, not a uniquely conservative phenomenon. It is a political strategy, not a partisan

position. It is a strategy to use and abuse history, because we can, even if we cannot make history precisely as we choose.

25. We patronize even the more affluent in ways that disempower them with "gated communities . . . metal detectors . . . treating academic failure as a kind of crime that someone must be held accountable for whether it be the student (no more social passing), teachers (pay tied to test scores), or whole schools (disband schools failing test scores)" (Simon 2006, chap. 1, 8). See also Johnson 2003; Baker 2003; White 2003; Bauman 2000.

26. "Hobbes captures our own experience today of an international realm wracked with terrorist violence and Third World desperation, as well as with the First World fear and uncertainty they breed. Weak local government, poverty, and religious fanaticism constitute a recipe for uncertainty; international predators, whether they are financial speculators, drug syndicate criminals, or enraged terrorists, leave billions of people in the world in a state of perpetual fear, unable to govern their own destinies, as frightened of their own government and sometimes their own neighbors as they are of distant superpowers that intimidate them with their splendor and their hegemony. Terrorism has now displaced fear from Third to the First World, giving those in Europe and America who have conquered anarchy within their own borders a taste of its grim rewards in the borderless world of interdependence that lies beyond" (Barber 2003, 71).

27. Taylor (1982) argues that one way to think about our love affair since Hobbes with the state as the one-size-fits-all solution to collective action problems is that this devotion to state agency itself has contributed mightily to the atrophy of alternatives to the state, in this case alternatives that focus on citizen agency within resilient communities as described by Boyte (1992), Barber (1984), and Altshuler (1970) or in the literature on social capital (Coleman 1988).

28. As one prominent conservative analyst put it, the transformation of America from the land of opportunity to the land of extreme inequality and intolerance has been hidden by the recurrence of the market utopianism animating the zero tolerance coalition—even as the transformation is driven by a powerful combination of public and private investment that demonstrates that free markets depend on government support rather than oppose it—and has "morph[ed] politics into a marketplace with barely hidden price tags."

> In just a little over two centuries the United States went from being a society born of revolution and touched by egalitarianism to being a country with the industrial world's biggest fortunes and its largest rich-poor gap. . . . [And free markets are] tied not only to government assistance, public policy, and [publicly financed] technology, but to the protective umbrella spread by more than a half century of American global economic hegemony. . . . Whereas liberal eras often fail through utopias of social justice, brotherhood, and peace, the repetitious abuses of conservatism in the United States in turn involve worship of market (the utopianism of the Right), elevation of self-interest rather than community. (Phillips 2002, xiv–xxi)

29. We are referring to Michael Moore's film *Bowling for Columbine.*

30. Social capital (see Coleman 1988) is like financial capital in that it is a resource. It is unlike financial capital in that it cannot remain a resource if it is separated from the relational networks within which it is interactively created. Social capital grows and inheres within reciprocal relationships and is available to the individuals who live and work within these relational networks. Social capital is an analytical tool for thinking about the relational basis of resilient communities and how to best invest in enabling the citizen agency and democratic stability constitutive of communities with the capacity to effectively prevent, resolve, or reduce the harms associated with conflict.

31. While conflict was seen as the consequence of difference, even violent (verbal, institutional, and physical) responses to conflict were simultaneously constructed as normal, again suggesting parallels to our vigilante tradition. The arguments advanced by Schattschneider (1975) with regards to conflict in general are consistent with those being articulated by scholars who study conflict management in schools today. This includes the pathbreaking work of Johnson and Johnson (1996, 327), who, like Schattschneider, argue that conflict is normal, that teaching children to fear conflict denies them opportunities to develop critical citizenship skills, and that a fear-filled culture where student-citizens lack these skills means their available approaches to conflict (call 911, use force, or withdraw) disempower them and reinforce state agency. See also earlier references to Stevahn 2004; Mayer and Leone 1999.

32. *Metro News,* 2004.

33. See Johnstone 2003 for a comprehensive examination of this trend in conflict management.

34. "Conflict-avoidant schools that try to reduce conflict by placing police in the hallways, searching students and their lockers, establishing 'zero tolerance' rules, suspending and expelling large numbers of students who present disciplinary problems, and increasing the punishment for small infractions may . . . become part of the problem rather than the solution because they decrease rather than improve students' ability to regulate their own behavior" (Johnson and Johnson 1996, 333–34).

References

Note on Sources

In order to fulfill commitments we made to protect the identity of students we interviewed as a part of the IRB process and commitments we made to the wonderful teachers and administrators we worked with at each school about keeping the identity of their individual buildings confidential, we have selectively altered aspects of each school and the communities each building is located within to preserve anonymity. This process involved disguising several sources that we cite in the book, such as newspapers, books written about the two towns, and historical documents that would identify the locations of these schools. All of these sources are available and on file with the authors. For these reasons, readers will note that our references to newspaper articles are simply to the (disguised) name of the papers, that some book-length manuscripts and historical documents are cited in footnotes (but not listed in the list of references) with manifestly fictitious, but consistent, names to allow readers to differentiate when references are from different sources.

Abel, Richard, ed. 1982. *The Politics of Informal Justice.* New York: Academic.

Adorno, Theodor, and Max Horkheimer. 1972. "The Culture Industry: Enlightenment as Mass Deception." *Dialectic of Enlightenment.* Trans. John Cumming. New York: Seabury Press.

Altshuler, Alan. 1970. *Community Control: The Black Demand for Participation in Large American Cities.* New York: Pegasus.

Aronowitz, Stanley, and Henry A. Giroux. 2003. *Education Still Under Siege.* Westport, CT: Bergin and Garvey Press.

Aronson, Elliot. 2000. *Nobody Left to Hate: Teaching Compassion after Columbine.* New York: W. H. Freeman.

Baker, Kevin. 2003. "We're in the Army Now: The GOP Plan to Militarize Our Culture." *Harper's Magazine,* October, 35–46.

Barak, Gregg. 1994. "Between the Waves: Mass-Mediated Themes of Crime and Justice." *Social Justice* 21, no. 3: 133–47.

Barber, Benjamin. 1984. *Strong Democracy: Participatory Politics for a New Age.* Berkeley: University of California Press.

———. 2003. *Fear's Empire: War, Terrorism, and Democracy.* New York: W. W. Norton.

Barthes, Roland. 1972. "Dominici, or the Triumph of Literature." *Mythologies.* Trans. Jonathan Cape. London: Jonathan Cape.

Bauman, Zybmut. 2000. "Social Issues of Law and Order." *British Journal of Criminology* 40:205–21.

Beckett, Katherine. 1997. *Making Crime Pay: Law and Order in Contemporary American Politics.* New York: Oxford University Press.

Beckett, Katherine, and Theodore Sasson. 2000. *The Politics of Injustice: Crime and Punishment in America.* Thousand Oaks, CA: Pine Forge Press.

Bennett, W. Lance. 1996. *News: The Politics of Illusion.* New York: Longman.

Bizzell, Patricia. 1994. "'Contact Zones' and English Studies." *College English* 56, no. 2: 163–69.

Black, Donald. 1971. "The Social Organization of Arrest." *Stanford Law Review* 23 (June): 1087–111.

Blumer, Herbert. 1933. *Movies and Conduct.* New York: Macmillan.

Blumstein, Alfred. 1993. "Making Rationality Relevant: The American Society of Criminology 1992 Presidential Address." *Criminology* 31, no. 1 (February): 1–16.

Bowers, William, Margaret Vandiver, and Patricia Dugan. 1994. "A New Look at Public Opinion on Capital Punishment: What Citizens and Legislators Prefer." *American Journal of Criminal Law* 22:77–150.

Boyte, Harry. 1992. "The Critic Critiqued." In *From the Ground Up: Essays on Grassroots Democracy and Workplace Democracy,* ed. George Bennello. Boston: Southend.

Broder, David. 2003. "Will Bush Succeed, Like FDR, or Fail, Like LBJ?" *Washington Post,* August 9.

Brown, Robert Maxwell. 1969. "Historical Patterns of Violence in America." In *The History of Violence in America,* ed. Hugh Graham and Ted Gurr, 154–226. New York: Bantam.

Cain, William E., and Gerald Graff, eds. 1994. *Teaching the Conflicts: Gerald Graff, Curricular Reform, and the Culture Wars.* New York: Garland.

Cassell, Mark. 2003. "Zoned Out: Distribution and Benefits in Ohio's EZ Program." *Policy Matters Ohio,* October. http://www.policymattersohio.org/enterprise_zones.htm.

Christie, Nils. 1994. *Crime Control as Industry: Toward Gulags, Western Style.* New York: Routledge.

Cohen, Joshua, and Joel Rogers. 1986. *On Democracy.* New York: Penguin.

Cohen, Richard. 1995. *Peer Mediation in Schools: Students Resolving Conflict.* Parsippany, NJ: Good Year Books.

Cohen, Stanley. 1985. *Visions of Social Control.* Cambridge: Polity.

Cohn, Steven, Steven Barkman, and William Halteman. 1991. "Punitive Attitudes toward Criminals: Racial Consensus or Racial Conflict?" *Social Problems* 38, no. 2 (May): 287–96.

Cole, David, and James Dempsey. 2002. *Terrorism and the Constitution: Sacrificing Civil Liberties in the Name of National Security.* New York: New Press.

Coleman, James. 1988. "Social Capital in the Creation of Human Capital." *American Journal of Sociology* 94:S95–120.

Covington, Jeannette, and Ralph Taylor. 1991. "Fear of Crime in Residential Neighborhoods: Implications of between- and within-Neighborhood Sources for Current Models." *Sociological Quarterly* 32, no. 2: 231–50.

Curtin, Mike. 1994. "The O'Neill-DiSalle Years, 1957–1963." In *Ohio Politics,* ed. Alexander Lamis, 42–59. Kent, OH: Kent State University Press.

Davey, Joseph Dillon. 1998. *The Politics of Prison Expansion: Winning Elections by Waging War on Crime.* Westport, CT: Praeger.

Davis, Mike. 1998. *Ecology of Fear: Los Angeles and the Imagination of Disaster.* New York: Vintage.

Dewey, John. 1966. *Democracy and Education.* New York: Free Press.

Diemer, Tom. 1994. "Ohio in Washington: The Congressional Delegation." In *Ohio Politics,* ed. Alexander Lamis, 196–233. Kent, OH: Kent State University Press.

Docuyanan, Faye. 2000. "Governing Graffiti in Contested Urban Spaces." *PoLAR: Political and Legal Anthropology Review* 23, no. 1: 103–21.

Donziger, Steven. 2002. "The Politics of Fear." Online interview. http://www.igc.org/deepdish/donziger.fear.html.

Douglas, Mary. 1992. *Risk and Blame: Essays in Cultural Theory.* New York: Routledge.

Dyson, Michael Eric. 2001. *Holler If You Hear Me: In Search of Tupac Shakur.* New York: Basic Books.

Eisenstein, Sergei. 1942. *Film Form: Essays in Film Theory.* New York: Harcourt.

Feeley, Malcom, and Jonathan Simon. "The New Penology: Notes on the Emerging Strategy of Corrections and Its Implications." *Criminology* 30:449–74.

Ferguson, Anne. 2000. *Bad Boys: Public Schools in the Making of Black Masculinity.* Ann Arbor: University of Michigan Press.

Foucault, Michel. 1977. *Discipline and Punishment.* New York: Pantheon.

———. 1988. "The Political Technology of Individuals." In *Technologies of the Self: A Seminar with Michel Foucault,* ed. Luther Martin, Huck Gutman, and Patrick Hutton, 145–62. Amherst: University of Massachusetts Press.

Fox, Thomas. 1990. "Basic Writing as Cultural Conflict." *Journal of Education* 172:65–83.

Frank, Thomas, and Matt Weiland, eds. 1997. "Why Johnny Can't Dissent." *Commodify Your Dissent: Salvos from the Baffler.* New York: Norton.

Fraser, Nancy. 1992. "Rethinking the Public Sphere: A Contribution to the Critique of Actually Existing Democracy." In *Post-Modernism and the Re-Reading of Modernity,* ed. Francis Barker, Peter Hulme, and Margaret Iversen, 197–232. New York: St. Martin's.

Freire, Paulo. 1973. *Pedagogy of the Oppressed.* Trans. Myra Bergman Ramos. New York: Continuum.

Frey, William. 2001. "Melting Pot Suburbs: A Census 2000 Study of Suburban Diversity." *Brookings Institution Census 2000 Series,* June.

Furedi, Frank. 1997. *Culture of Fear: Risk-Taking and the Morality of Low-Expectation.* Washington, DC: Cassell.

Gargan, John. 1994. "The Ohio Executive Branch." In *Ohio Politics,* ed. Alexander Lamis, 258–83. Kent, OH: Kent State University Press.

Garland, David. 1996. "The Limits of the Sovereign State: Strategies of Crime Control in Contemporary Society." *British Journal of Criminology* 36:445–71.

———. 2001. *The Culture of Control.* Oxford: Oxford University Press.

Giroux, Henry A. 2003a. *The Abandoned Generation: Democracy beyond the Culture of Fear.* New York: Palgrave Macmillan.

———. 2003b. *Public Spaces, Private Lives: Democracy beyond 9/11.* Lanham, MD: Rowman & Littlefield.

———. 2003c. "Democracy, Schooling, and the Culture of Fear after September 11." In *Education as Enforcement: The Militarization and Corporatization of Schools,* ed. Kenneth Saltman and David Gabbard, ix–xxiv. New York: RoutledgeFalmer.

Glassner, Barry. 1999. *The Culture of Fear: Why Americans Are Afraid of the Wrong Things.* New York: Basic Books.

Graff, Gerald. 1992. *Beyond the Culture Wars: How Teaching Conflicts Can Revitalize American Education.* New York: Norton.

Gramsci, Antonio. 1994. *Pre-Prison Writings.* Ed. Richard Bellamy. Trans. Virginia Cox. New York: Cambridge University Press.

Greene, Jack, and Stephen Mastrofski, eds. 1988. *Community Policing: Rhetoric or Reality.* New York: Praeger.

Greenhouse, Carol, Barbara Yngvesson, and David Engel. 1994. *Law and Community in Three American Towns.* Ithaca: Cornell University Press.

Habermas, Jürgen. 1989. *The Structural Transformation of the Public Sphere: An Inquiry into a Category of Bourgeois Society.* Cambridge, MA: MIT Press.

Haghighi, Bahram, and Jon Sorensen. 1996. "America's Fear of Crime." In *Americans View Crime and Justice: A National Public Opinion Survey,* ed. Timothy Flanagan and Dennis Longmire, 16–32. Thousand Oaks, CA: Sage.

Hall, Stuart. 1981. "Notes on Deconstructing 'The Popular.'" In *People's History and Socialist Theory,* ed. Raphael Samuel, 231–39. London: Kegan Paul-Routledge.

———. 1985. "Signification, Representation, Ideology: Althusser and the Post-Structuralist Debates." *Critical Studies in Mass Communication* 2, no. 2: 91–114.

———. 1989. "Cultural Identity and Cinematographic Representation." *Frame Works* 36:68–81.

Hall, Stuart, Chas Critcher, Tony Jefferson, John Clarke, and Brian Roberts. 1978. *Policing the Crisis: Mugging, the State, and Law and Order.* London: Macmillan.

Hanson, Russell. 1985. *The Democratic Imagination in America.* Princeton: Princeton University Press.

Harcourt, Bernard. 1998. "Reflecting on the Subject: A Critique of the Social Influence Conception of Deterrence, the Broken Windows Theory, and Order-Maintenance Policing New York Style." *Michigan Law Review* 97, no. 2: 291–389.

Harrington, Christine. 1993. "Community Organizing through Conflict Resolution." In *The Possibility of Popular Justice: A Case Study of Community Mediation in the United States,* ed. Sally Engle Merry and Neal Milner, 401–35. Ann Arbor: University of Michigan Press.

Haskell, Molly. 1974. *From Reverence to Rape: The Treatment of Women in the Movies.* New York: Holt.

Huaco, George. 1965. *The Sociology of Film Art.* New York: Basic Books.

Huesmann, L. R., and C. L. Podolski. 2003. "Punishment: A Psychological Perspective." In *The Use of Punishment,* ed. Sean McConville, 55–89. Devon, UK: Willam.

Hunter, James Davison. 1991. *Culture Wars: The Struggle to Define America.* New York: Basic Books.

Jackson, Chuck. 2000. "Little ,Violent, White: The Bad Seed and the Matter of Children." *Journal of Popular Film and Television* 28, no. 2 (summer): 64–74.

Jarratt, Susan C. 1991. "Feminism and Composition: The Case for Conflict." In *Contending with Words: Composition and Rhetoric in a Postmodern Age,* ed. Patricia Harkin and John Schilb, 105–23. New York: MLA.

Jarvie, I. C. 1970. *Movies and Society.* New York: Basic Books.

Johnson, Chalmers. 2003. "The War Business: Squeezing a Profit from the Wreckage of Iraq." *Harper's Magazine,* November, 53–58.

Johnson, David, and Roger Johnson. 1996. "Teaching All Students How to Manage Conflicts Constructively: The Peacemakers Program." In *The Journal of Negro Education* 65, no. 3 (summer): 322–35.

Johnson, Eric, and Eric Monkkonen, eds. 1996. *The Civilization of Crime: Violence in Town and Country since the Middle Ages.* Chicago: University of Illinois Press.

Johnstone, Gerry. 2003. *A Restorative Justice Reader: Texts, Sources, Context.* Portland: Willan.

Katznelson, Ira. 1976. "The Crisis of the Capitalist City: Urban Politics and Social Control." In *Theoretical Perspectives on Urban Politics,* ed. Willis Hawley and Michael Lipsky. Brunswick, NJ: Prentice Hall.

Kennedy, Paul. 1987. *The Rise and Fall of Great Powers: Economic Change and Military Conflict from 1500–2000.* New York: Random House.

Knepper, George. 1994. "Ohio Politics: A Historical Perspective." In *Ohio Politics,* ed. Alexander Lamis, 1–18. Kent, OH: Kent State University Press.

Krishnamurti, J. 1995. *On Fear.* San Francisco: Harper.

Krugman, Paul. 2003. *The Great Unraveling: Losing Our Way in the New Century.* New York: W. W. Norton.

Kymlicka, Will. 1989. *Liberalism, Community, and Culture.* Oxford: Clarendon.

Lamis, Alexander, ed. 1994. *Ohio Politics.* Kent, OH: Kent State University Press.

Leder, Drew. 1993. "Love from the Panopticon: Architecture and Power Revisited." *Lingua Franca* (July–August): 30–35.

Lu, Min-zhan. 1992. "Conflict and Struggle: The Enemies or Preconditions of Basic Writing?" *College English* 54:887–913.

Lyons, William. 1999. *The Politics of Community Policing: Rearranging the Power to Punish.* Ann Arbor: University of Michigan Press.

———. 2000. "Violence and the Politics of Law and Order." *Law and Society Review* 34, no. 1: 213–36.

Lyons, William, and Stuart Scheingold. 2000. "The Politics of Crime and Punishment." In *Criminal Justice 2000: The Changing Nature of Crime,* United States National Institute of Justice, 103–49.

Lyotard, Jean-Francois. 1985. *The Postmodern Condition: A Report on Knowledge.* Trans. Brian Massumi. Minneapolis: University of Minnesota Press.

———. 1999. *Postmodern Fables.* Trans. Georges Van Den Abbeele. Minneapolis: University of Minnesota Press.

Machiavelli, Niccolo. 1988. *The Prince.* New York: Cambridge University Press.

Macpherson, C. B. 1989. *The Life and Times of Liberal Democracy.* New York: Oxford University Press.

Mayer, Bernard. 2000. *The Dynamics of Conflict Resolution: A Practitioner's Guide.* San Francisco: Jossey-Bass.

Mayer, Matthew, and Peter Leone. 1999. "A Structural Analysis of School Violence and Disruption: Implications for Creating Safer Schools." *Education and Treatment of Children* 22, no. 3 (August): 24–39.

McDiarmid, Hugh. 1994. "The Gilligan Interlude, 1971–1975." In *Ohio Politics,* ed. Alexander Lamis, 84–101. Kent, OH: Kent State University Press.

Melossi, Dario. 1993. "Gazette of Morality and Social Whip: Punishment, Hegemony and the Case of the USA, 1970–92." *Social and Legal Studies* 2:259–79.

Metz, Christian. 1981. *The Imaginary Signifier.* Trans. Alfred Guzzetti et al. Bloomington: Indiana University Press.

Mill, John Stuart. 1975. *Three Essays.* Oxford: Oxford University Press.

Miller, Lisa. 2001. *The Politics of Community Crime Prevention: Implementing Operation Weed and Seed in Seattle.* Burlington, VT: Ashgate Dartmouth.

Miller, Richard E. 1994. "Faultlines in the Contact Zone." *College English* 56:389–408.

Monaco, Paul. 1976. *Cinema and Society.* New York: Elsevier.

Morrill, Calvin, Christine Yalda, Madelaine Adelman, Michael Musheno, and Cindy Bejarano. 2000. "Telling Tales in School: Youth Culture and Conflict Narratives." *Law and Society Review* 34, no. 3: 521–65.

Mulvey, Laura. 1975. "Visual Pleasure and Narrative Cinema." *Screen* 16, no. 3: 6–18.

Nader, Laura. 1993. "Controlling Processes in the Practice of Law: Hierarchy and Pacification in the Movement to Re-Form Dispute Ideology." *Ohio State Journal on Dispute Resolution* 9:1–25.

National School Safety Center Report. 2001. "School Associated Violent Deaths." Ronald Stephens. http://www.nsscl.org, 1–33.

Olweus, Dan. 1993. *Bullying at School.* Cambridge: Blackwell.

O'Neill, Barry. 1994. "The History of a Hoax." *New York Times Magazine,* March 6, 46–49.

Pateman, Carole. 1990. *Participation and Democratic Theory.* New York: Cambridge University Press.

Pear, Robert. 2004. "Education Chief Calls Union 'Terrorist,' Then Recants." *New York Times,* February 24. http://www.nytimes.com/2004/02/24/education/24GOVS.html.

Pearson, Geoffrey. 1983. *Hooligan: A History of Respectable Fears.* New York: Schocken Books.

Phillips, Kevin. 2002. *Wealth and Democracy: A Political History of the American Rich.* New York: Broadway.

Pleasantville. 1999. Dir. Gary Ross. New Line Cinema.

Powers, John. 2004. "Passion Show." *LA Weekly,* February 26. http://www.alternet.org/.

Pratt, Mary Louise. 1991. "Arts of the Contact Zone." *Profession* 91:33–40.

Profiles of America. 2002. Vol. 4: *Eastern Region,* 1458–59. 2d ed. Millerton, NY: Grey House.

Radway, Janice A. 1984. "The Institutional Matrix of Romance." *Reading the Romance: Women, Patriarchy, and Popular Literature.* Chapel Hill: University of North Carolina Press.

Rauch, Jonathan. 2003. "Politics—The Accidental Radical." *National Journal,* July 7.

Reiman, Jeffrey. 1995. *The Rich Get Richer and the Poor Get Prison: Ideology, Class, and Criminal Justice.* Boston: Allyn & Bacon.

Ricoeur, Paul. 1994. "Althusser's Theory of Ideology." In *Althusser: A Critical Reader,* ed. George Elliott. Cambridge: Blackwell.

Rousseau, Jean-Jacques. 1987. *The Social Contract.* Trans. Maurice Cranston. New York: Penguin.

Saltman, Kenneth, and David Gabbard, eds. 2003. *Education as Enforcement: The Militarization and Corporatization of Schools.* New York: RoutledgeFalmer.

Sampson, Robert, and Dawn Jeglum Bartusch. 1998. "Legal Cynicism and (Subcultural?) Tolerance of Deviance: The Neighborhood Context of Racial Differences." *Law and Society Review* 32, no. 4: 777–804.

Santos, Boaventura de Sousa. 1982. "Law and Community: The Changing Nature of State Power in Late Capitalism." In *The Politics of Informal Justice,* ed. Richard Abel, 249–66. New York: Academic.

Satcher, David. 2001. Youth Violence: A Report of the Surgeon General.

Scapp, Ron. 2003. "Taking Command: The Pathology of Identity and Agency in a Predatory Culture." In *Education as Enforcement: The Militarization and Corporatization of Schools,* ed. Kenneth Saltman and David Gabbard. New York: RoutledgeFalmer.

Schattschneider, E. E. 1975. *The Semisovereign People: A Realist's View of Democracy in America.* New York: Harcourt Brace.

Scheingold, Stuart. 1984. *The Politics of Law and Order: Street Crime and Public Policy.* New York: Longman.

———. 1998. "Constructing the New Political Criminology: Power, Authority, and the Post-liberal State." *Law and Social Inquiry* 23, no. 4 (fall).

Schiller, Zach. 2002a. "Ohio's Vanishing Corporate Franchise Tax." *Policy Matters Ohio,* October. http://www.policymattersohio.org/franchisetaxintro.htm.

———. 2002b. "Unmanaged Costs: Government Contracting by the State of Ohio." *Policy Matters Ohio,* April. http://www.policymattersohio.org/contractingintro.html.

———. 2002c. "Wal-Mart Special: Ohio Job Tax Credits to America's Richest Retailer." *Policy Matters Ohio,* July. http://www.policymattersohio.org/walmartintro.htm.

Schiraldi, Vincent, and Jason Ziedenberg. 2002. "School House Hype: School Shootings and the Real Risks Kids Face in America." *Justice Policy Institute.* http://www.cjcj.org/jpi/schoolhouse.html, 1–15.

Schlosser, Eric. 1998. "The Prison-Industrial Complex." *Atlantic Monthly* 282, no. 6 (December): 51–77.

Schor, Juliette. 2004. *Born to Buy: The Commercialized Child and the New Consumer Culture.* New York: Scribner.

Schumpeter, Joseph. 1943. *Capitalism, Socialism, and Democracy.* London: Allen and Unwin.

Sennett, Richard. 1970. *The Uses of Disorder: Personal Identity and City Life.* New York: Knopf.

Simon, Jonathan. 1995. "They Died with Their Boots On: The Boot Camps and the Limits of Modern Penality." *Social Justice* 22:25–48.

———. 1997. "Governing through Crime." In *The Crime Conundrum: Essays on Criminal Justice,* ed. Lawrence Friedman and George Fisher. Boulder, CO: Westview.

———. 2006. *Governing through Crime: The War on Crime and the Transformation of American Governance: 1960–2000.* New York: Oxford University Press. (Pagination in text references corresponds to unpublished manuscript edition).

Skogan, Wesley. 1988. "Community Organizations and Crime." In *Crime and Justice,* vol. 3, ed. Michael Tonry and Norval Morris, 39–67. Chicago: University of Chicago Press.

———. 1990. *Disorder and Decline: Crime and the Spiral of Decay in American Neighborhoods.* Berkeley: University of California Press.

———. 1995. "Crime and the Racial Fears of White Americans." *Annals of the American Academy of Political and Social Science* 539:59–71.

Skogan, Wesley, and Susan Hartnett. 1997. *Community Policing, Chicago Style.* New York: Oxford University Press.

Slack, Jennifer Daryl, and Laurie Anne Whitt. 1992. "Ethics and Cultural Studies." In *Cultural Studies,* ed. Lawrence Grossberg, Cary Nelson, and Paula A. Treichler, 571–92. New York: Routledge.

Stevahn, Laurie. 2004. "Integrating Conflict Resolution Training into the Curriculum." *Theory into Practice* 43, no. 1 (winter): 50–59.

Taqui-Edden, Khaled, and Dan Macalliar. 2002. "Shattering 'Broken Windows': An Analysis of San Francisco's Alternative Crime Policies." *Justice Policy Institute.* http://www.cjcj.org/jpi/windows.html, 1–12.

Taylor, Michael. 1982. *Community, Anarchy, and Liberty.* New York: Cambridge University Press.

Tocqueville, Alexis de. 1956. *Democracy in America.* Ed. and abr. Richard Heffner. New York: Mentor Books.

Tonry, Michael. 1995. *Malign Neglect: Race, Crime, and Punishment in America.* New York: Oxford University Press.

Tonry, Michael, and David Farrington, eds. 1995. *Building a Safer Society: Strategic Approaches to Crime Prevention.* Chicago: University of Chicago Press.

Tyler, Tom, and Robert Boeckmann. 1997. "Three Strikes and You Are Out, but Why? The Psychology of Public Support for Punishing Rule Breakers." *Law and Society Review* 31:237–65.

Vygotsky, L. 1978. *Mind in Society: The Development of Higher Psychological Processes.* Ed. Michael Cole, Vera John-Steiner, Sylvia Scribner, and Ellen Souberman. Cambridge: Harvard University Press.

Wacquant, Loic. 2002. "Deadly Symbiosis: Rethinking Race and Imprisonment in Twenty-first Century America." *Boston Review* 27, no. 2 (April–May). http://bostonreview.mit.edu/BR27.2/wacquant.html.

Walker, Samuel. 1984. "'Broken Windows' and Fractured History: The Use and Misuse of History in Recent Police Patrol Analysis." *Justice Quarterly* 1:75–90.

West, Cornell. 1993. "Nihilism." *Race Matters.* Boston: Beacon Press.

White, Curtis. 2003. "The New Censorship." *Harper's Magazine,* August, 15–20.

Wittgenstein, Ludwig. 1937. *Culture and Values.* Vol. 27. Chicago: University of Chicago Press.

Yngvesson, Barbara. 1993. *Virtuous Citizens, Disruptive Subjects: Order and Complaint in a New England Court.* New York: Routledge.

Zimring, Franklin, and Gordon Hawkins. 1997. *Crime Is Not the Problem: Lethal Violence in America.* New York: Oxford University Press.

Zinn, Howard. 1968. *Disobedience and Democracy: Nine Fallacies of Law and Order.* New York: Random House.

Index

DATE DUE

DEC 30			